VIRTUAL AMERICA

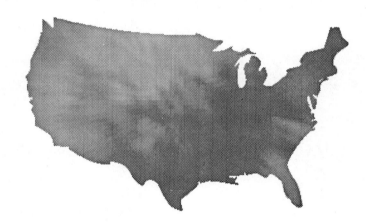

GEORGE BARNA

"George Barna has a very important message for every American, especially the body of Christ. To help us better relate to others and to communicate Christ more effectively, it is important that we keep abreast of prevailing attitudes and beliefs. *Virtual America* is a vital and necessary resource for that purpose."

– **Bill Bright**, *President,*
Campus Crusade for Christ International

VIRTUAL AMERICA

What Every Church Leader Needs to Know About Ministering in an Age of Spiritual and Technological Revolution

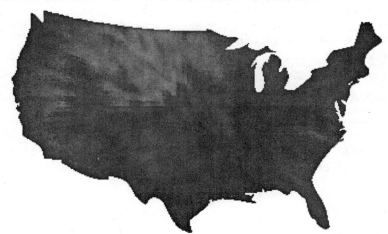

GEORGE BARNA

Regal Books
A Division of Gospel Light
Ventura, California, U.S.A.

Published by Regal Books
A Division of Gospel Light
Ventura, California, U.S.A.
Printed in U.S.A.

Scripture quotations in this publication are from the *New King James Version.*
Copyright © 1979, 1980, 1982, Thomas Nelson, Inc. Used by permission.

ISSN 1063-1437
ISBN 0-8307-1715-3

Rights for publishing this book in other languages are contracted by Gospel
Literature International (GLINT). GLINT also provides technical help for the adap-
tation, translation and publishing of Bible study resources and books in scores of
languages worldwide. For further information, contact GLINT, P.O. Box 4060,
Ontario, CA 91761-1003, U.S.A., or the publisher.

Contents

Section I: How We Live

Section II: How We Think

businesses to lower the federal deficit • Expediting divorce • Unisex weddings • Plight of abortion doctors/our views on legalized abortions • Teaching kids about sex • Underage kids moving away from family • Handling legal offenders • The right to die • Gambling

Section III: What It Means

Appendices

Acknowledgments

This book reports the findings drawn from interviews with more than 2,000 adults from across the United States. It also benefits from the insights of many more thousands of people in America who, over the past decade, have freely given of their time and opinions as we have sought to chronicle the American reality. Thank you to all of you who have enabled us to catch a glimpse of how our world is changing.

My friends at Gospel Light, through their Regal Books division, have once again been incredibly supportive partners in this endeavor. This is our fourth year of creating and marketing this project. I am indebted to them for their unflagging spiritual support, their constant emotional and professional encouragement, their commitment to building the Church and their friendship. I have worked most closely with Bill Greig III, Kyle Duncan, Gary Greig, Bill Denzel, Gloria Moss, Virginia Woodard and Bill Greig Jr. Working with them, though, is a team of committed believers and wonderful people. May God bless you all as you continue to seek His face and follow His leading.

My colleagues at Barna Research have again pulled through during my time away to write this book. Thanks are due to Cristina Banaag, Cindy Coats, Gwen Ingram and George Maupin, in particular, for their loyalty, their prayers and their partnership in our attempts to inform and serve the Church.

I was encouraged throughout this project by my pastor, colleague and friend, Shawn Mitchell. His words of encouragement and the opportunity to talk through issues and challenges with him have meant so much to me. Our working relationship at New Venture Christian Fellowship has helped to reignite my passion for the Church and for God's people. Thank God for leaders like Shawn who have been called and prepared by God for the daunting task of leading His people forward to victory.

As always, the people closest to my heart and work are my wife and daughter. They understandingly send me off to complete these tasks; they laugh and they cry with me over this work; they pray with me about our efforts to serve God; and they help me to put work in its proper perspective. Without the support of my family, this work would be flat and clinical. Through the fullness of experience and love we have together, this unusual ministry adventure has taken on true meaning and joy. May God restore to you both, a multiplied blessing for your goodness to me and your uninterrupted appreciation for God, for me and for the calling He has given to us.

Finally, I am indebted to God for giving me the financial resources, the information, the personal gifts and skills, and the opportunity to serve the Church in a novel manner. May this work, like all that I do, be my own sacrifice to be used by Him for building up the saints and for the expansion of His kingdom. There could be no greater honor than to be used by Him in ways that magnify His name.

Preface

One of the newest and more unusual technologies on the market these days is something called "virtual reality." By wearing special equipment (goggles, gloves and other paraphernalia), we may experience an environment that has been altered by these computer-driven mechanisms to give the illusion of existing in an altered world, even though we are physically present in the world that we know so well. It is a process of simulating a different form of reality that is loosely based on our known world, but is sufficiently different and unpredictable enough to seem like an entirely new life.

Living in America in the mid-nineties is much like that. We wake up, watch the morning news about events that seem close to what they should be but are off-center. We work in a marketplace that is almost the way we expect it to be, but not quite. We interact with family and friends but experience conversations, behaviors and expectations that are somewhat different from the norm. We engage in leisure activities that have a different flavor or character from the expected, not enough to ruin the experience but just different enough to distort our understanding of them.

In the '60s, we would have laughingly said we were living in the twilight zone. In the '70s, we would have compared our experiences to the adventures of the crew from *Star Trek*. Today, we might hear of others describing their lives as being slightly askew from their expectations or different from the past in bizarre ways, and we might tell them they are living in *Virtual America*.

We live in a time that is influenced by technology but in which technology, it seems, develops almost without restraint. People's values are undergoing radical changes, seemingly without a sense of purpose or direction underlying those changes. Personal relationships are operating in a different realm of expectations and parameters. Behaviors that used to be thought of as considerate, compassionate, loving and gentlemanly are passé, having been replaced by those that are selfish, protective, surprising, rude and cynical. Our perspectives on the role of work, faith and family have shifted so that they hold a very different place in our minds and hearts. The activities we engage in for relaxation and enjoyment have assumed a unique status, but even they are undertaken in a different light from ever before.

Perhaps you have had some illness that required you to take prescription drugs. To counteract the effects of the illness, the drugs may have been so powerful that they threw off your coordination or your sense of what was happening around you. You knew it was the drugs that were making you a little off-balance or slightly slower than everything that was moving around you, yet you were helpless to change your inability to keep up with your surroundings, or to get a clear sense of the swirl of activity. For many, that's what everyday life in America is like; it is so close to what we used to know and enjoy; it is virtually the America we have known and loved. But not quite.

The New Frontier

Historically, we have learned that as new regions of America's vast landscape were settled by the pioneers, they had to creatively adapt to the unknown and the unexpected. In much the same way, you and I will have to forge ahead and create new responses to our changing national conditions. Much like the pioneers, who often did not like the harsh conditions in which they found themselves, we must prepare for and understand how to cope with the new America, one in which what we knew in the old days is merely a memory, and what we experience today is simply a springboard to an almost unimaginable tomorrow.

Every aspect of American life is continuing to experience major change:

- How we spend our time.
- How we handle relationships and with whom we relate.
- Expectations and perceptions of major national institutions.

- Our reliance upon religion and the nature of the faith we believe in.
- The values that define our character and shape our behavior.
- The ways we utilize our resources, presumably toward achieving an ever-changing set of life goals.

The axiom "change is the only constant" has never been more accurate, and the reality of the axiom has never made life less predictable and less comforting.

In this book, we will explore the most current research we have conducted regarding these changes in America, and some of the implications of these shifts in thought, word and action. If it were not for the fact that this is the world in which you and I live, it might be a fascinating read, allowing us to mentally escape to this new America and chuckle at the adventures of those who must navigate these perilous and surprising paths.

But this is not the creative tale of a land created in the fertile mind of a fiction writer. This is our new world, and every indicator suggests that we will continue to experience substantial change in our daily reality.

It is my hope that by understanding this reshaped reality we can better exploit the opportunities we have to live a meaningful existence. You may not like the new reality, but you have to deal with it. And because the future does not just happen, but is formed by people who have made the structure of our daily experience their focus in life, we also have an opportunity to provide our own input into the mix. We are helpless in this emerging new creation only to the extent that we allow ourselves to be led into the new era originated for us by others.

Welcome to *Virtual America*.

Introduction

I live in Southern California. Perhaps the least valuable member of the television news team in this area of the nation is the weatherman (or weatherwoman). It doesn't take a trunk full of advanced degrees to get on screen each night and tell us that the coming day will bring sunshine, temperatures in the 70s, a slight breeze off the coast and a layer of smog holding it all in. Following this routine script would enable the weather predictor to be accurate more often than if he or she were to work through the complex calculations and estimates provided by the National Weather Service.

However, I spent the first quarter-century of my life living on the east coast, where the words of the weatherperson are greeted with only slightly less anticipation than were the words of Moses as he stumbled down the mountain after his encounter with God. Why does the weather forecast matter to those in most parts of the country where the weather changes from day to day? We have a preoccupation with the weather because we like to anticipate what is coming and be prepared to deal with it appropriately. We determine our clothing, what time we leave for work, what extracurricular activities we will schedule and even our general mood in accordance with the expected weather patterns.

This book is designed to provide a similar kind of forecast, one based upon the values, lifestyles, beliefs and religious practices of our society. By exploring what we can learn about how Americans live and think today, we may have a running start on preparing viable responses to a nation that is in search of meaning, purpose and fulfillment. Indeed, if you read the beginning portion of Matthew 16, you will find that Jesus

Himself used a similar analogy. "When it is evening you say, 'It will be fair weather, for the sky is red'; and in the morning, 'it will be foul weather today, for the sky is red and threatening.' Hypocrites! You know how to discern the face of the sky, but you cannot discern the signs of the times" (vv. 16:2,3).

This book is designed to facilitate more than mere understanding and prediction. Another key principle for ministry is delivered to us in Paul's writing in 1 Corinthians 9:19-25. In this passage, Paul exhorts us to contextualize our ministry so that we are able to maximize the hearing we receive from those who are not of the Christian faith. He reminds us that if we wish to gain the attention of those who view the world differently, we must understand them and, in a loving and truthful manner, present a biblical perspective on life to them. Unless we understand how people live, how they think and how they typically react to information, we may not fully exploit the opportunities we have to touch them with the fullness of God's truth and love. Ministry built upon such contextualized approaches is more than simple efficiency; it is obedience to God's calling that we be good stewards of all of the resources He has entrusted to us—including information and relationships.

The Source Documents

The information described in this book is derived from two large, nationwide studies my company conducted during the prior 12 months among adults in America. The first of the surveys was conducted in July 1993; the second, in January 1994. Using telephone interviews with random samples of adults, we probed their feelings, experiences, opinions and beliefs related to a variety of life dimensions. The results of our two surveys are provided for you in this book, with both analysis (i.e., the description of the results) and interpretation (i.e., my subjective viewpoint on the meaning of those results) provided for your consideration.

This is the fourth consecutive year we have published *The Barna Report*. Our goal—that is, the aim of Barna Research and Gospel Light—is to help those who care about people and who care about the Church to better understand what is happening and where we, as a society, are heading, so that we might be more effective and obedient servants of God. We have compared many of the measures reported this year to past results, thereby offering you more of a panoramic view of the changing characteristics of our nation.

If you are interested in more detail concerning who was interviewed, how they were selected or the estimated accuracy of such information, appendix 1 of this book contains such information.

The Terminology Trap

Throughout this book, you will be exposed to a variety of terms with which you may not be familiar. Although I tried to minimize the professional lingo and sociological or marketing language that might throw people off the trail, you will encounter a few terms that may need some explanation. Here are the ones that may catch you off-guard.

Baby busters. This is the generation of young adults emerging today. Born between 1965 and 1983, they are about 67 million strong. However, because our surveys address only adults, we have the views of roughly half of this generation—those who are 18 to 28 years of age.

Baby boomers. This is the fabled generation that rocked America. They are the people born between 1946 and 1964, currently about 79 million in number. This group encompasses people between the ages of 29 and 47. They are the largest of the four generations represented in this research.

Builders. This is the generation of adults born between 1927 and 1945. They are 48 to 66 years old.

Seniors. These are the oldest adults whom we interviewed, those 67 or older. They were born before 1926.

Evangelicals. These are a small proportion of adults characterized by unique religious beliefs. In our surveys, we classify people according to their spiritual beliefs, not according to the labels they assign themselves. Evangelicals are people who meet eight specific criteria:

1. Say religion is important in their lives;

2. Made a personal commitment to Jesus Christ that is still important in their lives today;

3. Believe that when they die they will go to heaven because they have confessed their sins and accepted Jesus Christ as their Savior;

4. Believe that God is the all-powerful, all-knowing Creator of the universe who rules the world today;

5. Reject the notion that if a person is good enough, or does enough good things during life, he or she will earn a place in heaven;

6. Believe that the Bible is accurate in all that it teaches;

7. Reject the notion that Satan is a symbol of evil rather than a living force;

8. Acknowledge that they, personally, have a responsibility to tell other people their religious beliefs.

Born-again Christian. These are people who meet two of the criteria described for evangelicals:

1. They have made a personal commitment to Christ that is still important in their lives today;

2. They believe that when they die they will go to heaven because they have confessed their sins and accepted Jesus Christ as their Savior. Note that an evangelical is always a born-again Christian, but a born-again Christian is not always an evangelical.

Non-Christian. People who do not meet the born-again criteria were classified as "non-Christian." This is based on the view that the Bible does not distinguish between born-again Christians and other Christians: Either you are born again (and, therefore, Christian) or not.

Hispanic. This is a designation that respondents chose for themselves. The Census Bureau provides information that is sometimes confusing because it places Hispanic people in two categories: white and Hispanic. In our research, we categorize people as one or the other, according to their own selection.

Reader's Guide

Here is how we have organized this book.

The book contains three sections. The first section deals with information pertaining to people's lifestyles. The second section contains chapters regarding people's attitudes, opinions and values. The third section offers an overview of what the preceding chapters have told us about the overall condition of the nation, and what we might expect in the future.

Each chapter opens with a brief summary of the highlights contained within its pages. The chapter itself includes commentary on the survey findings along with a few tables and a number of charts depicting the key findings. The final section of the book contains an appendix as well as an index. The appendix is composed primarily of the individual data tables from the surveys we conducted. Thus, depending on how detailed you wish to explore the data, you have everything at your disposal, from our running commentary on the data to summary data tables to charts and graphics displaying the information in a more visual format to the raw data in cross-tabulated form permitting you to perform your own analysis (if you so choose) to the index, which will make your use of this resource much easier.

A Closing Caution

A final word is in order about the perspective I embrace concerning the use of research and other sociological methods in relation to ministry.

God and His Church will be victorious. Although research and other tools are valuable means to a righteous and obedient end, they are fallible mechanisms whose sole purpose is to enable us to be better stewards of our time, money, energy, buildings, relationships and other resources. Estimations such as the number of Christians, or even the means used to categorize a person as a Christian are not meant to replace God's view; He alone knows our hearts, and He alone makes the perfect judgment.

In fact, we are not called to judge others at all. Research of the nature described in this book is not meant to divide people based on differences, but to create strategies for bringing people together in the common love and service of God. But, regardless of what the research shows, or what strategies emerge in response to such insights, we know only one certainty: God, and God alone, will reign eternally with those whom He has chosen to share that glorious existence. All other predictions are susceptible to error, and all human strategies for bringing about His kingdom are imperfect. In the end, we may try our best to serve Him, but He alone will determine the outcome of the world.

Research is a means to an end. The end is to bring glory and honor to God's name by serving Him more effectively by using the tools provided. If we utilize such information in ways that lead to compromising the gospel—the truths, the principles or the values clearly communicated in God's Word to us—then we lose the battle, no matter how clever the strategies and plans employed in the process.

The ability to win people's souls for eternity is a victory that only God can achieve. Resisting temptation and abstaining from all forms of evil are possible only in God's strength. Understanding truth and purity is possible only when filtered through God's wisdom. Pray that God will use the insights imparted in this book to better equip you for the challenges that face you as you serve Him in the coming days.

Section I

How We Live

In the three chapters in this section we will examine some indicators of how we live these days. The innovations of the past two decades have permanently reshaped the manner in which we cope with life and strive to enjoy it. Presently, millions of Americans are seeking to make sense of the blizzard of changes and new options in their lives; at the same time, they are attempting to squeeze all of the benefit, value and fulfillment from life they can possibly achieve. Juggling these challenging, and sometimes competing, interests makes for some interesting and unpredictable predicaments in our lives.

The chapters in this section explore our levels of satisfaction with contemporary life; examine some of the activities to which we devote our time, and other activities and organizations to which we commit our limited resources; and identify some of the religious and spiritual activities in which we engage.

Based on the trend data available from our past studies, we will discover that life is becoming more scattered and frenetic than it was five years ago; more people are less satisfied with the results; and our world is becoming increasingly individualized. As we struggle to make sense of the conditions within which we live—many of them intentionally created to facilitate joy and excitement in life—Americans are finding it harder and harder to remain enthusiastic about life. Part of this hardship may be attributed to our decreasing interaction with God.

Because our actions are usually an outgrowth of our attitudes, values and beliefs, we can understand the lifestyles described in this section to be a group of behaviors that have been developing for a decade or more. As we study the common responses to our environment and community, remember that our reactions have been conditioned by the perspectives we have embraced in the past. A vital question for us today, then, is: What emotional, intellectual and spiritual responses will we embrace in the coming years as a consequence of the lifestyles and life circumstances that define us today?

How's Life?

Chapter Highlights

- Six out of 10 adults say they are very satisfied with life these days. Such contentment is markedly higher among people who have certain lifestyles and backgrounds, including born-again Christians and the affluent.
- For every adult who said he or she was better off five years ago, four people asserted that they are more satisfied with their lives today.
- Interestingly, although people claim they are more satisfied with their own life, by almost a seven-to-one margin, Americans are more likely to say that America is doing worse than it was five years ago.
- When asked to compare life in America today with the way things were 10 years ago, adults contend that things are better than they used to be regarding people's political awareness, literacy, community involvement and showing compassion toward the needy. On the other hand, a preponderance of people believe that things are worse today in terms of moral values, spiritual commitment, honesty and integrity, job productivity, personal financial responsibility, selfishness and views about the family.

Prevailing Trends

If you turn on the televised news programs, or listen to talk radio or read the daily newspaper, you'd be hard pressed to describe what is going right in America these days. The headlines are chock-full of stories depicting gruesome crimes, political deception and maneuvering, economic woes, family misery, and cultural decay and decadence. The perspective conveyed by the mass media is that America is falling apart faster than we can understand the components of this collapse. It is amazing that anyone who absorbs these depressing signs of the times can arrive at work even moderately cheerful or conversant.

Yet, in spite of the mounting evidence that the world is in crisis and we are in the middle of it all, Americans are generally satisfied with

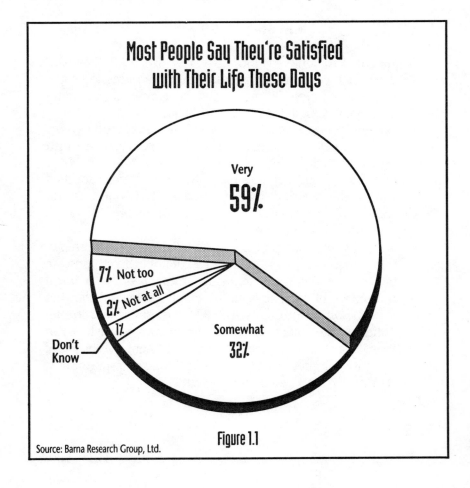

Most People Say They're Satisfied with Their Life These Days

Very **59%**

Somewhat **32%**

7% Not too

2% Not at all

1%

Don't Know

Source: Barna Research Group, Ltd.

Figure 1.1

life! Six out of 10 adults say that they are very satisfied with life these days, and the vast majority of the rest (32%) indicate that they are somewhat satisfied with life. Only a handful take on a gloomier perspective: 7% are not too satisfied, 2% not at all satisfied, and 1% don't know what to make of the world these days.

We also found that just over half of all adults (52%) say that they are more satisfied with life today than they were 5 years ago. Objective measures of cultural health dictate that people should be more disenchanted with life now than 5 years earlier; virtually every statistic evaluating the "good life" has been plummeting for the past 10 to 20 years. Yet, almost in defiance of logic, half are more satisfied with life now than they were in the past, one-third (36%) are equally satisfied, and just one out of every eight adults (12%) are less satisfied today than before.

Is Life Better These Days?

How can it be that in spite of the suffering, anguish and confusion that surround us, millions of Americans are generally at peace with life? Here are a few possibilities.

The Importance of Marriage
First, notice that certain groups of people are more comfortable than others with the way life is these days. Married people, for instance, are more likely to be satisfied with life than are single adults. In some cases, this appears to be because of the sense of companionship married people have with their spouses: They take a "we can make it through this together" perspective. Other married people seem more content because they have a more substantial resource base and believe that they can use their joint affluence to minimize the difficulties and obstacles they experience in life.

Money Matters
Second, we found that one of the strongest correlations with life satisfaction was household income. The higher the household income level, the more likely people were to feel satisfied with their lives. Less than half of those earning under $25,000 annually stated that they were very satisfied with life. Conversely, three out of four people living in homes with cumulative incomes of more than $50,000 said they were

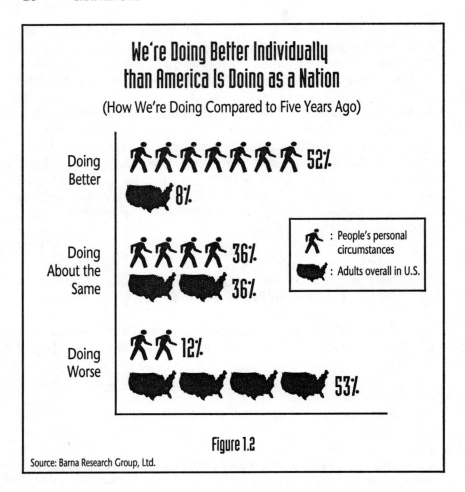

We're Doing Better Individually
than America Is Doing as a Nation

(How We're Doing Compared to Five Years Ago)

Doing Better — 52%
8%

Doing About the Same — 36%
36%

Doing Worse — 12%
53%

: People's personal circumstances
: Adults overall in U.S.

Figure 1.2

Source: Barna Research Group, Ltd.

very satisfied with life. Although many conservative analysts are uncomfortable stating that money buys happiness, some statistical support suggests that for many people, having economic security does, in fact, produce a higher level of satisfaction with life.

Ethnic Distinctions

Third, there are clear differences in perspective along ethnic and racial lines. We found that 6 out of every 10 Caucasian adults said they were very satisfied with life. However, only 4 out of every 10 black adults felt the same way, but more than 8 out of 10 Hispanic adults were very satisfied.

Why the dramatic distinctions? Black adults may be less satisfied with life because, in comparison to other ethnic segments, they are on the bottom rungs of the economic ladder; they have the highest incidence of broken families and single parenthood; they are the least likely to attain education or to have a professional career path; they are more likely to live in the inner city than in suburbs or rural areas, thus contending with crime and other urban problems on a daily basis; and they are more transient than either whites or Asians.

Why would Hispanics, who are not too much better off than blacks economically, be twice as likely as blacks to feel very satisfied with life? The answer may be related to the large proportion who have entered America through immigration. Having escaped from dire poverty and hopelessness in their homeland, many Hispanics have already achieved a higher standard of living in America than they could have ever realized in their native land. Shaped by a very different set of expectations than those held by black Americans, the Hispanic population appears to be content to live with economic circumstances similar to those of blacks, but to view their lifestyle from a different context for comparison. They are more likely to compensate for the deprivation in their lives through interaction with extended family and others who share their language, customs and lower material expectations.

Perspectives of Seniors and Busters
A fourth explanation for perspective on life has to do with the aging of the population. The older people are, the less likely they are to be satisfied with life these days in comparison to the past. However, the population curves are weighted so that we have many more adults under the age of 50 than over 50. In fact, we have almost 50% more adults ages 18 to 28 than people who are 65 or older. Older people have the greatest sense of the deterioration of life. Young adults are less dissatisfied because they have a very limited context for analyzing the world, and they operate with different standards for evaluation.

Spirituality Enhances Life
Finally, we also find that personal spiritual depth makes a difference in a person's perspective on life. The deeper the personal commitment to the Christian faith, the more satisfied the person is likely to be. Among the non-Christians we interviewed, 56% were very satisfied with life; among the born-again Christians, 63% were very satisfied; among the evangelical believers, 79%.[1]

Based on other research we have conducted, it is entirely likely that the various levels of satisfaction reported are not so much a reflection of the separate experiences of these three groups, but rather a reflection of the criteria through which those experiences pass before a judgment is made. Evangelicals, nonevangelical Christians and non-Christians, as a consequence (either direct or indirect) of their faith-influenced perspectives on life, each operate on the basis of their own unique standards for defining life-shaping perceptions such as "success" and "meaning in life."

At the same time, though, we have also discovered that the more committed the people are who are believers, the less comfortable they are in divulging any clues that insinuate they are disgruntled with the reality God has given them. It is almost as if they feel that concerns or complaints related to their daily experience would render them disobedient.

The Evangelical Equation

Simultaneously, evangelicals tend to evaluate their experiences in an entirely different frame of reference than do other people. Unintentionally, it seems, they redefine the very meaning of the adjectives used to convey their experience.

Thus, when we examine the reactions of evangelicals, in particular, we find that theirs is a curious mixture of trust in God and an unconscious, well-intentioned denial of their reality. In most cases, the result is a more sanguine commentary on life.

This analysis is meant neither as a compliment nor a condemnation of evangelicals, in particular, or of born-again Christians and non-Christians, to a lesser extent. Rather, it is simply a thesis designed to give context to the data we are studying. After examining dozens and dozens of studies and recognizing that something is idiosyncratic about the lives of evangelicals, in particular, it is my best attempt at getting beneath the surface and making sense of the very different world in which evangelicals seem to live. My contention is that their views and experiences are just that—different. Not necessarily good, not necessarily bad, not better or worse than the filters and frameworks and sensitivities of others, but certainly different.

Yes, in the final analysis, as the faith-impervious data imply, evangelicals probably *are* "happier" and more "satisfied" with life than are their peers who are less tuned-in to Jesus Christ. But these summary concepts mean something profoundly different among true evangelicals than they mean to the rest of the public. The equation employed by evangelicals when it comes to determining joy, fulfillment, satisfaction, happiness, fullness, sadness, disappointment and despair is built with an entirely different lexicon of symbols and concepts than others use. From what we can discern, evangelicals are not cognizant of this novel and divergent filter on reality that they, alone, seem to possess. Perhaps they possess this naïveté because the end result is the same, mundane representation of human experience: happiness, fulfillment, satisfaction and so on.

It's Personal

We also studied people's views on the condition of America as a nation. As was expected, we discovered that people were far more likely to feel that America is worse off today than it was five years ago. In fact, the proportion of people who said the country is in worse shape these days outpolled those who said it is in better shape by almost a seven to one ratio (53% versus 8%). About one out of every three adults believed that the state of affairs has remained about the same since 1989.

More extensive probing helped to explain this bleak view of the unfolding of America's condition. When we asked people to tell us if specific elements of our corporate life have gotten better, worse or remained about the same in the past 10 years, the reasons for people's concern became clear.

Overall, people had positive views regarding several aspects of our existence. Adults were more likely to say things have gotten better than worse in terms of the public's political awareness, demonstrations of compassion to needy people, people's ability to read or write and levels of involvement in community matters (see Table 1.1). There was general indecision regarding how we have changed in terms of exhibiting tolerance toward people who are different from us: one-third said we have gotten better in this regard, one-third said things are about the same as a decade ago and one-third said it has gotten worse.

In seven key areas, however, adults were more likely to say things have deteriorated, rather than improved. These dimensions included people's financial responsibility, levels of personal spiritual commitment, job productivity, views about the family, people's selfishness, people's honesty and integrity, and the nation's moral values. Notice that a majority of Americans believe things are worse today than they were a decade earlier regarding selfishness, honesty and integrity, and moral values.

What we are witnessing, then, is a nation that recognizes that the character of the people is disintegrating! Once again, such concern is felt most extensively among that small, but distinctive, evangelical population. As can be determined from Table 1.2, for every one of the dozen indicators of change tested in our survey, evangelicals had the least optimistic view of the change that has occurred in America in the past decade. More than three-quarters of evangelicals interviewed suggested that things have declined in the areas of honesty and integrity, people's selfishness and moral values.

Especially interesting is that among the 12 issues studied, the public's consensus is that moral values have been the element experiencing the greatest demise. Thus, the concerns raised in the mass media that the warning of national moral decline is a fabrication of the political right, the evangelical zealots or the conservative Protestant movement is, itself, a fabrication. The evidence is quite clear that a majority of Americans not only believe that we are losing our national moral solvency, but also that people are vitally concerned about this undermining of the moral foundation of the republic.

Reconciliation

How, then, is it possible for people who describe the nation as being in a state of moral and emotional decline to simultaneously feel pretty good about their own lives?

Somehow, Americans have learned to cope with the despair, deterioration and evil in their midst by creating two separate and impenetrable worlds: the "out there" world and their own personal sphere of activity. Most of the exposure people have to violence, theft, assault, deception, poverty, ill health, family dissolution, war, famine and other daily tragedies is impersonal; it is experienced through the media or through verbal accounts from other people. Consequently, using this distant, impersonal reality as the standard for comparison, many people emerge with the impression that, compared to how bad it could be, they are actually surviving quite adequately.

What a change from the 1950s, when people were likely to believe they could create a world without limits, become a nation of overachievers and establish a lifestyle of material comfort and emotional stability. In contrast, as a defense mechanism to simply get by these days, people now measure their existence against a different standard:

sustainable survival. Given the widely understood incapacity for millions of people to reach that modified standard of success and comfort, the average adult concludes that life may not be all they had once hoped for but, in the ever-changing context of life, their own circumstances are certainly endurable.

Table 1.1
How Have Things Changed in the Last 10 Years? (N=691)

Aspect of life evaluated	Gotten Better	Stayed Same	Gotten Worse	Net Change
People's political awareness	50%	30%	17%	+33 pts.
Showing compassion to the needy	45	34	18	+27
People's ability to read, write	37	28	29	+ 8
Involvement in community matters	33	39	22	+11
Tolerance toward people who are different than we are	33	31	31	+ 2
Personal financial responsibility	19	34	42	-23
Personal spiritual commitment	21	36	37	-16
Job productivity	21	34	40	-19
Views about the family	21	28	47	-26
People's selfishness	9	35	52	-43
Honesty and integrity	9	35	53	-44
Moral values	9	22	65	-56

Table 1.2
Are Evangelicals Less Forgiving About the Changes in Our Society Over the Last 10 Years?* (N=691)

Aspect of life evaluated	All	Evan-gelicals	Born Again	Non-Christians
People's political awareness	+33	+28	+36	+33
Showing compassion to the needy	+27	+12	+26	+27
People's ability to read, write	+8	0	+14	+3
Involvement in community matters	+11	-4	+11	+12
Tolerance toward people who are different than we are	+2	-15	+7	-1
Personal financial responsibility	-23	-38	-26	-21
Personal spiritual commitment	-16	-44	-17	-15
Job productivity	-19	-21	-19	-18
Views about the family	-26	-57	-31	-23
People's selfishness	-43	-82	-48	-40
Honesty and integrity	-44	-77	-50	-40
Moral values	-56	-85	-65	-51

*The figures in the tables represent the difference between those who said things have gotten better and those who said things have gotten worse during the last 10 years. A plus sign (+) before the number means that, overall, people felt things have gotten better. A minus sign (-) before the number means that, overall, people feel things have gotten worse.

Note
1. The definitions of evangelicals and born-again Christians are provided in the introduction of this book. The terms "evangelical" and "born again" are not posed to respondents in order to classify them as belonging inside or outside of these groups. Each is determined according to people's religious beliefs and perceptions. Evangelicals are considered to be born-again Christians, but not all born-again Christians are classified as evangelicals. In fact, only 20% of the born-again Christians are included in the evangelical category.

Making the Most of Our Time

Chapter Highlights

- Some lifestyle activities are on the decline. In a typical week, people are less likely than they were in the past to read a book for pleasure or to volunteer their time to a nonprofit or charitable organization. The decline in the proportion of pleasure readers is one of the most startling and rapid behavioral changes we have ever witnessed. In 1991, 75% read a book in a typical week; today, barely half do so!
- Some lifestyle activities are more common than you might expect. For instance, one out of every three adults watches an R-rated movie during the course of a typical week.
- People are continuing to restructure their time allocation during the week. Among the activities that are gaining more of our time than in the past are family activities, working on the job, exercising, listening to the radio and discussing the meaning and challenges of life. Endeavors that are less popular than in the past include watching television, pursuing religious activities and volunteering time.
- Compared to a few years ago, fewer people these days claim they have a philosophy of life that helps them organize their reality and make good decisions.

- Most people believe it is getting harder to develop strong, meaningful friendships.
- A swing back seems to be occurring from the leisure-lust syndrome that characterized the '80s and early '90s to a greater focus upon getting ahead in a career.

Prevailing Trends

Literally millions of dollars worth of research has been conducted on exploring how much time people spend with their most beloved friend: the television. Currently, adults spend more than four hours every day paying rapt attention to what their immobile, wired, stationary talk box has to show and tell. Our study last year found that the typical adult spends the equivalent of two complete months of each year—that's 61, 24-hour days—mesmerized by the television.[1]

Volunteerism
Our research this year explored some of the other common, and not so common, activities of Americans. Among other things, we learned that volunteerism continues a very slow but consistent decline. A substantial proportion of adults—one out of every five—commits some time in a typical week to help a nonprofit or charitable organization other than a church. This is a drop from 24% in 1991. Volunteerism is most commonly practiced among college graduates and registered voters.

Pleasure Reading
Sadly, but not surprisingly, we also discovered that people are less apt to be reading for pleasure during the course of a typical week. Currently, about half of all adults (53%) claim that they read part of a book for pleasure during the week. This is down from close to three-quarters of the population just three years ago, and two-thirds of the adult group just two years ago. Accordingly, we also observed that just one out of every seven adults (14%) claims to have borrowed a resource from a public library during the week prior to their interview. Librarians report that the number of people who now borrow alternative media—such as compact discs, audiocassettes and prerecorded videocassettes—is rising, at the expense of borrowing books.

The rapid decline of pleasure reading is one of the fastest-changing

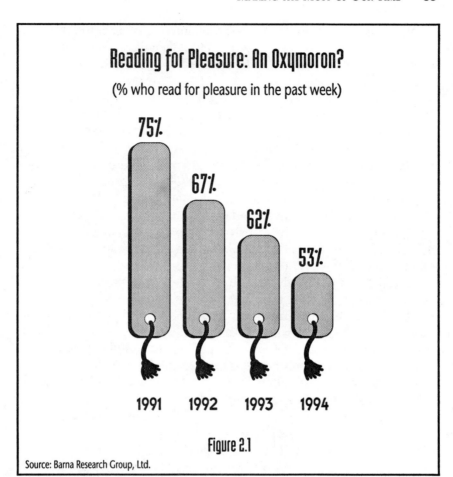

Reading for Pleasure: An Oxymoron?

(% who read for pleasure in the past week)

75%

67%

62%

53%

1991   1992   1993   1994

Figure 2.1

Source: Barna Research Group, Ltd.

behaviors we have seen in the last two decades. With the availability of a myriad of less mentally demanding media to people these days—movies, television programs, video games, computer games, CD-ROM, laser discs, compact discs, audiocassette players, et cetera—and with literacy levels dropping like a boulder in the ocean, the decline of extracurricular reading is far from surprising.

The "Post-Literate Age"

One study, issued in 1993 by the U.S. Department of Education, reported that nearly half of all American adults are functionally illiterate.[2] Even so, the decline in the number of people reading for the fun of it does reflect the continuing shift from a literate mass to a culture based

on the communication of digested and interpreted information conveyed in bite-size pieces (e.g., sound-bite journalism). Some analysts
now refer to ours as the "post-literate age."

Movies and Television

The emphasis upon the convenience and speed of delivery of a wide
range of products is evident in the apparent growth of other activities.
For instance, movies are no longer an experience enjoyed only at
movie theaters. In addition, people may now purchase or rent movies
for home viewing, order them through on-demand satellite and cable
delivery systems, or see them as scheduled telecasts on network or cable
TV. All of these new delivery processes provide the in-home movie
quickly and relatively inexpensively. One consequence of the new
delivery environment is that 1993 saw the movie industry break the
all-time record for annual revenue.

According to our study, one-third of the adult population (34%)
watch an R-rated movie during the course of a typical week. This is
more than double the proportion measured just 12 years ago. Born-
again Christians are less likely than non-Christian adults to watch
such fare. However, the behavioral gap between the born-again and
non-born again segments is not as large as might have been expected:
26% of the born-again adults watch R-rated movies in a given week,
while 38% of non-born again adults do so.

Simplicity and convenience are the hallmarks of the direct-market-
ing industry. As evidence of the acceptance of shopping by mail or telephone, we also found that one out of every eight people (13%) calls an
800 number each week to order a product or service. And, although
you may laugh at, or at least flip past, the omnipresent home-shop-
ping channels that litter the television landscape, 4% of all adults say
that they ordered a product or service from such a channel in the past
week. Projected across the aggregate adult population, that is 7 to 8
million people each week calling in to buy a cubic zirconium diamond,
fitness video or other product seen on a shopping channel.

Incidentally, the same proportion of people (4%) attend a meeting of
a recovery group or 12-step group during the course of a typical week.

Rearranging Our Schedules

The survey also discovered that people are still trying to decide how to use their limited time in the most appropriate and fulfilling way. When we asked adults to estimate if they are spending more time, less time or the same amount of time on each of 11 different activities than they were one year ago, we found that at least half of the population has changed the proportion of time allocated to 9 of these endeavors. For the other 2 activities, more than 4 out of every 10 adults indicated that they have shifted the amounts of time devoted to these undertakings.

Winner Activities
You may be surprised by some of the activities that are gaining a larger share of our time. Among the winners these days are spending time at home with the family (for which 38% said they are spending more time than one year ago and 14% are spending less time, for a net gain among 24% of the population), discussing the meaning and challenges of life with family and others (a net gain among 18%), listening to the radio (a net increase among 12%), working at one's job (a net gain realized among 11%), exercising or working out physically (a net rise among 9%), and reading for pleasure (a net rise among 8%).

Loser Activities
Five endeavors are getting the short end of the stick these days. Losers in the time derby were television viewing (15% claim they are spending more time watching, 38% say they are watching less, for a net loss among 23%), involvement in activities at one's place of religious activity (down among 10%, net), volunteering (net drop among 10%), spending time with friends (net decline among 6%), and time spent in formal educational activities (net loss among 5%). (See Table 2.1.)

Solitary Endeavors
Notice the pattern of activity indicated in this reassignment of our waking hours. The activities that are getting more time tend to be solitary endeavors, in which we are isolated from the world or from people other than family. The activities we are shying away from are those that take place in corporate settings or that require group involvement. There are exceptions, but this seems to be the general tone of the changes taking place.

We asked the same question of a similar national sample of adults three years ago. The figures in Table 2.2 show how things have changed in the last three years. Overall, very little change has occurred. Perhaps the most dramatic insight is simply that people are now less likely to be changing their time allocation than was true just three years ago. At that time, for the nine activities measured in common in 1991 and 1994, we see the proportion of people who have devoted roughly the same amounts of time to this group of activities as averaging 40% in 1991, but increasing to 47% in 1994.

Family Is Important
Digging into the data a bit more deeply, some encouraging patterns are emerging in the continuing struggle to find the most satisfying time arrangement. For instance, men are more likely than women to state that they are now spending more time with family than previously. Past studies have noted the relative paucity of time millions of men have committed to nurturing their families; this is, indeed, a welcome development.

In the same manner, the fact that black adults were even more likely than whites to state that they are allocating more time to family is heartening, given the difficulties faced by black families, from a macroperspective. The fact that our youngest generation of adults (i.e., baby busters) is struggling with the amount of time they spend watching television is positive. Residents of the western states are more likely to be spending more time with their friends than less time—a contradiction of the national pattern. This is important because new trends and lifestyle patterns often originate in the west. In a nation beset by loneliness and social isolation, perhaps we are witnessing the early stages of a new relational revolution.

Some Red Flags to Watch

On the other hand, some red flags are waving, too.

Parents of Young Children Working More
For instance, among the people groups spending greater amounts of time working are parents of young children. The age group that is conspicuous for spending less time involved in activities at a religious center is the busters. Many of them are currently forging the lifestyle patterns that will carry them into parenthood and beyond, so this pattern does not bode well for their future affiliation with the institutional church.

Less Volunteerism Among Born-Again Christians
Note, too, that born-again Christians are more likely to be cutting back

on the time they are volunteering than to be increasing that donation of time. This, of course, is a signal to churches that the labor pool for ministry activity may be shrinking rather than expanding.

Decline in Pleasure Reading

The statistics regarding pleasure reading bear special mention, as we noted earlier that the decline in pleasure reading is a major indicator of the deterioration of our culture's health.

Compared to one year ago, we find that about one-third of adults are devoting more time to pleasure reading, almost half have kept their reading commitment constant and one-fourth are putting less time into reading than before. These figures do not conflict with the information described earlier in this chapter, showing that fewer people than in prior years are reading for pleasure in a given week. Together, these bits of information simply suggest that fewer people, in total, are reading for pleasure these days. Among the smaller base of adults who do read for pleasure, a larger share of readers are providing increased amounts of their free time for that activity than are restricting their reading schedule.

What may be most interesting about these findings regarding reading patterns relates to how population subgroups are reacting. Who is behind the reported increase in the amount of time being set aside for pleasure reading? It is people from the generations for whom reading is both a common skill and a long-awaited luxury. People 50 or older are almost three times as likely to invest more time in reading now than they are to be designating less of their time to this activity. It is among the younger generations—boomers and busters—that pleasure reading is less common and less robust.

People are still searching for the right balance that will allow them to achieve the desired outcomes they deem important and satisfying. Clearly, a majority of adults are still experimenting with different allocation strategies.

Giving It All Away

Another interesting facet of the American lifestyle pertains to our propensity to donate money to organizations involved in not-for-profit work. It is estimated that America has approximately 800,000 nonprofit organizations that are supported by donations from individuals, corporations, the government and foundations. The tendency to give money to these organizations is uniquely American; no other nation of people willingly forfeits as much of its earnings to charitable endeavors. No other nation on earth has as many nonprofit or charitable organizations in place to receive and distribute these funds, or to organize and deploy volunteers in performing charitable work.

Our most recent measures indicate that almost two-thirds of all adults (64%) make a financial contribution to a nonprofit organization or a church within a typical month. To the credit of the American people, this proportion barely changed in lean economic times during the early '90s, when it would have been easy to cease all charitable giving in order to ease the burden of tough times.[3]

Giving Makes a Difference
The reason such giving continued uninterrupted was that Americans are motivated to give, primarily by a desire to help other people when possible and to make a lasting, positive difference in the world. Although some have cynically argued that people give to receive tax breaks, our research on financial donations suggests otherwise. When people see a need and have the ability to help, when they believe that the organization through which they will offer their money is honest and efficient, and when they can feel as though they are part of something that satiates a personal interest and makes them feel good about the act of giving, Americans will give.[4]

Nonprofit Groups Rank High in Integrity
Amazingly, people donate more than $100 billion each year to charitable and religious causes. Very few adults (10%) have *ever* asked any of the organizations to which they have contributed for a financial statement. This is especially surprising because most donors are somewhat skeptical about the integrity of nonprofit organizations. Overall, we discovered that only 6% of all adults say they can trust nonprofit and charitable organizations "a lot"; 6 out of 10 (59%) say they feel they can trust them "somewhat"; one-quarter trust them "not too much"; and 9% do not trust them at all.

Trust in Religious Organizations
What kinds of nonprofit organizations did people entrust their money to during the past year? By far the most popular recipient of donor dollars were churches and other religious centers. Among donors, three-

How Much Do We Trust the Leaders of Nonprofit Organizations?

59% Somewhat

6% A lot

23% Not much

9% Not at all

3% Don't know

Figure 2.2

Source: Barna Research Group, Ltd.

quarters (74%) gave money to a church, synagogue or other house of worship. Next most popular were health care and medical research organizations: 44% gave some money to such organizations. Three out of every 10 donors contributed funds to community development organizations (31%) or to wildlife and environmental entities (29%). About one out of every four donors supported the work of religious organizations other than churches or other worship centers (27%), colleges or other educational organizations (26%), one-fifth helped political parties or advocacy groups (21%), and 15% gave to music, arts or cultural organizations.

Born-Again Christians Are Generous
Which people gave the highest proportion of their household incomes

to religious or charitable work? Born-again Christians. Which segment gave to the greatest number of nonprofit organizations? Born-again Christians. In fact, we discovered that a person's religious beliefs and behavior are perhaps the best predictors of their inclination to donate money and their tendency to maintain their giving over a given period of time.[5]

Table 2.1
Compared to One Year Ago, Changes in How We Are Spending Our Time (N=603)

Activity	Amount of time currently spent on this activity:		
	More	Same	Less
At home with your family	38%	47%	14%
Discussing the meaning and challenges of life with family and other people	34	48	16
Working at your job	34	40	23
Exercising/working out physically	32	44	23
Reading for pleasure	31	45	23
Listening to the radio	30	51	18
Gaining additional formal education	23	46	28
Being with your friends	23	48	29
Volunteering your time	20	48	30
Participating in activities at your church or place of religious involvement	17	54	27
Watching television	15	47	38

Table 2.2
A Comparison of How We Are Changing
How We Spend Our Time,
1991 Versus 1994

| Activity | Amount of time currently spent on this activity: | | | | | |
| | — 1994 — | | | — 1993 — | | |
	More	Same	Less	More	Same	Less
At home with your family	38%	47%	14%	43%	41%	14%
Working at your job	34	40	23	39	39	17
Exercising or working out physically	32	44	23	34	37	28
Reading for pleasure	31	45	23	34	38	27
Gaining additional formal education	23	46	28	30	37	34
Being with your friends	23	48	29	26	42	30
Volunteering your time	20	48	30	22	45	32
Participating in activities at your church or place of religious involvement	17	54	27	20	44	33
Watching television	15	47	38	18	40	42
Sample size		603			1,005	

Notes
1. George Barna, *The Barna Report, Absolute Confusion* (Ventura, CA: Regal Books, 1993), pp. 112-115.
2. "Adult Literacy in America," National Center for Education Statistics, U.S. Department of Education, 1993.
3. This measure is part of an ongoing series of evaluations of charitable giving among Americans conducted by Barna Research in conjunction with the *Non-Profit Times*.
4. For a more detailed explanation of who gives to charity, how much they give, how many organizations they support and the motivations underlying their gifts, see "The Mind of the Donor" by George Barna, a report produced by the Barna Research Group, Ltd., Glendale, CA, 1994.
5. Ibid, chapters 4 and 6.

The Role
of Religion

Chapter Highlights

- Almost every measure of religious behavior we have available is currently at, or near, its low point for the past decade. This includes church attendance, Bible reading, adult Sunday School attendance, and small-group participation.
- Large proportions of the population remain attuned to Christian media, especially Christian television. However, there is reason to question the accuracy of people's responses to inquiries about their exposure to "religious" media.
- More than 9 out of 10 households own at least one Bible; the median number of Bibles owned is three. The most commonly owned version is the *King James Version (KJV)*—by a wide margin. Evangelicals were the group most likely to use the *New International Version® (NIV®)*.
- Most people believe they have, at some time in their lives, experienced God's presence. Among those who have experienced it, two-fifths say they experience His presence on a daily basis; at the other end of the continuum, one-fifth say they have felt it only once or twice in their entire lives.
- Among all adults who typically attend a Protestant or Catholic church, 39% say they "always" or "usually" feel as if they are personally experiencing God's presence at their church's wor-

ship services. The same proportion rarely or never experience God during those services.
- The adjectives most commonly used by adults to describe their church's worship services are inspiring, refreshing, Spirit-filled, participatory and traditional. Fewer than 1 out of every 10 describes them as disappointing or embarrassing.

Prevailing Trends

It is a competitive market out there. People have many options for how to spend their time. As we saw in chapter 2, a constant reassessment is taking place in terms of how to maximize a person's time. Religious activity has traditionally been one of the consistent recipients of several hours of people's time each week. Is this pattern holding true even as the battle for people's attention and involvement reaches a feverish pitch?

The answer is yes—and no. Yes, Americans continue to devote significant amounts of their time to religious pursuits. However, it appears they are devoting a shrinking share of their time to religious endeavors. Although most Americans continue to describe themselves as "religious," and retain the attitude that religion is important in their lives, their behavioral patterns are less perfectly aligned with their attitudes than used to be the case.

Attending Church Services

A clear pattern is evident regarding church attendance, and it is not a pleasing one for the Christian Body. For the third consecutive year, we have witnessed a decline in the proportion of adults who had attended a church service during the week prior to their interview. Currently, we stand at 42% having attended in the past week—the lowest point since we began measuring this behavior in 1986.

Why is this figure declining? Here are several of the key reasons.

- More baby busters are being added to the "adult population" (i.e., 18 or older) each year. More than other generations, busters are prone to abandon the Christian faith in favor of

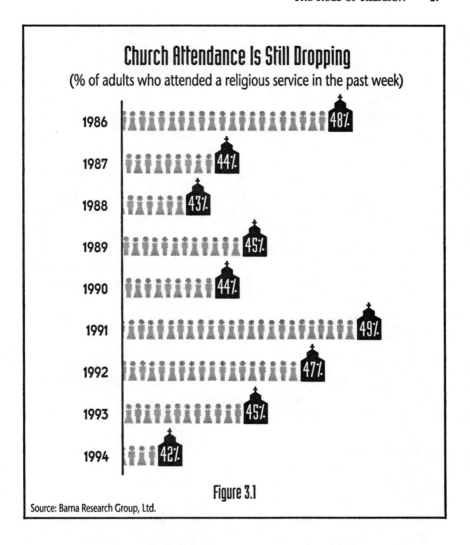

Church Attendance Is Still Dropping
(% of adults who attended a religious service in the past week)

1986 — 48%
1987 — 44%
1988 — 43%
1989 — 45%
1990 — 44%
1991 — 49%
1992 — 47%
1993 — 45%
1994 — 42%

Figure 3.1

Source: Barna Research Group, Ltd.

other religious faiths. They are a generation greatly interested in spiritual development, but are not necessarily inclined to embrace Christianity as their natural faith.[1] As busters come to reflect a larger proportion of the adult population, their lack of attendance at church services continues to pull down the national average. Currently, only 33% of busters attend services on a given Sunday; 44% of older adults attend.

• Between 1988 and 1991, baby boomers were in the midst of a search for God and were anxious to evaluate what the Church had to offer. Since that time, after several years of experiencing and evaluating the Church, they have departed in record numbers, deciding that the Church did not have enough benefits to justify the resources required to be part of the Church (e.g., their time, money, energy, etc.). Today, 41% of boomers are attending church services on a given weekend. This is down from 52% in 1991, the high point of the boomers' search for God.

- The Hispanic population has, unexpectedly, distanced itself from the Church. Many of the Hispanics in America—about two-thirds—are Catholic. However, millions of Hispanics in America are wrestling with acculturation, trying to decide once and for all if they are Hispanic people merely living in America, or American people with a Hispanic heritage. This struggle for national identity and cultural security influences their religious choices. For the moment, at least, many have chosen to sidestep the question and are not involved in any church activities, including attending services on the weekend. Hispanics represent 1 out of every 10 Americans, so their absence from the religious sphere is keenly felt.

The challenge to church leaders is obvious. Unless clear and compelling motivations are provided to these critical population groups to reverse their apparent decision to reject church life, we might expect to see the downward pattern continue into the future.

Monthly Attendance
The good news about church attendance is that people who do attend services are most likely to attend services every week. Among adults who attend any church services at all during a typical month, 6 out of 10 will attend *every* weekend. Women were more likely than men to attend every week (64% versus 48%, respectively). Other population segments more likely than average to attend every week included senior citizens (72% of those who attend services at all during a month attended every week) and those 50 to 65 years of age (65%), residents of the South (63%), registered Republicans (63%) and evangelicals (96%).

Convincing certain subgroups of the value of consistent involvement in church life will prove to be a particular challenge. The people least likely to attend religious services at all during a month included residents of the western states (43%), adults who are not registered to vote (39%), men (35%) and singles (35%). The groups that reflected the greatest ambivalence toward attending—that is, those who were likely to attend during a typical month, but irregularly—were baby boomers, midwesterners, the affluent and Hispanics.

Bible Saturation

Trying to find households that do not own a Bible is a real challenge. More than 9 out of every 10 homes (92%) contain at least one Bible. Among the Bible-owning households, the average number of Bibles possessed is three. Interestingly, that is one Bible per household more than the number of people living in that household!

One of the keys, of course, is what people do with their Bibles. The most basic inquiry concerns whether or not people read their Bible during the week. Here, again, the results are not encouraging. Less than two out of every five people (37%) had read from the Bible, not including when they were at a religious service, during the week prior to their survey interview. This represents a small, but statistically insignificant, gain from 1993 (34%), but a substantial tumble from the level of 1992 (47%).

Who Reads the Bible Most?

Some very clear patterns emerged in regard to Bible reading. People over the age of 50 were the most likely to read the Bible; the youngest adults were the least likely and the boomers fell in between. The lower the household income, the more likely the person was to read the Bible. Residents of the South were considerably more likely to read the Bible than were people from other parts of the country. Women were more avid readers of Scripture than were men. Black adults were more likely to read the Word than were people from any other ethnic group. Protestant adults were twice as likely as those aligned with a Catholic church to have read the Bible in the past week.

Popular Bible Versions

Many people may be reluctant to read the Bible because they have a version that is not conducive to comprehend for someone of their religious background, training and literacy level. We found that among those people who say they own a Bible, 38% said they usually read the *King James Version (KJV)*. This was eight times as many people as claimed to read the next most popular versions of Scripture, which were the *NIV®* and *The Living Bible*. However, given what experts tell us about

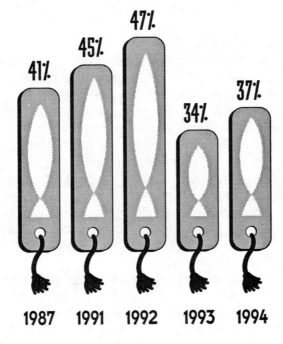

Bible Reading Has Slipped

(% who read from the Bible, other than at church, in the past week)

41%   45%   47%   34%   37%

1987   1991   1992   1993   1994

Figure 3.2

Source: Barna Research Group, Ltd.

the literacy level of adults, we know that a large proportion of Americans presently are incapable of deciphering the language used in the *KJV*—a circumstance that would certainly affect a person's desire to read the Bible.

On the other hand, we discovered that among the people who own a Bible and can identify the version they usually read, a growing proportion are moving away from the *KJV*. Currently, some 41% usually read a version other than the *King James Version*. Table 3.1 shows that versions other than the *KJV* are preferred in greater proportions by baby busters (47%), parents with children under 18 (45%) and evangelicals (49%). Also note that three particular segments have little clue what version they are reading: non-Christians (44% of whom admitted they don't know what version they use when they do read from the Bible), residents of the northeast (45%) and baby busters (56%). This is a further indication that people from these segments are less likely to read the Bible and, that when they do, it may not be taken as seriously as by other subgroups.

Sunday School Is Hanging On

Church attendance and Bible reading are efforts that win people's attention when it comes to assessing the health of the Christian Church in this country. But many other measures are worth exploring, as well.

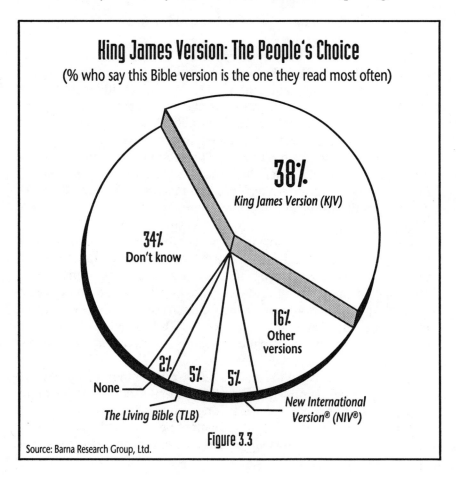

King James Version: The People's Choice
(% who say this Bible version is the one they read most often)

38% King James Version (KJV)

34% Don't know

16% Other versions

2% None

5% The Living Bible (TLB)

5% New International Version® (NIV®)

Figure 3.3

Source: Barna Research Group, Ltd.

Sunday School involvement has traditionally been one of the hall-marks of a healthy and vibrant church. Sunday School has been de-emphasized in many churches in recent years though. Several Protestant denominations have recently pumped substantial resources into rebuilding the strength of their Sunday School programs, both for adults and for young people.

Adult attendance has remained relatively static in recent years. In 1991, 23% of all adults attended a Sunday School class in a typical week. The 1994 finding was 21%. The same basic demographic patterns have held up over time concerning the most likely attenders: women, married adults, parents, lower- and middle-income adults, southerners, blacks and evangelicals.

Small Groups Are Shrinking

Small groups, those that meet regularly for Bible study, prayer or Christian fellowship, but that are not a church service, Sunday School class or 12-step group, have continued to decline in number. In the late '80s, it appeared that small groups would serve as the foundation for a new burst of church growth and stability. Many in the American Church became infatuated with the explosive growth of South Korean churches, such as that pastored by Paul Yonggi Cho, and sought to model their ministries after the structure and programs that helped those churches to grow beyond 100,000 members. A cadre of church growth consultants began to promote small groups as the new means to growing a church.

After a few years of growth in the numbers of people involved in small groups, however, America has experienced a sharp and consistent decline in the proportion of adults involved in cell ministries. In 1982, before much attention was focused on the value and development of small groups within the local church, 10% of adults were active in such a group. The late '80s and early '90s brought forth an explosion in small-group participation, with as many as one out of every four adults involved in such meetings.

Today, it appears that the air has been let out of the small-group balloon, at least temporarily. After the proportion of adherents fell to just 16% in 1993, the numbers for 1994 are even lower at 12%. This decline does not indicate that small groups cannot be successful as a means to growing a church, but simply that the way many churches have

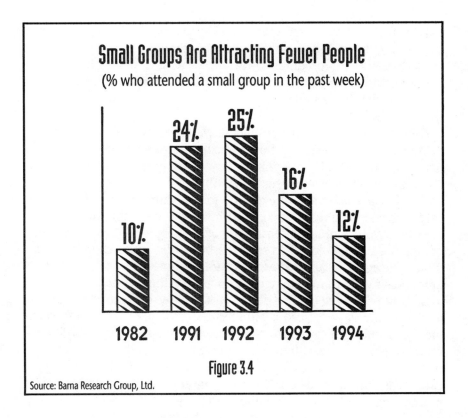

Small Groups Are Attracting Fewer People
(% who attended a small group in the past week)

10% 24% 25% 16% 12%

1982   1991   1992   1993   1994

Figure 3.4

Source: Barna Research Group, Ltd.

attempted to create a viable small-group ministry has been unsuccessful.

Who left the small groups behind? Comparing the demographic profiles of those who were in small groups two years ago with those who are presently involved in a small group, we discovered that people from virtually every subgroup examined have fled in significant numbers. The segments of the population that have departed at above-average rates were those from the builder generation (currently ages 48 to 66), people from lower-income households, residents of the South, blacks and born-again Christians.

The Motivation Behind the Abandonment of Small Groups
Perhaps even more importantly, it is useful to zero in on the reasons people have left small groups so rapidly and in such dramatic numbers. Based on companion studies we have recently conducted, we conclude that small groups may have grown too quickly for their own good. Desperate for a means to help people deepen their faith and

solidify their relationships within the community of believers, many churches embraced the small group as a panacea to compensate for weak discipleship procedures within the church. Hopeful leaders, anxious to foster both numerical and spiritual growth, enthusiastically supported the development of a system of small groups within their church body.

Unfortunately, our research suggests that many of the laity who participated in the program were sadly disappointed with what they experienced. Many felt that the promises made were never delivered upon. Six primary deficiencies existed in small groups:

1. *Bad teaching.* One of the driving forces behind people deciding to get involved in a small group is the ability to spend more time analyzing God's Word. Unfortunately, many of the people who teach in small groups are neither skilled as teachers nor sufficiently schooled in the Bible. The result is group sessions that become exercises in sharing ignorance rather than challenging times of gaining insight.

2. *Lack of leadership.* The absence of quality leaders in the small-group setting is widespread. Manifestations of poor leadership commonly include indecisiveness regarding future directions, poor follow-up on absent members, failure to maintain continuity from session to session, lack of a sense of focused purpose, insensitivity to people's special needs, refusal to deal with inappropriate behaviors and the mismanagement of the group's limited time together.

3. *Disconnection from the church.* Most small groups are, to some extent, an outgrowth of the church attended by the group members. One frequent problem is that people fail to sense a connection between the small group and the life of the mother congregation. Effective groups enable people to feel as though the small group is an extension of the larger body. Dysfunctional groups tend to operate in isolation from, or indifference to, the larger church.

4. *Confusion of purpose.* The typical small group attempts to cover too many bases with too few resources. Most groups allocate time for teaching, worshiping, praying and building relationships. Given a 90-minute block of time, however, and the lack of adequately trained and supervised leaders and teachers, many small-group participants feel as if the group does not give enough time to any one of those endeavors, and does not do an effective job in any one area.

5. *Child care.* Many of the people most interested in a small-group experience are parents of young children. Unfortunately, most groups do not have a means of addressing child-care needs, leaving the par-

ents to fend for themselves. For many parents, child care is an issue of cost and inconvenience. Consequently, attendance is inconsistent and loyalty to the group wanes.

6. *Unwieldy size.* In some churches, "small" groups average from 15 to 20 people. This is simply too large to permit for the kind of positive and intimate group dynamics small groups are generally conceived to provide.

For many adults, then, the bottom line is: What value and benefits do the small groups offer? Judging by the recent demise of small-group involvement, people seem to be saying that small groups do not have enough value and benefit to merit continued involvement.

My Time Is the Church's Time

Because time has become such a major issue in people's lives, one of the best determinants of the vitality of the Church is to measure how much time people commit to both the inreach and the outreach of their church. As for the outreach side of the equation, this year's study found that one-quarter of all adults (25%) said they had volunteered their time to church work within the past week. This is on par with what we have found in each of the previous three years.

The profile of church volunteers supports the axiom "if you want something done, ask the busiest person." The adults most likely to offer their services to their church are people 50 or older, married people, parents of young children and adolescents, the higher educated and evangelicals. This group was also more likely than others to volunteer their time and energy to other causes in which they believe.

Experiencing God's Presence

One of the fundamental reasons we encourage people to attend church services is so they will have the opportunity to corporately experience God's presence. Do they have such an experience?

Two out of every three adults (68%) who describe themselves as Protestant, Catholic or Christian say that at some time in their lives they felt as if they were in God's presence. The people most likely to make such a claim were women, boomers and seniors, middle- and lower-income people, Protestants, born-again Christians and evangeli-

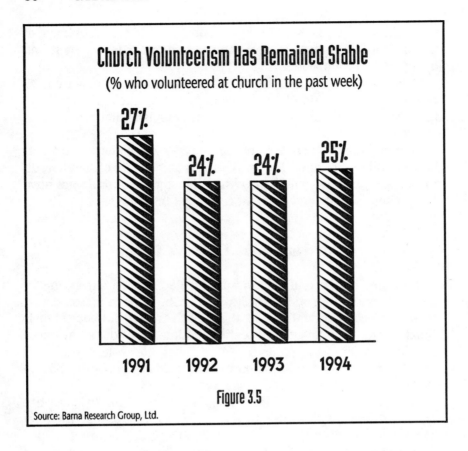

Church Volunteerism Has Remained Stable
(% who volunteered at church in the past week)

27%

24%   24%   25%

1991   1992   1993   1994

Figure 3.5

Source: Barna Research Group, Ltd.

cals. Surprisingly, more than half of all non-Christians who described their church affiliation as Protestant, Catholic or Christian (58%) also indicated that they have felt they have been in His presence.

Among the surprises emerging from the responses to these questions about worship was the finding that one out of every six born-again Christians (17%) said he or she has never experienced God's presence. Given how people are categorized in our research as born-again Christians (i.e., they claim to have made a "personal commitment to Jesus Christ that is still important in [their] life today" and believe that when they die they "will go to heaven because [they] have confessed [their] sins and have accepted Jesus Christ as [their] Savior"), it is heartbreaking to discover that there may be 10 to 15 million people who believe in Christ and have committed their lives to Him, but have never had any sense of a personal encounter with Him.

In addition to the many born-again Christians who have never experienced God's presence, it is worth noting that millions of baby busters who have been involved with Christian churches have also lacked any personal experience with God. The survey revealed that among the busters who associate with Christian churches, 40% have never felt His presence at any time in their lives.

Unexpectedly, we discovered that many adults claim to feel His presence daily. Overall, among those who describe their church as being Protestant, Catholic or Christian, one out of every four (25%) said he or she feels God's presence every day, 6% said they experience it at least once a week, 21% said they sense His presence occasionally, but not regularly, one out of every eight (13%) has felt God's presence one or two times in their lives and 32% have never sensed His presence in their

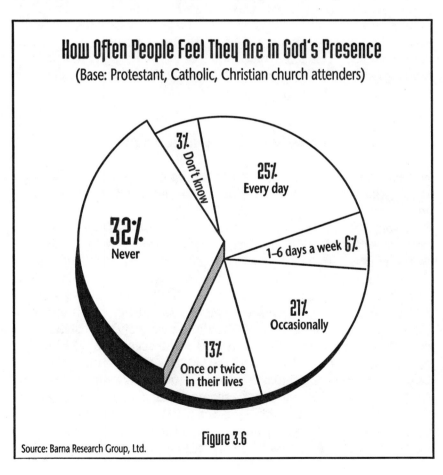

How Often People Feel They Are in God's Presence
(Base: Protestant, Catholic, Christian church attenders)

- 3% Don't know
- 25% Every day
- 1–6 days a week 6%
- 21% Occasionally
- 13% Once or twice in their lives
- 32% Never

Figure 3.6

lives. The two subgroup's figures that stand out are black adults, among whom 44% said they feel God's presence daily, and born-again Christians, among whom one-third (32%) have either never felt God's presence or have sensed it only once or twice in their lives!

Do We Worship at Worship Services?

Calling a church service "a time of worship" does not always make it so, according to people who attend Christian churches. Among those who attend Protestant or Catholic churches, only two out of every eight adults (27%) contend that they "always" sense God's presence at their church's worship services, another one out of eight "usually" feels His presence (12%). Two out of eight churched adults (24%) have "sometimes" or "rarely" experienced God's presence during worship services, while the remaining three out of eight (34%) said they had never experienced God's presence. Once again, black adults reflected the high point of experiencing God's presence, almost half (49%) either always or usually sense Him in their midst during their corporate worship times.

Christian Media Reach People

Not everyone relies upon church services for an entire diet of Christian input. Millions of adults have exposure to Christian teaching and perspectives through the Christian media.

In spite of the shenanigans of some high-profile televangelists in the past, and the reduction in television time devoted by broadcast networks and independent stations to religious programming, one-third of the adult population (35%) claims to have watched a Christian television program during the week prior to answering our survey questions.

The other four media we examined also reached prolific numbers of adults. In total, one-quarter of all adults said they had listened to a radio program featuring Christian teaching or preaching (27%) or had read a book about the Christian faith (27%), and one-fifth of the adult population claimed to have listened to a radio station that plays only Christian music (22%) or to have read a Christian magazine (22%).

And, as the figures in Table 3.2 point out, surprisingly large numbers of non-Christians have willingly exposed themselves to each of these Christian media. Projected to the aggregate population of nonbeliev-

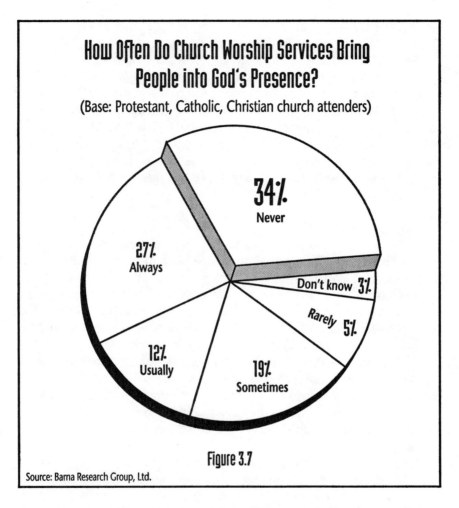

How Often Do Church Worship Services Bring People into God's Presence?

(Base: Protestant, Catholic, Christian church attenders)

34%
Never

27%
Always

Don't know 3%

Rarely 5%

12%
Usually

19%
Sometimes

Figure 3.7

Source: Barna Research Group, Ltd.

ers, these figures intimate that about 50 to 55 million non-Christian adults (41%) have interacted with some form of Christian media in the past week!

Before you get excited and start to think a national revival has taken root, realize that one minor problem comes into play: These figures cannot possibly be an accurate portrayal of reality. If we carefully evaluate the audience size that would exist if these data were accurate, the outcome would necessitate nothing less than a revolution within the nation's mass media environment. Put quantitatively, if these proportions of adults were, in fact, exposed to Christian media during the past week, then, close to 90 million adults would have interacted with one or more of these Christian media during the previous seven days. We know that this simply is not the case.

Take the Christian television statistic as an example. Clearly, 35% is an overestimation of such viewing. If that were an accurate depiction of adult viewing of Christian programming, the cumulative audience would be substantially greater than that of the highest-rated network television show! Although there is no doubt that tens of millions of Christians watch television at any given time of the day, it is implausible to posit that about 65 to 70 million adults watch a church service, Christian teaching or other kind of televised Christian program during a typical week.

Honest Deception?

Why do we get inflated figures in response to a question regarding Christian media? Apparently, many people continue to believe that being associated with viewing such programs is still a socially desirable characteristic. Perhaps many of them *mean* to watch these programs; maybe many others watch *occasionally*, but not on a regular basis. Or it may be that some of these people watch Christian programming *for a few moments* as they "channel surf"—gliding from station to station with their remote control in hand, stopping at a channel only long enough to assess a program's content and appeal before scrutinizing the next offering. Naturally, some people are simply lying or posturing, seeking to convey an image they desire, although it conflicts with their actual behavior. Probably all of these explanations are in effect to some extent.

Related research we have conducted may provide yet another insight into why the discrepancy between people's claims and their behavior is so consistently large. We know that all of the Christian magazines that rely upon paid subscriptions for their circulation reach fewer than five million people among them. If you add the base of recipients of nonpaid, ministry-centered periodicals, we might add another five million people to the list. At best, then, no more than 10 million people receive Christian periodicals. If we then assume that there are two adults per household (another overestimation), and that both of those people are reading these publications (another assumption we know to be false), we get an aggregate base of 20 million people. This is a gross exaggeration of the existing base, but simply points out the outrageous character of the 22% readership figure (which represents more than 40 million adults).

But our qualitative follow-up research has shown us that many people define "Christian" media differently from what we had assumed. For instance, one study we conducted discovered that the most widely read "Christian" magazine was *Reader's Digest*. Another study revealed that among the most listened to "Christian" radio programs were "The Paul Harvey Report" and Rush Limbaugh's talk-radio program. In other words, what people consider to be "Christian" media these days may be something quite different from what church leaders define as "Christian" media.

So how many people truly watch Christian television, listen to Christian radio, read Christian books or read Christian magazines? The answer is that it depends on how you define "Christian" media, and even after you have clarified the definition, nobody really knows.

Table 3.1
What Version of the Bible Do Bible Owners Usually Read? (N=552)

Population segment	KJV	Other	None	Don't Know
All adults	38%	26%	2%	34%
Men	39	23	4	34
Women	36	30	*	34
Baby busters (age 18-28)	20	18	6	56
Baby boomers (age 29-47)	43	28	2	27
Builders (age 48-66)	42	30	1	27
Seniors (67 or older)	45	26	*	29
Parents of kids under 18	34	28	3	35
No kids under 18	40	25	1	34
Northeast	30	22	3	45
South	44	29	*	27
Midwest	37	27	4	32
West	37	24	2	37
Evangelicals	47	45	*	8
Born-again Christians	46	34	*	20
Non-Christians	32	21	3	44

(* indicates less than one-half of 1% gave this answer)

Table 3.2
A Comparison of How Many Christians and Non-
Christians Claim Exposure to the Christian Media
(% of adults exposed to the medium within the prior seven days)

Medium	Evan-gelicals	Born Again	Non-Christians
Television show featuring a church service, Christian teaching or other type of Christian activity	62%	52%	25%
Radio program featuring Christian teaching or preaching	70	44	17
Book about the Bible or Christian principles or activities	59	42	19
Radio station that plays only Christian music	56	36	14
Magazine devoted exclusively to Christianity or activities of special interest to Christians	54	34	15
Christian TV or radio	92	69	31
Any of the five media above	97	83	41
Subgroup size	83	428	778

Note
1. For more information about the characteristics, belief patterns and idio-syncrasies of the emerging generation known as the baby busters, refer to George Barna, *Baby Busters: The Disillusioned Generation* (Chicago, IL: Northfield Publishing, 1994). (This book was previously published with the title *The Invisible Generation: Baby Busters.*)

Section II

How We Think

As life becomes more complicated, people often cope by adopting more sophisticated and complex methods of organizing information, arriving at decisions and relating their thinking processes to their behavior. Accordingly, people's attitudes and values serve as useful predictors of their future behavior. In the same way, understanding their thoughts can help untangle the motivations underlying their lifestyles and other activity patterns.

Each of the five chapters within this section explores a different dimension of people's attitudes, values and expectations. By seeking to understand what is going on in their heads, we may arrive at a clearer notion of how the changing conditions in our culture are likely to evolve in the coming years. Armed with such insight, we may then have a heightened probability of exerting a positive influence upon the contours of the American experience.

Specifically, this section includes a chapter focusing upon how adults rate the performance of various institutions and change agents (chapter 4). The following chapter studies the current values that are dear to people, and attitudes that influence people's perspectives (chapter 5). In chapter 6 you will discover what people think about religion, followed by chapter 7, which examines the prevailing religious beliefs of Americans. The closing portion of this section (chapter 8) explores some of the public policy decisions toward which individuals would be most supportive.

In general, the widespread confusion and inconsistency that have marked people's worldview behavior over the last few years has remained firmly entrenched. We continue to be harsh judges of how professionals and key institutions do their work; at the same time, we say we count on them to handle our needs. As we move even farther away from moral absolutes and traditional values, we are frustrated that nobody seems to be playing by the rules that were designed to protect us. Although we think of religion as important and useful, we question many of the fundamental elements that make Christianity the powerful and life-transforming influence it has proven to be throughout the course of human history. As we look to the future, we yearn for changes in established life patterns and regulations, rejecting the likelihood that many of those transitions will bring hardship upon us.

Life in America in the '90s is truly bewildering. Adjectives such as inconsistency, complacency, irreverence, selfishness, disloyalty, skepticism, fear, loneliness, as well as hope, satisfaction, compassion and achievement are all, to some extent, accurate descriptions of common feelings and behavior in our culture. These elements have been mixed together in a bizarre concoction that defines the American people. Hang on as we try to untangle some of the key threads of this gnarled mass of assumptions, concepts, dreams, values, ideas and expectations to make some sense of the prevailing cultural chaos.

Rating the World's Performance

Chapter Highlights

- Adults are not overly impressed with the quality of the job done by most people. *None* of the nine people groups whose overall performance of responsibilities was evaluated were accorded an "excellent" performance rating by even one out of every five adults. The top-rated groups were military leaders (14%) and doctors and other medical professionals (11%). The other seven groups evaluated each received "excellent" scores in the single-digit range.
- When people evaluated how well needs are taken care of by a variety of public service organizations or individuals, the highest rated entities were public libraries and churches. Farther down the list were hospitals and the local police. Relatively low levels of support were accorded to local public schools, local cable TV companies, local government officials and congressional representatives.

Prevailing Trends

Pleasing Americans is a challenging task these days. If you don't believe it, you haven't examined people's attitudes about the performance of other people who have a diverse range of responsibilities, from parenting to policing to preaching. In this year's surveys, we uncovered a deepening sense of mistrust toward both people and institutions. This lack of confidence in others is nothing new; our trust levels have been dropping for more than a decade. These latest measures simply confirm that the confidence slide is not yet over.

Who Does Excellent Work?

We asked respondents to rate the performance of nine groups of people. These groups ranged from those whose work affects the entire nation (e.g., political leaders) to those who influence our local activities and lifestyle (e.g., local police) to those whose efforts shape intimate institutions such as the family (e.g., parents).

Military Leaders and Medical Professionals Rated Highest

The revelations began in earnest when we discovered that *none* of these nine groups of people was accorded an "excellent" performance rating by even one out of every five adults. The top-rated group—military leaders—was awarded the highest of the four rating levels by just 14% of the public. The only other group evaluated that won top ratings from at least 1 out of every 10 adults was doctors and other medical professionals. That group was deemed to do an excellent job, overall, by 11% of the population.

Political Leaders Rated Lowest

The remaining seven groups evaluated each received "excellent" scores in the single-digit range. These runners-up included the clergy (9% said the clergy was doing an excellent job within their areas of responsibility), public school teachers (also 9%), parents (6%), college professors (5%), journalists (4%), business leaders (3%). At the bottom of the ladder were national political leaders, whom only 2% of the public described as doing an excellent job in governing the country.

The figures outlined in Table 4.1 show yet another response pattern concerning people's assessment of the performance of these nine groups. Notice that a majority of the population feel that seven of these nine groups are doing either an excellent or good job in their respective areas of activity. Although Americans are "tough graders," they are not unreasonable; they are generally inclined to give other people the benefit of the doubt, but concurrently strive to maintain a sense of control or a standard that keeps others on edge and in check.

Parents and National Political Leaders Doing Poor Job
Who were the two people groups *not* viewed by the majority as doing at least a good job? Parents (47% awarded today's parents a combined excellent or good rating) and our national political leaders (32%).

The diverse perspectives and expectations of various population segments became evident through the different ratings accorded to the nine test groups. Among the trends we found were that among the three major ethnic groups, Hispanics awarded the most positive scores to seven of the nine groups—unusually high scores in six cases. In fact, all nonwhites tended to offer a more positive assessment of each group than did the white respondents.

The older the respondents, the less likely they were to give favorable ratings to a group. Parents of children under the age of 18 also tended to offer a more generous assessment of a group's performance than did adults without young children in their home. There were relatively minor differences between the views of Christians and non-Christians, across the regions of the country, according to gender and related to household income.

Clergy Approved by Younger Adults
Evaluations of the clergy provided a couple of surprises. Senior citizens, a segment usually thought of as being most sympathetic to the institutional church and its leaders, actually gave clergy comparatively inferior evaluations: Barely half (53%) gave the clergy positive ratings, compared to more than two-thirds of all other adults (68%) describing the clergy as doing either excellent or good work. The clergy also received lower marks from people in lower-income households, men, adults without children under 18 and residents of the western states.

At Your Service

Our survey also evaluated people's perceptions of how well their needs

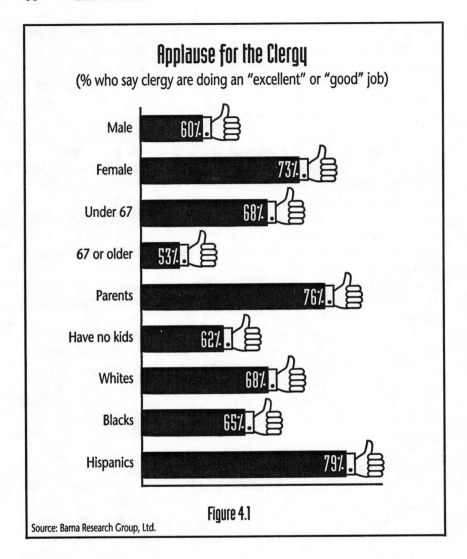

Applause for the Clergy
(% who say clergy are doing an "excellent" or "good" job)

Male — 60%.

Female — 73%.

Under 67 — 68%.

67 or older — 53%.

Parents — 76%.

Have no kids — 62%.

Whites — 68%.

Blacks — 65%.

Hispanics — 79%.

Figure 4.1

Source: Barna Research Group, Ltd.

are taken care of by a variety of public service organizations or individuals (all but one of which were nonprofit entities). Once again, the public emerged as a tough judge of public servants.

Libraries and Churches Doing Very Well
The highest rated entity—public libraries—was deemed to serve people's needs "very well," the highest accolade, by less than half of the

public (45%). Next highest was churches, which one-third of the public felt were serving the people's needs very well, followed by hospitals and the local police, each accorded the highest rating by one out of four adults (26%).

Public Schools Get Positive Ratings

The other four entries—local public schools, local cable TV companies, local government officials and congressional representatives—were viewed as serving people very well by fewer than one out of every five adults. (See Table 4.2 for the listing of reactions to each group.)

Following the same pattern as in the prior question, however, we noted that half of the eight entities evaluated by respondents were given positive marks (either "very well" or "pretty well"). One group—public schools—generated positive response among exactly half of the respondents. The other three entities—cable companies, local officials and congresspersons—all received favorable evaluations from a minority of adults.

Churches Receive Favorable Ratings

There were surprisingly few distinctions across demographic subgroups regarding how churches were rated. The significant differences related to educational achievement (the more educated the people, the less likely they were to assign a positive rating to churches) and region (southerners had a much more favorable assessment of churches than did others; westerners provided, by far, the least favorable ratings).

Oddly, when the scores for doing "very well" and "pretty well" are combined, one of the audience segments most positive toward churches is baby busters: 84% gave one of these ratings, compared to 69% of all older adults. When the combined scores are examined, non-Christians reflect a less sanguine view of churches: 65% gave one of the upper ratings, compared to 78% of the born-again adults providing a similar evaluation.

The encouraging sign is that 7 out of 10 adults (70%) claim that local churches are doing an above-average job at serving people's needs. In fact, at least 6 out of every 10 people from each of the 32 subgroups whose answers we analyzed provided such a favorable rating for churches. The only other entity tested that could make that same claim was public libraries.

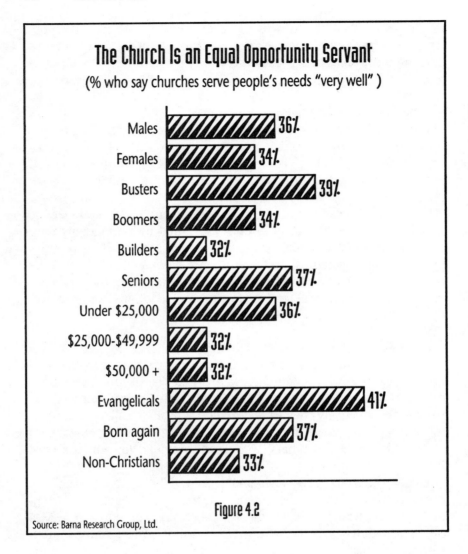

The Church Is an Equal Opportunity Servant
(% who say churches serve people's needs "very well")

Group	%
Males	36%
Females	34%
Busters	39%
Boomers	34%
Builders	32%
Seniors	37%
Under $25,000	36%
$25,000-$49,999	32%
$50,000 +	32%
Evangelicals	41%
Born again	37%
Non-Christians	33%

Figure 4.2

Source: Barna Research Group, Ltd.

All Is Not Fair

In our 1993-1994 report, we indicated that America is a seething cauldron of racial tension waiting to boil over. In this year's research, we found that there may be a substantial level of resentment or callousness toward specific people groups, too. Relatively few adults believe that every person has an equal likelihood of getting ahead. Most adults believe that certain people groups generally have an edge toward achieving financial success, while other groups operate at a disadvantage. (See Figure 4.3 for the comparisons we tested.)

Indeed, social scientists have evidence to suggest that some groups do have a better chance of getting ahead financially. Maintaining the perception that life is not absolutely fair to people regardless of their background, in itself, is not indicative of prejudice against specific people groups, although the predisposition that such inequalities exist may precede or facilitate cross-cultural biases.

The Importance of College to Get Ahead Financially
Who do Americans believe are the people most likely to get ahead financially? The most lopsided perspective underscores the reason millions of parents are so dogmatic about their children attending college, even though the cost of a college degree puts great stress on many families. According to the survey respondents, a college graduate is far more likely to be a financial success than someone who has finished only high school: 82% would bet on the college graduate, only 3% on the high school graduate, and 14% said it probably wouldn't make any difference. Even among those who have a high school diploma but no college degree, just 4% would bet on the high school graduate. None of the college graduates felt the high school graduate was more likely to be a financial success.

Having Children Hinders Financial Success
Interestingly, most adults view children as a permanent financial noose around the parents' necks. By nearly a four-to-one margin, people were more likely to believe that a person who did not have children was more likely to be a financial success than were adults who had children (65% versus 18%, respectively). Parents who responded to the survey were even more likely to assume this point of view than were adults without children! The subgroup most likely to view a childless person as being the probable financial victor was baby busters. By a 12-to-1 margin, young adults predicted that having children would hamper an adult's financial potential.

Men Have the Financial Advantage
Women's liberation, the working mom and the rise of the professional female notwithstanding, most Americans are persuaded that men are more likely to get ahead financially than are women. Overall, 65% sided with the chances of men getting ahead, while 13% cast their lot

with women—a five-to-one differential. Just 20% believed that gender provides no advantage in the accumulation of financial spoils. People who earn larger amounts of money tend to be even more convinced that men will emerge victorious in the battle for financial ascendancy. Overall, the views of men and women on this matter were identical.

Racial Realities Regarding Fiscal Success

Most people refute the contention that establishing a positive economic outcome is detached from racial realities. For every one adult who said a black person is likely to be more successful financially, 12 people said a white adult would have greater fiscal success. One-third of all adults said it would make no difference. Of interest was the fact that in the South, where many social analysts contend that racism and prejudice are strongest, the greatest proportion of respondents (40%) said people of both races had an equal opportunity to succeed financially. Blacks were only slightly more likely than whites to anticipate that white adults would do better economically.

A similar outcome was predicted regarding income of white and Asian people. By a four-to-one margin, adults predicted that a white adult would be more likely to succeed financially than would an Asian adult. What makes this conclusion so fascinating is the fact that census data show Asian households have a higher annual median income than do Caucasian households—by more than 30%! Whether it is inaccurate stereotypes or ethnic prejudice that have led most people to this conclusion, many would certainly be surprised to discover that the white population is not the most financially successful ethnic or racial segment in America.[1]

When asked to decide who would have the upper hand, blacks or Hispanics, a plurality (38%) said there would be no difference, while one out of every three (32%) said blacks would have the advantage, and one out of every five (20%) had confidence in Hispanic adults.

Interestingly, blacks were more likely to say that black adults would emerge with the advantage. Hispanic respondents tended to say neither group would have a comparative edge. Whites were twice as likely to expect blacks to have the advantage or to expect no difference as to predict that Hispanics would prevail financially.

Church Attendance as a Financial Advantage

Although most adults in this nation are churched, respondents were divided about whether being active in a church would provide a finan-

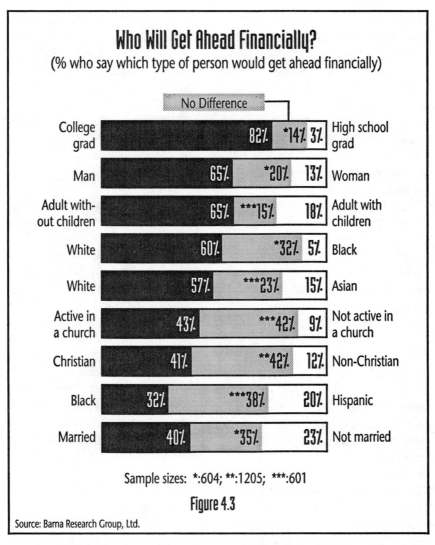

Who Will Get Ahead Financially?
(% who say which type of person would get ahead financially)

	No Difference	
College grad	82% *14% 3%	High school grad
Man	65% *20% 13%	Woman
Adult without children	65% ***15% 18%	Adult with children
White	60% *32% 5%	Black
White	57% ***23% 15%	Asian
Active in a church	43% ***42% 9%	Not active in a church
Christian	41% **42% 12%	Non-Christian
Black	32% ***38% 20%	Hispanic
Married	40% *35% 23%	Not married

Sample sizes: *:604; **:1205; ***:601

Figure 4.3

Source: Barna Research Group, Ltd.

cial advantage or make no difference. Only a few argued that not being active in a church would give a person a financial advantage. However, equal numbers of adults said being active in a church would make no difference financially as said such involvement would provide an economic advantage. The older the people were, the more likely they were to perceive church involvement as leading to financial benefit: 30% of the busters felt an active church person would have an advantage, 43% of the boomers agreed, 50% of the builder generation joined in and 53% of the senior citizens espoused this view. Residents of the southern states were twice as likely as those in the northeast to anticipate church attenders as having an easier time financially.

The more educated the respondents, the less likely they were to see church participation as a financial boon. Born-again Christians were more likely than non-Christians to define church activity as advantageous financially, though the margin (50% versus 39%, respectively) was smaller than might have been expected.

Economic Benefits of Being a Christian Versus a Non-Christian

Almost the same figures were derived in regard to the economic benefit of being a Christian or a non-Christian. Respondents were evenly divided between seeing Christians as having an advantage and believing that their faith commitment would not make a difference financially. Only 12% felt that being a non-Christian would provide some kind of financial advantage. The subgroups most likely to believe that being a Christian is financially advantageous included seniors (60%), southerners (54%) and Hispanics (57%).

The views of Christians and non-Christians, themselves, varied significantly. Half of the nonbelievers said a person's faith commitment would make no difference, while 4 out of 10 said Christians would have an advantage. Among Christians, nearly half felt believers would have an easier time financially, but a large proportion (20%) felt the pendulum would swing in favor of the non-Christian adult. That's three times the proportion of nonbelievers who felt they would have a financial advantage.

Single Versus Married Status for Financial Ascension

Respondents were almost evenly divided regarding whether single adults (35%) or married people (40%) would have the advantage financially, with one-fourth of the adults (23%) assuming there would be no difference based solely upon marital status.

When it comes to financial ascension, millions of people are battling perceptual odds as well as cultural expectations and societal barriers. Often, the grass looks greener in the other person's pasture. And, in many instances, it is.

Table 4.1
How Adults Rate the Job Done by Others (N=691)

Type of Performer	Performance Rating				
	Excellent	**Good**	**Not Too Good**	**Poor**	**Don't Know**
Military leaders	14%	61%	13%	5%	7%
Doctors/medical professionals	11	62	17	7	3
Clergy	9	58	15	7	11
Public school teachers	9	52	22	10	7
Parents	6	41	36	15	2
College professors	5	53	15	7	19
Journalists	4	47	29	16	5
Business leaders	3	49	31	12	5
National political leaders	2	30	37	27	3

Table 4.2
How Well Do Various Industries Serve People's Needs? (N=604)

Industry	Very Well	Pretty Well	Only Fair	Not too Well	Poorly	Don't Know
Local public libraries	45	36	8	2	1	8
Local churches	35	35	17	2	1	9
Local police	26	40	21	3	7	4
Hospitals	26	40	20	6	6	3
Local public schools	18	32	27	8	10	5
Cable TV companies	11	22	29	14	12	12
Local government officials	8	21	32	16	18	4
Congress	7	20	29	19	20	4

Note
1.   "Money Households," Census Bureau, 1992.

The Values and Attitudes That Define Us

Chapter Highlights

- Almost two-thirds of all adults believe "life is too complex these days."
- One out of every six people agreed that "sometimes, it feels like life is not worth living."
- Three out of every five adults (61%) agreed that "the main purpose of life is enjoyment and personal fulfillment." What may be most disturbing about this finding is that half of all born-again Christians (50%) and more than one-third of all evangelicals (37%) believe that life's purpose is enjoyment and self-satisfaction.
- Three-quarters of all adults (72%) agreed that "there is no such thing as absolute truth; two people could define truth in totally conflicting ways, but both could still be correct." A similar percentage claim that "when it comes to morals and ethics...there are no absolute standards that apply to everybody in all situations." Compared to three years ago, people are more likely today to reject absolute truth than they are to accept its existence.
- The most desirable attributes for life in the future were identified as good health, a clear purpose for living, close friends, a close relationship with God and a comfortable lifestyle.

- The consistently above-average and higher-intensity rejection of traditional and prevailing cultural norms by the baby busters suggests that we may be immersed in a transitional period in which the moral and spiritual boundaries of our culture are being permanently reshaped in ways that conflict with traditional Christian perspectives.

Prevailing Trends

In a constantly changing world, people are continually absorbing, analyzing and responding to new information about life and the possibilities it presents to them. To help make meaningful and self-defining decisions that, hopefully, lead to productive and positive activity, people rely upon the worldview they have developed. That worldview acts as a filter through which they see the world and the challenges that are before them. It is comprised of the values and attitudes that shape how they will respond to those challenges and opportunities.

It is natural for people to incessantly recalibrate their worldview in light of the new information and conditions that emerge from moment to moment. However, the aggregate perspective typically remains relatively stable and the recalibrations reflect minor tinkering rather than a major overhaul of a person's thinking and responses. This fine-tuning assumes that people are generally at peace with the worldview they have embraced and the changes they make are designed to perfect rather than replace their understanding of the world, what is important personally and how to make the most of life in any given circumstance.

Most adults these days have backed into their worldview; that is, they did not consciously sit down and determine the fundamental values and critical attitudes that define them and influence their reactions to daily events. Conscious or not, the lifestyles that describe American society today are a result of the values and attitudes that seem to have settled into place for most adults.

Although four out of five adults (83%) claim they "have developed a clear philosophy of life that consistently influences the decisions [they] make and the way [they] live," most Americans struggle with the articulation of the elements that comprise that philosophy of life. In this chapter, we will examine some of the perspectives that reside within the hearts and minds of Americans and act as either the determinants or residuals of their worldview.

The Macroperspective

Making sense of life in a fast-paced, increasingly sophisticated global environment is a real challenge. Just how challenging is evident from the big picture most Americans possess regarding the nature of life in the mid-nineties.

Technological Advances Create Tensions

Almost two-thirds of all the adults we interviewed (64%) admitted that they believe "life is too complex these days." We have found that people expect change to take place and are anticipating a future that is even more rapid-paced and sophisticated than the culture we have today. But people are saying, "I'm being left behind. Technology is outgrowing me, lifestyles are leaving me behind, and the most popular strategies for living a comfortable and successful life bewilder me. It's too much, too fast; I cannot absorb it all." At the same time that we encourage innovation and creativity, we are drowning in the sea of breakthroughs and transformations that have already been left behind in our society's unending quest for "progress."

The ways various people groups cope with these changes and challenges is fascinating. Boomers and builders—the generations responsible for the bulk of the technological discoveries and creations in the past two decades—are the very ones who struggle the most with the complexities of life today. The tensions and pressures that people between the ages of 30 and 65 wrestle with pertaining to the complications of our culture represent a classic case of the creation engulfing the creator.

Why aren't senior citizens suffering even more acutely than others from the stress and embarrassment of striving to understand and master the nuances and applications of the numerous technological advances, restructured lifestyles and nontraditional worldviews that have emerged in these last two decades? Mostly, because they have decided to live their final years without exploiting the possibilities offered by most of these newfangled creations. Their response is that they will make the most of those elements that can be easily integrated into their lives, but will simply ignore the rest.

Progress Produces Psychological Anxieties

Complexity in life is not simply related to technological development. Women were more likely than men to agree that life is too complex these days (69% versus 58%). Their reactions were often a reflection of the time pressures they live with from day to day—juggling the multiple roles of wife, mother, chief of the household, employee, spiritual leader of the household, friend, church activist, community servant and so on.

The psychological anxieties we feel resulting from the rush of progress that sweeps over and around us is compounded by the sense that the globalization of the marketplace is undermining our world standing as Americans and, ultimately, as a significant person. Four out of five adults (81%) contend that "American businesses are losing ground in the global marketplace." The only subgroup at odds with this perspective was senior citizens—some of whom were out of touch with current global economics, but many of whom simply maintained a different standard for assessing the strength of American business.

What makes the demise of the American business standing in the marketplace seem more important is the pride most people have for America.

The Big Picture: How Are We Doing?

(% who agree)

Life is too complex these days	**64%**
American businesses are losing ground in the world marketplace	**81%**
Overall, the U.S. is the most powerful nation on earth today	**80%**
The main purpose of life is enjoyment and personal fulfillment	**61%**

Figure 5.1

Source: Barna Research Group, Ltd.

Four out of five Americans maintain that "overall, the United States is the most powerful nation on earth today." It is typically more disheartening to be the leader and lose that standing, than to be an "also-ran" gaining on the leader. There is an emerging sense that many adults fear becoming an also-ran as the world becomes more complex and uniform.

Why Live?

An alarmingly high proportion of people—17%, nearly one out of every five adults—agree that "sometimes, it feels like life is not worth living." This state of disenchantment is most acute among the elderly (22% of those 67 or older), those from lower-income households (24%), people who are not registered to vote (30%) and blacks (20%).

From a biblical perspective, we might argue that many people question the value or viability of life because of their standards for living. For instance, we discovered that three out of every five adults (61%) agreed that "the main purpose of life is enjoyment and personal fulfillment." This view remains as deeply entrenched as it was three years ago, when we first asked people to agree or disagree with that statement. What is perhaps most disturbing about the results is that half of all born-again Christians (50%) and more than one-third of all evangelicals (37%) remain wedded to this notion of life's purpose.[1]

Truth and Morality

In each prior edition of *The Barna Report*, we noted that people's views on truth are heavily weighted toward the perspective that all truth is relative, determined by the person's convictions, perspectives and the prevailing circumstances. It has been my contention that this way of dealing with reality, more than any other component of our worldview, explains much of the deterioration of our nation—morally, spiritually, relationally, emotionally as well as economically.[2]

More Liberal Views on Absolute Truth in 1994
This year's research confirms that things are *not* moving toward a more conservative, biblical perspective on truth and morality. We found, for instance, that nearly three-quarters of all adults (72%) agreed that "there is no such thing as absolute truth; two people could define truth in total-

To Increasing Numbers, Absolute Truth Is Bogus

(Reaction to the statement: "There is no such thing as absolute truth; two people could define truth in totally conflicting ways, but both could still be correct.")

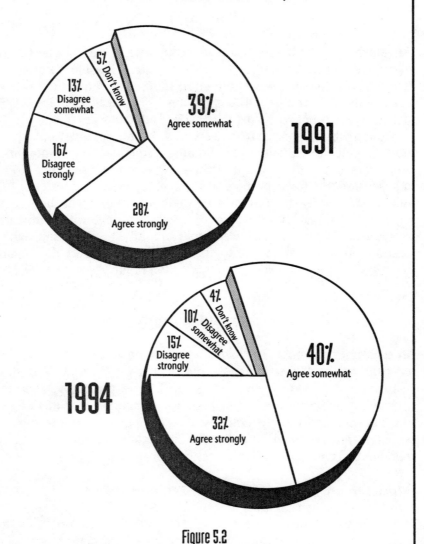

Figure 5.2

Source: Barna Research Group, Ltd.

ly conflicting ways, but both could still be correct." This is actually a larger proportion of adults who embrace this outlook than was the case just
three years ago, when 67% concurred with the statement tested.

Men and women equally embrace relative truth. Three years ago, we
found that although a majority of women bought into relativism, they
were less likely than men to do so. Today, men and women are equally likely to embrace relative truth rather than absolute truth.

Older people more accepting of relativism. Three years ago, we noted that
the older the people were, the more likely they were to believe in situa-
tional truth. Today, that pattern is still in place, but we find that older
people are more accepting of relativism than was previously the case. The
oldest adults, who represent perhaps the last generation who could force-
fully defend absolutes, are acquiescing to the dominant views of the day.

In 1991, only 59% of the builder generation accepted the notion that
truth is relative, eight percentage points less than the national norm.
Today, 71% of the builders embrace relativism, virtually identical to the
national norm and a jump of 12 percentage points during the period
when the increase nationwide was smaller (five points).

Believers are now buying into relativism. Three years ago, one of the dan-
ger signs was that most born-again Christians (52%) sided with the
national majority in accepting relative truth as the standard. Sadly, an
above average acceptance of relativism among believers has occurred in

Christians Are Abandoning Absolute Truth

(% who agree "there is no such thing as absolute truth")

	1991	1994
All adults	67%	72%
Evangelicals	N/A	42%
Born-again Christians	52%	62%

Figure 5.3

Source: Barna Research Group, Ltd.

the intervening years. Currently, 62% of all born-again adults say there is no such thing as absolute truth. Amazingly, close to half of all evangelical Christians (42%) also reject absolutes when it comes to truth.

No absolute standards apply to everybody. Americans are fairly consistent in this reaction to absolutes. The same proportion of people agreed with a statement that approached truth views from a different angle. Seventy-one percent agreed that "when it comes to morals and ethics—what is right and wrong—there are no absolute standards that apply to everybody in all situations."

This outlook holds true across the board, characterizing almost equal proportions of every subgroup of the population we analyzed. The exceptions were those people who have a divergent faith commitment from the norm. Born-again Christians were less likely than non-Christians to refute the possibility that absolute moral and ethical standards exist, but they did not differ by much. In fact, a majority of Christians (64%) agreed with the statement we tested—significantly fewer than the 77% of the nonbelievers, but an alarming proportion nevertheless.

The majority is not always right. Is there any hope of seeing this moral decay subside? Perhaps. One of the bright spots we encountered was that only about one out of three adults contends that "as it turns out, the majority is almost always right." However, to point to this response as evidence that people have not gone too far in their abandonment of absolute standards is truly a stretch. It may be encouraging that people do not automatically assume the majority is always right, but this measures an attitude that is radically different and removed from people's views on absolutism.

The Values Translation

So how do these views on truth and the meaning of life get translated into daily practice? For a growing number of people, these perspectives serve as the intellectual justification of aberrant or irresponsible behavior. Currently, one out of every three adults (31%) believes that "it is almost impossible to be a moral person these days." People of different backgrounds had some divergent views on this matter. Adults who had never attended college were almost three times as likely as college graduates to concur with this sentiment. People from lower-income households were nearly twice as likely as the wealthiest respondents to accept this statement as valid.

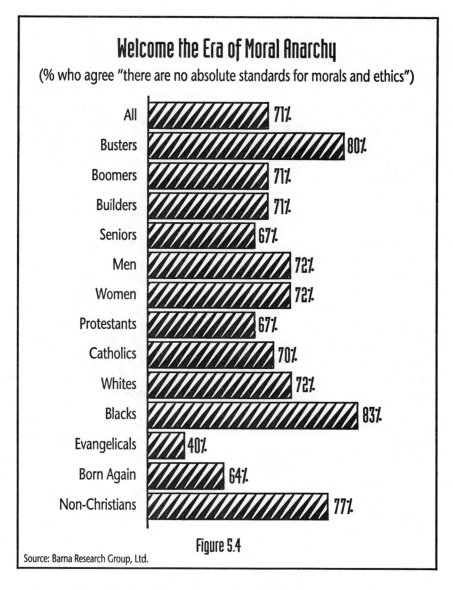

Welcome the Era of Moral Anarchy

(% who agree "there are no absolute standards for morals and ethics")

All	71%
Busters	80%
Boomers	71%
Builders	71%
Seniors	67%
Men	72%
Women	72%
Protestants	67%
Catholics	70%
Whites	72%
Blacks	83%
Evangelicals	40%
Born Again	64%
Non-Christians	77%

Figure 5.4

Source: Barna Research Group, Ltd.

Some of our thinking is probably shaped by the exposure we have to the mass media. One-third of the respondents (35%) said they believe that "the values and lifestyles shown in movies and television programs generally reflect the way that most people live and think these days." Not only were the less educated and lower income adults more likely than others to agree with this statement, but nonwhite adults were also 50% more likely to support this contention than were whites.

Rules Are Made to Be Broken

The bottom line is that we increasingly live by a "rules are made to be broken" philosophy. Half of our adult population (47%) agreed that "to get by in life these days, sometimes you have to bend the rules for your own benefit." Some may see this as a harmless perspective in which people are admitting that in a complex world you can make the most of your talents and opportunities by interacting in creative ways with an ever-changing world.

Placed in the context of the other information at our disposal, however, our interpretation is that Americans are more and more likely to view survival in this culture, given our ultimate ends, as a no-holds-barred confrontation in which it is every person fighting for all he or she can get. In this perpetual fight for survival, no rule is too sacred to withstand challenge; no person is too insignificant to superimpose his or her views on others; no faith is so superior that it can be defined as the "one true faith"; no lifestyle is so righteous that it is to be appreciated more than any other.

It bears mentioning that we consistently see the young adults of our nation (i.e., the busters) ranking highest in terms of nontraditional perspectives. Consider the following comparisons of the views of busters and all other adults on the values and perspectives explored thus far.

Perspective	Baby Busters	All Other Adults
Sometimes, it feels like life is not worth living	20%	16%
The main purpose of life is enjoyment and personal fulfillment	73%	59%
There is no such thing as absolute truth	78%	70%
When it comes to morals and ethics, there are no absolute standards	80%	69%
It's almost impossible to be a moral person these days	35%	30%
To get by in life these days, sometimes you have to bend the rules for your own benefit	66%	44%

Transformation of Acceptable Behavior and Values

Are these views simply a demonstration of the usual disrespect for authority that characterizes young people, and a reflection of the natural desire they have to test the limits of the culture they will inherit? Undoubtedly, this plays some role in developing such comparatively extreme attitudes. However, the consistency of these attitudes, the levels of intensity busters assign to these views, and the aggregate lifestyle perspectives and practices of this emerging generation suggest that we are witnessing something more than the traditional, predictable youthful rebellion. More likely, we are in the midst of a transformation of the boundaries of what our culture will encompass as constituting acceptable behavior and reasonable values.

Not Heartless Toward the Helpless

Although a society that rejects absolutes is one that is moving ever closer toward anarchy, it is encouraging to note that some of the relativistic and selfish tendencies of Americans are developing within an atmosphere of wanting to remain sensitive to those who are in need. Almost 9 out of 10 Americans (88%) stated that they "personally, have a responsibility to share what [they] have with others who are poor and struggling." The desire to reach out and help someone was especially strong among women (91%), blacks (94%) and evangelicals (97%).

To put this finding in context, however, recall that a much smaller proportion of people actually apply tangible resources to the needs of others. Not quite two-thirds of all people give money to charitable causes during a typical month. Less than one out of every three adults volunteers time to a nonprofit organization or church during a typical month.

Significant Relationships

In past studies, we found that substantial numbers of Americans would like to have more close, personal friends, and to have deeper, more intimate relationships with the friends and family who are currently part of their lives.[3]

However, one of the perspectives that may well be restraining adults from achieving closer friendships is the ingrained belief that "the most

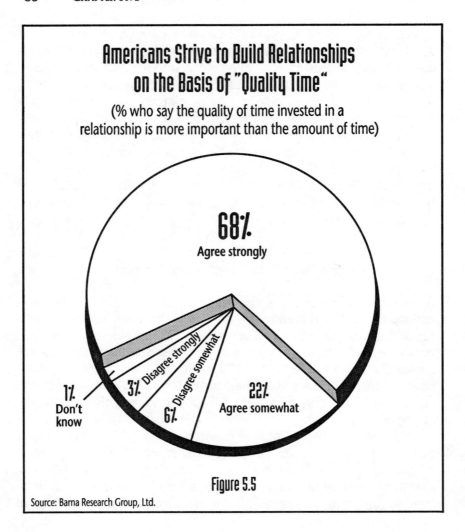

Americans Strive to Build Relationships on the Basis of "Quality Time"

(% who say the quality of time invested in a relationship is more important than the amount of time)

68%
Agree strongly

1%
Don't know

3% Disagree strongly

6%

Disagree somewhat

22%
Agree somewhat

Figure 5.5

Source: Barna Research Group, Ltd.

important thing in a relationship is not how much time you spend together, but the quality of time spent together." Nine out of 10 adults believe this—the same proportion who held that perspective three years ago.

This may help to explain why most people (58%) are of the opinion that "it is getting harder and harder to make lasting friendships." Interestingly, this perspective is even more entrenched among born-again (62%) and evangelical (73%) Christians than among nonbelievers (55%).

Apparently, being part of a community of believers does not, by itself, automatically provide people with the network and opportunities for developing lasting friendships.

Taking Chances

Most people describe themselves as followers rather than leaders. Most people abstain from taking risks if they can pursue a safer route. In short, people strive to minimize pain and maximize pleasure. Taking risks is generally seen as a strategy at odds with living comfortably.

Two out of every three adults (67%) told us that if they "had to make a choice, [they'd] rather play it safe than take risks in life." The people more open to taking a chance were men (36% of whom said they'd be more apt to take risks than play it safe), baby busters (45% of whom would take risks), the wealthiest respondents (38%), residents of the western states (37%), college graduates (41%) and Catholics (40%). Notice, however, that a majority of every subgroup examined was more likely to play it safe than to take risks.

The Ideal Life

What is it that Americans are looking for in life? In the midst of a swiftly changing culture, are we also redefining what we want out of life every few years?

Good Health
The data in Table 5.1 suggest a general consensus about what factors constitute the good life these days. The most important factor among the 13 tested was having good health, deemed very desirable among more than 9 out of 10 adults (92%). This characteristic was of slightly lesser appeal to young adults (of whom many treat good health as a given) and nonwhite adults.

A Clear Purpose for Living
Eight out of every 10 adults described having a clear purpose for living and having close, personal friendships as very desirable commodities for their lives. Having a clear purpose for living was almost a defining characteristic among evangelicals: 97% labeled this as very desirable.

Unexpectedly, we also discovered that a much smaller proportion of black adults (66%) identified close friendships as a very desirable element for their future.

A Close Relationship with God

Three out of every four adults indicated that they view a close relationship with God (74%) and having a comfortable lifestyle (72%) as very desirable attributes to achieve. Having a close relationship with God ruptured the sense of unanimity across subgroups that existed for most of the characteristics tested. Notice the following distinctions, by subgroup, in terms of finding a close relationship with God to be very desirable.

Subgroup	Very Desirable
Males	66%
Females	82
Adults under 50	69
Adults 50 or older	82
Southerners	88
Westerners	63
Midwesterners, Northeasterners	70
Whites	72
Blacks	90
Born-again Christians	94
Non-Christians	61

Not surprisingly, women, older adults, residents of the South, blacks and born-again Christians expressed a more intense desire to have a close relationship with God. Do not lose sight of the fact, though, that even among non-Christians three out of every five people felt that being more intimate with God would be a very desirable reality.

A Comfortable Lifestyle

As for the desire to lead a comfortable lifestyle, the data inform us that one of the segments least likely to promote this as a key hope for the future was baby boomers! Just two-thirds of them (65%) said comfort was a goal, compared to three-quarters of all other adults.

Why the break from the well-publicized possession-mad lifestyle of the boomers? For some, it is the recognition that a decade of unrestricted greed left them unsatisfied. For others, it is endemic to their life cycle, as many of them now enter a time of wanting to scale back and remove some of the financial stress with which they have lived for so long. For others, their reaction is a result of already having achieved material affluence and comfort, so this need not be one of their future goals.

Living Close to Family
The subgroup analysis of the desire to live close to family and relatives reminds us of some of the stereotypes regarding family relationships. Women are more likely than men to want to be close to their families. Older adults (i.e., grandparents) have a greater desire to live closer to relatives than do younger adults. Blacks have the greatest desire of all groups to live close to family.

Living a Long Life
A majority of Americans are hoping to live a long life (57%). This is especially true for the adults who are nearing the end of their lives: 67% of the senior citizens interviewed described this as a very desirable condition.

An Active Sex Life
The only other element that at least half of the nation (51%) coveted was an active sex life. Actually, this component would have been much higher if older adults had been excluded from the base—56% of those under 67, or 61% among busters and boomers.

Being Part of a Local Church
Not quite half of the respondents (49%) said being part of a local church would be very desirable. This is intriguing because a larger proportion of adults are already affiliated with some kind of church. The fact that a smaller proportion define such a relationship as very desirable does not bode well for churches in the days ahead.

Some very significant differences of opinion emerged related to church affiliation. Women were over 50% more likely than men to describe being part of a church as a very desirable characteristic (59% versus 39%, respectively). Busters and boomers were much less likely than older adults to strongly desire a church relationship in the future (45% versus 56%). And had it not been for the South, where a church is much more desirable (64%), the national average would have been much lower. Naturally, we also saw born-again Christians (73%) much more likely—in fact, more than twice as likely—to describe a partnership with a church as very desirable than did non-Christians (34%).

The relationship between wanting to be close to God and wanting to be part of a local church provides important insights into the mind of the typical American. Although most people want to relate to God more intimately, comparatively few people are willing to pursue a deeper level of involvement with a local church. This perspective can be found among born-again Christians (almost one-quarter of whom want a deeper relationship with God, but are not very anxious to pursue church involvement), but especially among non-Christians (among whom half who want to be more intimate with God do not express a similar desire to pursue church involvement).

A High-Paying Job
Among the lifestyle attributes evaluated as being very desirable by less than half of the adult population were having a high-paying job (43%), influencing other people's lives (39%), owning a large home (30%) and achieving fame or public recognition (10%).

One People, One Mind

The survey showed that both Christians and non-Christians seem driven to achieve the same basic end results and lifestyles. In Table 5.2, notice that the only attributes for which there were significant distinctions between the desires of believers and nonbelievers were having a clear purpose in life (which the vast majority of both groups desire, Christians to a somewhat greater extent), having a close relationship with God (which, again, both segments generally desire, but more Christians exhibit such a hope), being part of a local church (which Christians were twice as likely as non-Christians to seek), and having influence in other people's lives (somewhat more characteristic of the Christian segment). Non-Christians were slightly more interested in having an active sex life, but that may be attributed to the age differential between Christians and non-Christians (i.e., Christians tend to be somewhat older) more than faith perspectives.

Not Everything Is Changing These Days

Although many aspects of life are undergoing rapid and fundamental change, what most people are seeking out of life has changed surprisingly little in the past three years. In Table 5.3, you will see that only four significant changes have occurred in people's most pressing desires for the future. In general, these changes—increases in the desire to have more friends, a comfortable lifestyle, a high-paying job and to own a large home—move in the direction of having a broader experience of "the good life." There is no evidence of a push for more intensive spirituality, heightened altruism or deeper family ties.

Table 5.1
What Conditions Would Be Most Desirable in Life?
(N=690)

Condition	Very	Some-what	Not Too	Not at All	Don't Know
Have good health	92%	7%	1%	0	0
Have a clear purpose for living	80	14	2	1	3
Have close, personal friendships	79	15	3	2	2
Have a close relationship with God	74	18	2	4	2
Have a comfortable lifestyle	72	22	4	1	1
Live close to family and relatives	63	27	5	3	2
Live to an old age	57	31	7	3	3
Have an active sex life	51	31	5	10	3
Be part of a local church	49	29	10	9	2
Have a high-paying job	43	31	11	12	2
Influence other people's lives	39	40	9	8	3
Own a large home	30	32	20	17	1
Achieve fame or public recognition	10	26	30	33	2

Table 5.2
Christians and Non-Christians Are Generally Striving
for the Same Things in Life
(N=690; % who described the condition as "very desirable")

Condition	Born-Again Christian	
	Yes	No
Have good health	92%	91%
Have a clear purpose for living	89	75
Have close, personal friendships	81	78
Have a close relationship with God	94	61
Have a comfortable lifestyle	74	72
Live close to family and relatives	63	63
Live to an old age	60	54
Have an active sex life	45	55
Be part of a local church	73	34
Have a high-paying job	42	44
Influence other people's lives	48	33
Own a large home	25	32
Achieve fame or public recognition	13	7

Table 5.3
What We Want from Life Hasn't Changed Much Since 1991
(N=690; % who described the condition as "very desirable")

Condition	1994	1991
Have good health	92%	93%
Have close, personal friendships	79	73
Have a close relationship with God	74	72
Have a comfortable lifestyle	72	59
Live close to family and relatives	63	67
Live to an old age	57	51
Be part of a local church	49	50
Have a high-paying job	43	36
Influence other people's lives	39	40
Own a large home	30	23
Achieve fame or public recognition	10	10

Notes
1. For context, it is my contention that the Bible challenges us to live not for our own joy and self-gratification, but for the glory of God (see 1 Cor. 10:31). This means that our primary purpose in life would be to have a personal and growing relationship with God, in which we demonstrate our love for Him by committing our lives to His service. Although it is quite feasible to gain a sense of "enjoyment and personal fulfillment" by devoting ourselves to God's purposes, we know from our research that most Americans interpret this question in light of the personal benefit they receive from life through a focus on self-gratification in a material and emotional, rather than spiritual, sense.

2. For more insight into past exploration of the absence of absolutes and eternal truth principles, see the three previous Barna Reports by George Barna (Regal Books, Ventura, CA): *What Americans Believe* (1991), *America Renews Its Search for God* (1992) and *Absolute Confusion* (1993). Other recent perspectives on the rejection of moral absolutes and the consequences of such a life view are found in *The Body*, Chuck Colson and Ellen Vaughn (Dallas, TX: Word Inc., 1993); *The American Hour*, Os Guinness (New York, NY: Free Press, 1993) and *Warning: Nonsense Is Destroying America*, Vincent Ruggiero (Nashville, TN: Thomas Nelson Publishers, 1994).

3. The relevant figures can be found on pages 128-130 in *American Renews Its Search for God: The Barna Report, 1992-1993*, George Barna (Ventura, CA: Regal Books, 1992).

Attitudes and Perspectives on Religion

Chapter Highlights

- Not quite half of all adults (45%) strongly agreed that the Christian faith is relevant to the way they live today; another one-third (34%) offered moderate agreement with that notion.
- People were more likely to perceive Christianity to be relevant than to describe the Christian churches in their area as relevant. Overall, just 33% strongly agreed and 38% agreed somewhat that their local churches were relevant.
- Half of all adults agreed that "most churches are more interested in raising money than in helping people."
- Two-thirds of all churched adults said they were very satisfied with their ability to worship God at their church. Overall, 95% of all churched people said they were either very or somewhat satisfied with the ability to worship at their church.
- When asked to rate the worship experience at their church, people's perspectives were unusually positive. The most commonly selected adjectives from the list of 13 provided were the terms inspiring (92%), refreshing (90%), Spirit-filled (85%), participatory (82%) and traditional (78%).

Prevailing Trends

Six out of every 10 Americans claim that religion is very important in their lives these days, so you would expect to find overwhelmingly positive sentiment toward churches, the Christian faith and the role of religion in our culture. Hold on...

Religious Relevance

One of the notions baby boomers, in particular, brought to the fore of the discussion about the role of the Church has been the concept of relevance. Boomers and, in their wake, busters, have raised questions about why churches engage in many of the behaviors they practice. In some quarters of the church world, the term "relevance" has become an unwelcome word, based on the assumption that for a ministry to be relevant it must compromise its fundamental principles and values to become more accessible to those who hold different core concepts. At the same time, however, many of the fastest-growing and most influential churches are those that have understood the cry for relevance to be the younger generations' appeals for meaning and depth—but not theological compromise—in a contextualized manner.

Is the Christian faith itself relevant to the way people live these days? In response to that question, 45% strongly agreed that it is, and 34% agreed somewhat. The remaining one-fifth of the population either disagreed (18%) or did not know what to make of the relevance of Christianity (4%).

Continuing an established pattern, adults were more likely to perceive Christianity as relevant than to describe the Christian churches in their area as relevant. Overall, just 33% strongly agreed and 38% agreed somewhat that their local churches were relevant; 23% disagreed and 5% abstained from commenting.

The Relevance of the Christian Faith Is Stable
Compared to people's answers to these same questions in 1991, there has been no change in the perceived relevance of the Christian faith, and a small increase in the proportion who feel that the Christian churches in their locale have become more relevant to the way people live these days. Overall, given the slow but steady decay in religious activity identified in chapter 3, this stability is a more favorable cir-

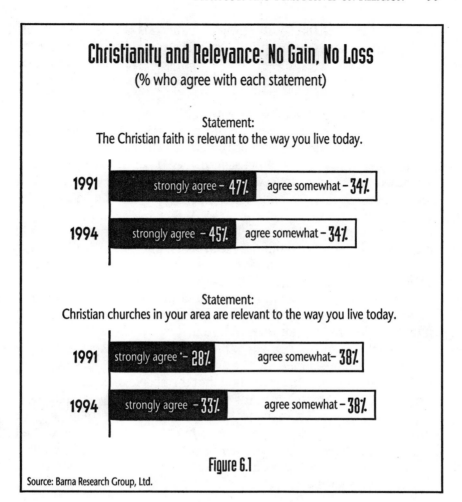

Christianity and Relevance: No Gain, No Loss
(% who agree with each statement)

Statement:
The Christian faith is relevant to the way you live today.

1991 | strongly agree – 47% | agree somewhat – 34%

1994 | strongly agree – 45% | agree somewhat – 34%

Statement:
Christian churches in your area are relevant to the way you live today.

1991 | strongly agree – 28% | agree somewhat– 38%

1994 | strongly agree – 33% | agree somewhat – 38%

Figure 6.1

Source: Barna Research Group, Ltd.

cumstance than might have been hoped for.

The expected subgroup patterns were evident. The younger the people, the less likely they were to describe Christianity as relevant. Residents in the northeast and west were the harshest judges of Christianity. Intriguingly, registered Republicans were twice as likely as registered Democrats to view Christianity as relevant. Nine out of 10 evangelicals (86%) and three-quarters of all born-again adults (72%) strongly agreed that Christianity is relevant to today's people; less than one-third of the non-Christians concurred (29%).

Those who were most firmly convinced that the Christian churches in their area were relevant included women (38%), senior citizens

(49%), residents of the South (45%), Republicans (44%), evangelicals (56%) and born-again Christians (48%). The people least likely to view local churches as relevant were men (29%), baby boomers (25%), people in the northeast (27%) and west (25%) and non-Christians (25%).

Attitudes About Churches Remain the Same as 1991
In assessing the shifts that have occurred since 1991, it is disappointing to discover almost no real change in attitudes about local churches. In the months that intervened between the 1991 and 1994 studies, it is estimated that more than 5,000 new Christian churches were launched and in excess of $100 billion was spent on domestic ministry by American churches.

One of the most visible signs of change in churches was the dramatic acceptance of more contemporary and accessible "praise and worship" music in church services, either replacing or supplementing the traditional hymns and other forms of music that have been used in churches for centuries.[1] During that same time period, we found a small increase in the proportions of busters and builders who strongly agreed that their local churches were relevant, but no change whatsoever among either boomers (for whom most contextual changes in churches were made!) or seniors.

Also of interest was the revelation that the people most likely to have responded more favorably to the changing tenor of the church these days were believers. Between 1991 and 1994, a seven percentage point increase occurred in the proportion of believers who strongly agreed that the Christian churches in their area were relevant to today's people. Concurrently, a four-point increase occurred in such sentiment among nonbelievers.

Sign Me Up

Membership in any kind of organization or communal gathering—from book clubs to zoos to churches to families—has not been looked upon with great favor by boomers or busters. Concerned that "joining" any group would limit their options, most of the adults under 50 have steadfastly ignored organizations that require membership—unless the benefits so far outweighed the potential restrictions that they could easily justify breaking their own rule of abstaining from membership in anything.

Church membership carries with it both negative and positive baggage in people's minds. Overall, half of the adults interviewed said they strongly agreed that being a church member is important, another one-quarter agreed somewhat. The people most likely to affirm the importance of joining a church were women, people over 50, lower-income people, people who had not attended college, nonwhites, evangelicals and born-again Christians.

What emerges, then, is a picture of the people who are relatively downscale or who are already most active in the church, promoting the importance of church membership. These are important segments to reach and to integrate into the fabric of the community of faith. However, this profile reflects a rather unbalanced representation of the people who are part of a church, or who have an interest in experiencing the benefits available through church involvement.

Searching for Souls and Sawbucks

One of the common stereotypes about churches is that they are more interested in a person's financial support of the church than they are in the person's spiritual well-being.

The survey data lend only moderate support to this axiom. We discovered that half of all adults (49%) agreed that "most churches are more interested in raising money than in helping people." The profile of those who were most likely to have this view included older adults (57% of those 48 or older), perhaps because they are treated by many churches as the resident wealth holders and represent the financial core of the congregation. Other segments disproportionately likely to agree that churches are money hungry included the least affluent, the least well-educated and blacks (73%!).

Amazingly, non-Christians were no more likely than born-again Christians to express the feeling that churches place money over service. It is also fascinating to notice that although baby busters are not avid enthusiasts of the Christian faith or its churches, they were the generation least likely to criticize churches for their financial focus: two-thirds disagreed that most churches emphasize money instead of outreach.

Worship in the Church

As noted in chapter 3, the focal point of most church activity is the weekend worship service. This high-profile event receives the lion's share of the typical church's budget, staff time, physical space and emotional energy. It is also the activity that draws the largest number of people.

We discovered that two out of every three churched adults claim they are very satisfied with their ability to worship God at their primary church. In fact, 95% of all churched people said they were either very or somewhat satisfied with the worship capacity at their church.

The survey did, however, raise several significant red flags.

Is Worship Really Satisfying?

The first warning signal had to do with people's understanding of "worship." When we asked people to define the meaning of worship for us, we learned that 36% provided a reasonable assessment of what worship means; 25% provided answers that were too generic to evaluate; and 39% offered explanations that were clearly erroneous. Thus, a substantial proportion of the worship population—perhaps even a majority of it—appears to be unclear about what it is they venture to the church to accomplish each weekend. This ambiguity, in turn, calls into question the value or validity of having satisfied people's expectations regarding a worship experience.

Second, recognize that the question was only asked among people who currently attend church services on a regular basis. Many of the people most likely to harbor dissatisfaction with the worship experience would therefore be excluded from the sample, assuming that they may have stopped attending churches (at least partially) because their need to worship was not adequately met.

Third, the data point out that there are substantial differences in perspective depending upon the denominational affiliation of the respondent. People associated with Catholic and mainline Protestant churches were the least satisfied with their worship experiences. People attending independent evangelical, charismatic and Baptist churches were notably more pleased with their worship experiences.

A Great Report Card

When people who attend churches were asked to rate the worship experience at their church, using any of 13 suggested adjectives that seemed appropriate, the evaluation was overwhelmingly favorable. Better than three out of every four adults selected the terms inspiring (92%), refreshing (90%), Spirit-filled (85%), participatory (82%) and tradition-al (78%).[2] A majority also selected the terms modern or contemporary (70%), challenging (67%) and life transforming (58%).

Five adjectives that were not so complimentary were posed to peo-ple, and small proportions chose each of those to describe their church worship experience. Fewer than one out of every seven adults said their services were outdated, just a performance or boring. Fewer than 1 out of 10 called their church's worship time disappointing or embarrassing.

Christians and non-Christians who regularly attend worship services displayed a great number of differences in their evaluations of church worship services. The following chart indicates that believers invariably had a more positive perspective about the worship experience.

| | Born Again? | |
Attribute	Yes	No
Inspiring	97%	88%*
Refreshing	95	85*
Spirit-filled	92	79*
Participatory	85	79
Traditional	79	77
Modern or contemporary	65	75*
Challenging	77	57*
Life transforming	70	48*
Outdated	7	19*
Just a performance	8	17
Boring	6	18*
Disappointing	5	9
Embarrassing	3	4
Sample size	161	180

(* indicates a statistically significant difference between the born-again and non-born again respondents.)

One of the more tantalizing tidbits in this chart pertains to the expression "life transforming." Given that nonbelievers had never made a commitment to Christ that resulted in their belief in grace as

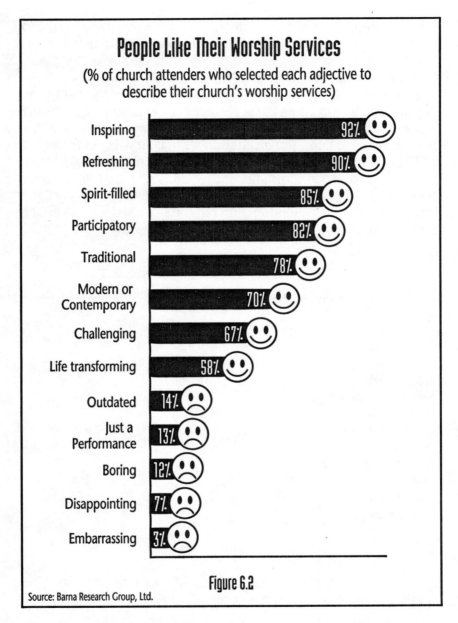

People Like Their Worship Services

(% of church attenders who selected each adjective to describe their church's worship services)

Inspiring — 92%
Refreshing — 90%
Spirit-filled — 85%
Participatory — 82%
Traditional — 78%
Modern or Contemporary — 70%
Challenging — 67%
Life transforming — 58%
Outdated — 14%
Just a Performance — 13%
Boring — 12%
Disappointing — 7%
Embarrassing — 3%

Figure 6.2

Source: Barna Research Group, Ltd.

the means to eternal salvation, it is perplexing what kind of life transformation would have engulfed them in their church worship services. Naturally, people's lives can be radically influenced through a service in many ways beyond coming into a life-changing relationship with

Jesus. It would be fascinating to discover what the nature of those life transforming experiences have been for nonbelievers, and how they compare with the life-transforming experiences alluded to by the believers.

Notes
1. For more information about the changes that have taken place in the format of church services, including the introduction of contemporary Christian music, praise and worship music, live drama, video, liturgical dance and healing, see pages 94-96 of *Today's Pastors*, George Barna (Ventura, CA: Regal Books, 1993).
2. In retrospect, it seems plausible that many of the survey respondents heard the term "Spirit-filled" over the telephone line and interpreted the phrase to mean "full of energy, vigor and spirit" as opposed to "permeated by God's Holy Spirit."

Religious Beliefs

Chapter Highlights

- Two-thirds of all adults have an orthodox Judeo-Christian view of God.
- Roughly one-third of all adults (35%) are born-again Christians, based on having made a personal commitment to Christ and trusting in God's grace, rather than their own best efforts, to merit His eternal forgiveness. This is a slight decline from the levels of the past two years.
- Among those most likely to be Christians were baby boomers; among those least likely were senior citizens.
- In comparison to their proliferation in the national population, the two segments that were significantly overrepresented among the ranks of the born again were women and people from the South.
- Only 24% of the busters are born again. People usually accept Christ as their Savior before reaching the age of 18; thus, a very real possibility exists that the proportion of born-again adults will continue to decline in the future as the remainder of the emerging buster generation becomes more numerous and the generations with higher proportions of Christians start to recede.
- The proportion of adults classified as evangelicals has slipped from 12% to 9% in our July 1993 survey and to just 7% in the latest survey (January 1994).

Prevailing Trends

Given the general downward trend in religious activity, it would not be surprising to find that some of the traditional Christian standard beliefs that defined the spiritual condition of America would have deteriorated as well. In meeting with church leaders around the country, I regularly encounter some of them who challenge the validity of research about people's religious beliefs. These leaders find it hard to accept the possibility that people might change their core beliefs from time to time. One of the most difficult notions for some to embrace is that a person who is classified as a born-again Christian, or perhaps as an evangelical, might eventually be reclassified as somewhat less committed to Christ and to God's grace as the means of salvation.

Two key factors are useful to help understand how such classification changes can occur.

God, Not Surveys, Knows a Person's Relationship with Him

The first factor is to recognize that surveys do not determine a person's relationship with God; only the true nature of their hearts can determine where they stand with Him. Research, such as we perform, is merely an approximation of where people stand with God. We do not have sufficiently sensitive tools, nor the right, to judge another person's faith: that is God's prerogative, and His alone. Our measures are crude representations of what might be happening in America spiritually and are conducted to better enable us to minister effectively, efficiently and compassionately.

Many Are Dabbling in Spirituality

Second, realize that some adults are absolutely committed to serving God with every resource and opportunity they have available. But that makes them an aberration. In contrast, most Americans merely dabble in spirituality. They use it as a quick fix during crisis points, as a sedative to assuage their guilt or as a means to a worldly end.

Most adults will freely tell you, if prompted, what they believe about God, Jesus Christ, eternity, the Church and so forth. But because spiritual matters are not part of their core being, many of the religious views and spiritual perspectives people possess are susceptible to change. Sometimes it doesn't take much to precipitate that change. As new information, new life experiences and various pressures to reformulate their worldview come to pass, one consequence is a modified belief system.

Because most adults lack the big picture of how Christ and the story of life contained in the Bible fits into our lives, transitions from one faith perspective to another may have little more significance to a person than whether they finally decide to buy a Toyota, a Nissan or a Honda.

Many Changing Core Beliefs on Spiritual Perspectives

We can be thankful, though, that Americans do change their religious perspectives with some facility. Indeed, if people's religious beliefs did not change, there would be little reason to invest personal resources in evangelism, discipleship, Bible reading, worship, prayer or the practice of any of the spiritual disciplines—all of which, in some fashion, have the function of transforming us or those with whom we come in contact. If we did not demonstrate the capacity to change our spiritual perspectives, life for millions and millions of people would certainly be hopeless—and they would be helpless.

Knowing God

More than 95% of Americans profess that they believe in God or a universal force. Only two out of three Americans (67%), however, define their god as "the all-powerful, all-knowing Creator of the universe who rules the world today." Although this outcome is consistent with last year's result, it is a drop from the 73% who described God in an orthodox manner in 1992.

How else do adults define God? Ten percent called God "a state of higher consciousness"; 8% said He is the "total realization of all human potential"; 8% offered other descriptions ("everyone is God," "there are many gods," "there is no such thing as God") and 7% did not know what God means.

Our analysis of the answers provided by various population subgroups shows that the people least likely to maintain a classical Judeo-Christian view of God are men (60% see Him as the omniscient, ruling Creator), baby busters (63%), upper-income adults (58%), people in the northeast (56%) and non-Christians (54%).

Getting Straight with Jesus

As has been the case for close to a decade, two-thirds of all adults pro-

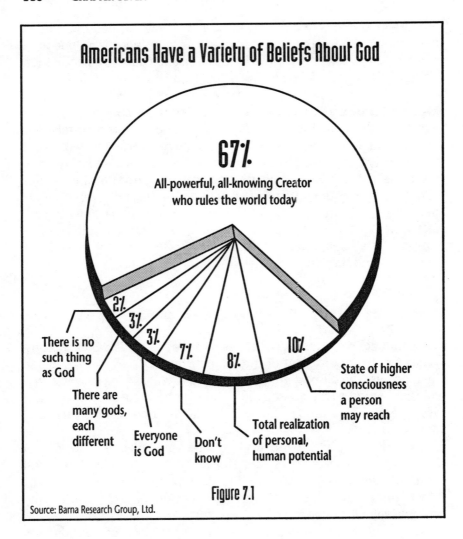

Americans Have a Variety of Beliefs About God

67%
All-powerful, all-knowing Creator
who rules the world today

2%
There is no
such thing
as God

3%
There are
many gods,
each
different

3%
Everyone
is God

7%
Don't
know

8%
Total realization
of personal,
human potential

10%
State of higher
consciousness
a person
may reach

Figure 7.1

Source: Barna Research Group, Ltd.

claim that they have made a personal commitment to Jesus Christ that is still important in their lives today. The nature of a person's commitment has many significant demographic distinctions. The chart below summarizes the primary differences.

High levels who made a commitment to Christ		Low levels who made a commitment to Christ	
Women	71%	Men	57%
Builders	71%	Baby busters	52%

High levels who made a commitment to Christ		Low levels who made a commitment to Christ	
Marrieds	69%	Singles	58%
Southerners	73%	Northeasterners	52%
Blacks	73%	Hispanics	51%
Registered voters	67%	Not registered	55%
Protestants	78%	Catholics	60%

It is also noteworthy that among the people who are not classified as born-again Christians, nearly half (44%) say they have made an important, personal commitment to Jesus Christ. Other data tell us that these people are relying upon their own good behavior and best efforts to "earn" God's favor and forgiveness, or that they believe in a universal salvation.

Among the 64% of adults who have made some kind of important, personal commitment to Christ, about half (55%) believe that when they die on earth, they will go to heaven because they have confessed their sins and have accepted Christ as their Savior. The other half of those who made a personal commitment either believe they will gain a place in heaven by their good works (16%), because God will have mercy on all people (9%), are not sure what will happen when they die (15%) or hold some other point of view (5%).

Which people groups are most, and least, likely to be born again, according to these two questions? The following chart lists the segments that stand out at each end of the scale.

High percentage of born-again Christians		Low percentage of born-again Christians	
Women	41%	Men	31%
Boomers, Builders	40%	Busters	24%
Seniors	30%	Singles	29%
Marrieds	41%	Northeasterners	24%
Southerners	50%	High school graduate or less	32%
Attended college, did not graduate	42%	Hispanics	18%
Blacks	42%	Not registered	27%
Registered voters	39%	Catholics	25%
Protestants	52%		

The surprising born-again boomers. Among the surprises emerging from the list is that boomers, of all people, are among the most likely to be Christians while senior citizens, the archetypal traditionalists around whom so much of today's church policies, structures and outlook were built, are among the least likely to know Christ in a significant way.

Born-again Catholics increasing. The data confirm that not only are many Catholics born again (one-quarter of the lot), but Catholic Christians are also slowly increasing in number. This is quite different from the pattern among Protestants, who are more likely to be Christians, but among whom there is no evidence of numerical expansion.

High percentage of women and southerners are born again. Did you notice that two groups are significantly overrepresented among the ranks of the born again, compared to their incidence in the national population? Women constitute 51% of the population, but 59% of the born-again community. In like manner, although the South is home to just 33% of the nation's adults, it is the area in which 47%—almost half—of the born-again population resides.

Independents are born again, too. An oddity pointed out by the survey is that one out of every eight born-again believers (13%) does not claim to be a Protestant or Catholic. Many of these people either classify themselves simply as "Christian" or utilize other labels, such as independent or nondenominational.

Few busters claim to be born again. But perhaps the most significant insight relates to the fact that only 24% of the busters are born again. We know that more than 7 out of every 10 believers accepted Christ as their Savior before reaching the age of 18; thus, the Church does not do well at leading people into a transforming relationship with Christ once they reach adulthood. Given the fact that so few busters are Christians, this raises the possibility that the proportion of born-again adults will continue to decline in the future as the remainder of the buster generation reaches adult status and as older adults (who were more likely to be Christian) pass away.

The Invisible Army

If you pay attention to the secular media accounts, you would be led to believe that the evangelical slice of America is a massive, cohesive, unified core of zealots poised to battle anyone who disagrees with the

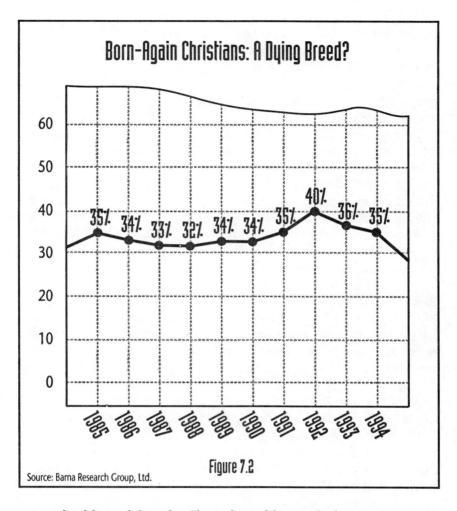

Born-Again Christians: A Dying Breed?

35% 34% 33% 32% 34% 34% 35% 40% 36% 35%

1985 1986 1987 1988 1989 1990 1991 1992 1993 1994

Figure 7.2

Source: Barna Research Group, Ltd.

evangelical line of thought. The only problem with that assessment is that none of it is accurate.

Massive? The size of the evangelical corps depends on how you define evangelicals. Using a series of questions based on how the National Association of Evangelicals defines their beliefs and perspective, we currently find only about 7% of the population could be classified as evangelicals.* That, incidentally, is a decline from 12% in 1992 and 9% in 1993.

Cohesive and unified? The evangelicals do not have a singular leader, a coalescing organization or a sense of being united for a focused, succinctly defined purpose. There is no comprehensive list of evangelicals, no machinery that effectively mobilizes them to act in unison, no issues that efficiently bring their energy to bear on those with authority and power to respond in a given manner.

In fact, as noted earlier, we cannot even find a sizeable number of people who can define who or what an evangelical is—including those whose beliefs and actions classify them as evangelicals!

Homogeneous group. One of the most powerful characteristics evangelicals have going for them, fragmented and disconnected as they may be, is that they tend to think and behave in very similar ways. This trait may suggest cohesion and unity. However, that unanimity of thought and deed is spontaneous and is largely attributable to how responsive and faithful these folks are to their religious views and convictions. Perhaps more than any of the other three dozen subgroups we have tracked in these studies, evangelicals may be the most homogeneous group we have studied, but they are not necessarily tightly knit as a result.

Beliefs of the Day

When it comes to the beliefs we study in our surveys that are used to identify evangelicals, the movement of the data suggests that we may see a continued shrinking of the ranks of evangelicals in the immediate future, short of a miraculous outpouring of God's Spirit upon the people of our land.

As outlined in Table 7.1, just 4 out of every 10 adults contend that the Bible is accurate in all that it teaches. Only one out of every four firmly rejects the notion that good people can earn their way into heaven (nearly twice as many strongly believe this is possible). Not quite one in four adults rejects the idea that Satan is merely symbolic (again, close to twice that number strongly agree that the devil is a symbolic device). About 3 out of every 10 adults say that they have a responsibility to share their religious beliefs with others, and almost 4 out of every 10 respondents vigorously rejected the thought that Christ made mistakes.

The statistics in Table 7.2 provide a sense of the movement related to these beliefs in the last three years. The trends for two of the items—the accuracy of the Bible and the personal importance of religion—are certainly pointed downward. Response to the other two items that were originally evaluated in 1991—defining Satan as a symbolic presence and having a sense of personal responsibility to share one's faith with others—have remained virtually unchanged in the four years that have elapsed since the initial *Barna Report* was published.

As the accompanying figure indicates, though, several population segments are more in line with an evangelical perspective. These segments include women, builders, married adults, parents of young children, residents of the South and blacks.

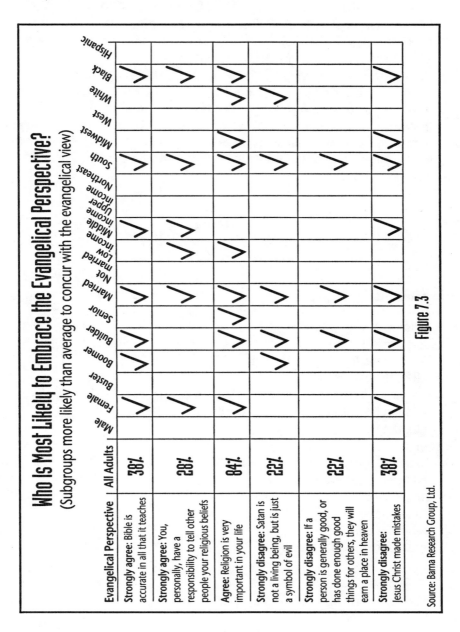

Figure 7.3

Source: Barna Research Group, Ltd.

Other Beliefs

The surveys also found that, for the most part, people claimed to be absolutely certain that in a time of crisis God could be counted on to take care of them. This was strongly admitted to by 63%, and another 22% concurred somewhat—that's more than four out of five people believing that God would take care of them when necessary. Strength of conviction was deepest on this matter among women, southerners, those with limited formal education and Christians.

To add a bit of confusion to the mix, we also uncovered the fact that most people (56%) disagreed that what you do for other people is more important than what you believe about Jesus Christ. Again, the segments that were most likely to express disagreement with this included women, married adults, the least affluent, those from the South and Midwest, and Christians.

Table 7.1
What Do Americans Believe?

Statement	Agree		Disagree	
	Strong	Some-what	Some-what	Strong
Religion is very important in your life	62	22	9	7
The Bible is totally accurate in all of its teachings	38	21	21	15
If a person is generally good, or does enough good things for others during life, they will earn a place in heaven	37	24	12	22
The devil, or Satan, is not a living being but is a symbol of evil	36	23	12	22
You, personally, have a responsibility to tell other people your religious beliefs	28	17	24	29
Jesus Christ made mistakes	12	24	15	38

Table 7.2
How Americans' Beliefs Have Changed Since 1991
(% who strongly agree)

Statement	1991	1992	1993	1994
Religion is very important in your life	59%	69%	65%	62%
The Bible is totally accurate in all of its teachings	47	56	42	38
If a person is generally good, or does enough good things for others during life, they will earn a place in heaven	—	—	39	37
The devil, or Satan, is not a living being but is a symbol of evil	35	—	—	36
You, personally, have a responsibility to tell other people your religious beliefs	28	—	31	28
Jesus Christ made mistakes	—	—	18	12

Note
* The Statement of Faith of the National Association of Evangelicals states:
    1.   We believe the Bible to be the inspired, the only infallible, authoritative Word of God.
    2.   We believe that there is one God, eternally existent in three persons: Father, Son and Holy Spirit.
    3.   We believe in the deity of our Lord Jesus Christ, in His virgin birth, in His sinless life, in His miracles, in His vicarious and atoning death through His shed blood, in His bodily resurrection, in His ascension to the right hand of the Father, and in His personal return in power and glory.
    4.   We believe that for the salvation of lost and sinful man, regeneration by the Holy Spirit is absolutely essential.
    5.   We believe in the present ministry of the Holy Spirit by whose indwelling the Christian is enabled to live a godly life.
    6.   We believe in the resurrection of both the saved and the lost; they that are saved unto the resurrection of life and they that are lost unto the resurrection of damnation.
    7.   We believe in the spiritual unity of believers in our Lord Jesus Christ.

Creating the Future

Chapter Highlights

- When asked to take a stand on a variety of public policy matters, we discovered that a majority support voluntary prayer in public schools, limits on the sale of information about people's background and buying habits, and euthanasia. People generally opposed efforts to outlaw pornography, simplify divorce proceedings, legalize homosexual marriages and sentence abortion doctors to prison for committing murder. People were evenly divided on the prospect of fining households if they did not recycle all recyclable materials.

- When asked to choose among various policy options on other high-profile public issues, the people's will showed favor for abortion under limited, specified conditions; allowing public schools to teach sex education, without promoting abstinence as the most appropriate strategy; prohibiting children under 18 from moving out of their parents' home to live independently, at the discretion of the child; introducing a mandatory death penalty for those who commit premeditated murder; and permitting doctors to assist in euthanasia.

- Evangelicals consistently stood out as being at odds with the general mood of the public on many of the issues examined.

Prevailing Trends

Government by the people, for the people. Many debate whether we have a democracy in which this is what truly happens. Some argue that, even though we have the form of democracy, we are at the mercy of a lumbering bureaucracy that has taken on a life of its own. Others contend that we have a government that caters to the desires of those with the financial means to bully their way through the policy labyrinth.

Most people have little confidence in the government and its representatives. What would happen if we had a system in which the majority opinion truly dictated government policy? To some, this is a freeing concept, representing a means to true self-determination. To others, this is a tragedy waiting to happen, a nightmarish mistake that would wreak havoc on the entire society. Apart from the logistics of how to implement such a system, if this approach to policy-making were unleashed, what kinds of legislation and laws would we see put in place?

Prayer in Schools

Many leaders might be surprised by some of the choices the people would lean toward. For instance, the matter of school prayer is not much of a struggle to most people. Nearly 9 out of 10 adults (87%) said they would favor allowing prayer in public schools, as long as it is done on a voluntary basis. At least 4 out of 5 adults from every one of the three dozen subgroups we analyzed favored this approach to prayer in public schools. (Table 8.1 outlines people's responses to each of the issues alluded to in this section.)

Keeping Things Private

Although the level of agreement was not quite as substantial, two-thirds of all adults (68%) indicated that they favored outlawing the distribution of information about themselves and the products they purchase without obtaining the person's permission to distribute that information. This would have extraordinary repercussions for the $200 billion direct-marketing industry, whose lifeblood is the trail of information acquired from a wide range of sources concerning people's demographics, lifestyle preferences and product purchase patterns.

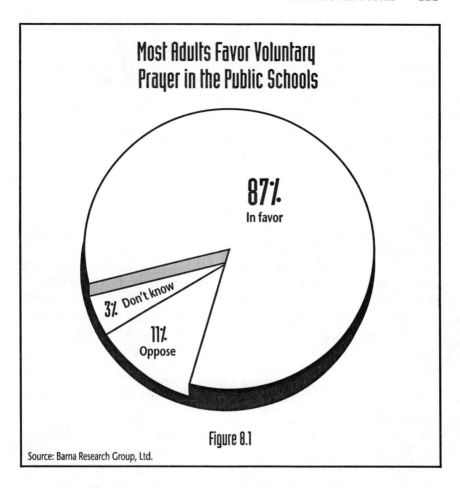

Most Adults Favor Voluntary Prayer in the Public Schools

87% In favor

3% Don't know

11% Oppose

Figure 8.1

Source: Barna Research Group, Ltd.

Nevertheless, the recent escalation of concerns about personal privacy has made information a commodity that millions of people want to have regulated. Incredibly, the very people whose ideas and behavior both created and continue to fuel direct marketing—baby boomers—are those most zealous in the desire to regulate the marketing information industry.

Legal Suicide?

The majority of adults also desire legalizing euthanasia, described for respondents as allowing adults to "end their lives through the use of special drugs if they are physically impaired or suffering." Nearly 6 out of 10 adults supported such a practice. Although a majority of most subgroups favored such a policy, those who defected from the majority included blacks (55% of whom opposed such a policy), Protestants (who were evenly split on this matter), evangelicals (two-thirds of whom protested this possibility) and born-again Christians (among whom a 49% plurality prevailed).

Save the Planet

Quick, stash your trash, it's the garbage police! That was the reaction of half the public when asked if they would support a policy of fining people who fail to recycle materials that could be recycled. In total, 48% favored such an approach and 49% opposed it. True to expectations, the older the people, the less likely they were to favor this requirement. However, even a surprisingly small proportion of the baby busters (56%), the generation widely regarded as having revived environmental concern in recent years, favored such a legislated approach to recycling.

Permitting Pornography

One of the most unexpected and inexplicable outcomes from our surveys was the majority of adults rejecting legislation that would outlaw the distribution of "sexually explicit or pornographic" movies and magazines. Despite substantial documentation indicating that pornography has no socially redeeming value, millions of adults apparently view this as an issue of free speech and censorship and would prefer to risk moral decay and physical abuse than hinder anyone's "right" to communicate any images they desire.

The distribution of pornography was one of the issues that stirred the greatest disharmony across subgroups. For instance, while men opposed such a policy by a 56% to 38% ratio, women favored it by a 49% to 45% outcome. Boomers and busters had nearly identical views (a cumulative 56% opposed such a policy, 38% approved of it), while two-thirds of those in the 48 to 66 age range preferred to prohibit pornography (63% versus 32%).

A majority of born-again Christians favored the policy of outlawing the distribution of pornography (54%) while a majority of non-

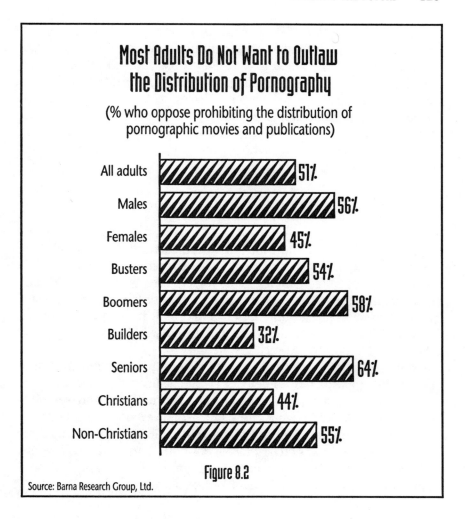

Most Adults Do Not Want to Outlaw the Distribution of Pornography

(% who oppose prohibiting the distribution of pornographic movies and publications)

All adults	51%
Males	56%
Females	45%
Busters	54%
Boomers	58%
Builders	32%
Seniors	64%
Christians	44%
Non-Christians	55%

Figure 8.2

Source: Barna Research Group, Ltd.

Christians opposed it (55%). Perhaps the least expected result was noting that among parents of children under the age of 18, 50% opposed such a policy while 45% supported it. This distribution was no different from that among adults who did not have young children in their homes.

Passing the Buck

An issue that did not generate a majority reaction one way or another concerned raising taxes of businesses to pay for the federal government's deficit. In total, 49% opposed such a move, while 44% accepted it. This issue, too, generated many contrasts among subgroups. Men opposed it; women favored it. Married people opposed it; singles preferred it. Parents of young children supported the concept, but adults without young kids in their homes rejected it. Lower-income respondents liked the idea; upper-income people were among its biggest detractors. Among the four regions, only those in the northeast favored passage of such legislation. Whites generally dismissed the notion, but blacks and Hispanics liked it.

Expediting Divorce

In past studies, we found that most people said they would like the approval of divorce to be more difficult. That may be where people's hearts are, but when it comes to the nuts and bolts of divorce, a large minority of people (42%) actually sided with a system in which divorce would be made quicker and easier to accomplish, by filing notarized papers, rather than working through the courts. A slim majority (51%) stated their opposition to such a system.

The most notable discrepancies by subgroups were that men supported the proposal, but women didn't; people under 50 liked it, people over 50 vehemently rejected it; residents of the northeast and west gave the idea their blessing, while those in the Midwest and the South were significantly opposed. For every evangelical Christian who voted for this option, five registered their opposition. Born-again Christians rejected the notion by a two-to-one margin; a slight plurality of non-Christians (48% versus 43%) favored such a system.

Unisex Weddings

Another marriage proposal dealt with legalizing marriage between homosexual adults. By a two-to-one ratio (62% to 29%), adults defeated this alternative. The younger the respondents, the more likely they were to support the idea: 42% of the busters saw this as an acceptable strategy, compared to just 11% of senior citizens. Once again, faith commitment influenced the person's views on this issue. While more than one-third of the nonbelievers (35%) sided with the right of gays to marry each other, only half as many born-again Christians shared that

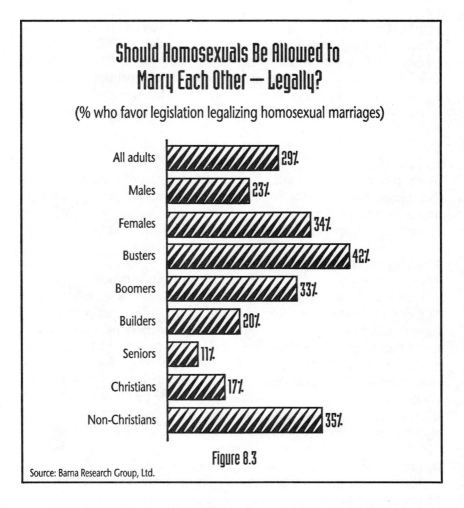

Should Homosexuals Be Allowed to Marry Each Other — Legally?

(% who favor legislation legalizing homosexual marriages)

All adults	29%
Males	23%
Females	34%
Busters	42%
Boomers	33%
Builders	20%
Seniors	11%
Christians	17%
Non-Christians	35%

Figure 8.3

Source: Barna Research Group, Ltd.

viewpoint (17%), and only 3% of the evangelicals supported the notion of homosexual marriages.

The Plight of Abortion Doctors

Although people's views on abortion may well be confused at the moment, there was little indecision about how they would like the doctors who perform abortions to be treated. About 7 out of every 10 adults (68%) said abortion doctors should not be sentenced to prison for murder. One out of every four adults (26%) said they would support such legislation. The only subgroups from which more than one-third supported a prison penalty were Hispanics (54%), Catholics (36%), born-again Christians (36%) and evangelicals (57%). Notice that even within the born-again community a tremendous division exists between those who are evangelicals and those who are born again but not evangelical.

Rewriting the Rules

In our January 1994 survey, which comprised part of the database for this report, we approached a half dozen social issues and policy permutations from a different angle. Many of these issues stirred the juices of the public. Consider some of the stands people take on these matters.

The Legal Parameters for Abortion
Abortion has been a high-profile issue for nearly two decades. Last year's research discovered that three out of every five adults believed that the issue gets more attention than is merited.[1] Other research we have conducted on the matter suggests that most adults have heard a lot of the discussion but still have not determined what they believe about abortion, other than that they would not have one.

Currently, nearly half of the public (49%) believes that abortions should be legal only under limited, specified circumstances. Three out of every 10 people say abortion should be legal under any circumstances, the choice being left to the individual. One out of every six people are at the other end of the continuum, suggesting that abortion be prohibited regardless of the circumstances.

The legalization thrust gets its greatest intensity of support from residents of the northeast (where 42%, a plurality, support unrestricted abortion legalization). The movement to ban all abortions is most fervently supported by evangelicals (35%). Among evangelicals, just 3% favor unrestricted legalization; among non-Christians, 37% favor such a policy.

Teaching Kids About Sex
A related topic is sex education and how public schools handle adolescent sexuality. Our survey pointed out two key outcomes. First, three-quarters of all adults believe that public schools should be teaching sex education to students; only 18% contend that sex education is the sole responsibility of the parents; 6% don't know what to make of the issue.

Evangelicals Are at Odds with Non-Christians on Many Public Policy Issues

In favor of

Opposed to

Issue	Evangelicals	Non-Christians	Evangelicals	Non-Christians
Euthanasia	28%	66%	68%	24%
Pornography	59%	38%	40%	55%
Notarized divorce	16%	48%	78%	43%
Gay marriage	3%	35%	97%	52%
Imprison abortion doctors	57%	20%	37%	74%
Legalize all abortions	3%	37%	92%	59%
Make all casinos illegal	54%	8%	39%	82%

Figure 8.4

Source: Barna Research Group, Ltd.

Second, in the matter of how to address sexuality, widespread disagreement prevailed over the best strategy. Three out of 10 adults (28%) said schools should teach sex education but promote sexual abstinence as the proper behavior. The same proportion went in a different direction, exhorting the schools to not only teach sex education, but also to make birth-control devices available to students who request them.

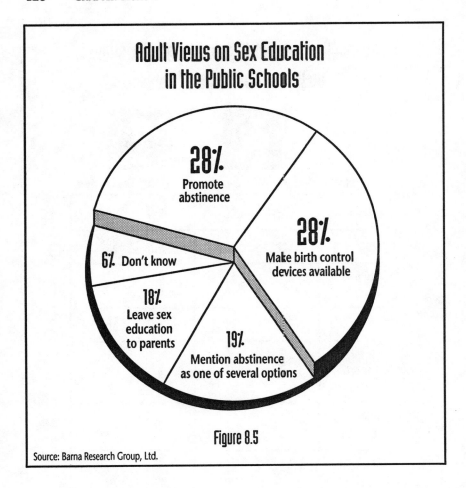

Adult Views on Sex Education in the Public Schools

28%
Promote abstinence

28%
Make birth control devices available

6% Don't know

18%
Leave sex education to parents

19%
Mention abstinence as one of several options

Figure 8.5

Source: Barna Research Group, Ltd.

A third option, chosen by one out of every five parents, was for schools to teach sex education and include sexual abstinence among the options available to youths. Overall, notice that nearly half of the adults interviewed indicated that while it is permissible to mention abstinence as a possibility, it should not be promoted as the most appropriate strategy for sexual relations.

Leaving "sex ed" to parents was twice as popular among those 50 or older (28%) as among younger adults (14%). Evangelicals also had a very different response profile than any other subgroup: 58% supported sex education that promoted abstinence, 35% preferred leaving all sex education activity up to the parents, and only 6% had some other opinion. No other segment we studied had nearly the same degree of internal consensus on this issue. Non-Christians were substantially different from Christians on this matter, too. Two-thirds of the born-again contingent selected parental responsibility or promoting abstinence, whereas only half as many nonbelievers chose those routes. The preference in the eyes of non-Christians was teaching sex education and making birth-control devices available to students (35%).

Freedom from Family

What about the notion of children under the age of 18 moving out of their parents' home and living independently, as is permitted (with government assistance!) in several other nations? Few Americans see the wisdom in this idea. Two-thirds said this should be permitted only if there is proof that the child is suffering from neglect or physical abuse. One out of every 10 adults was fully supportive of youthful independence, while a similar proportion (12%) said separating the child from the family should not be permitted under any circumstances.

One interesting aside on this matter is that blacks and Hispanics were twice as likely as whites to say adolescent independence should be permitted under any circumstances. One hypothesis to explain this outcome is that the family friction and emotional abuse that occurs within a comparatively large proportion of black and Hispanic families has led many people from these ethnic communities—especially younger adults—to condone restructuring lifestyles and family responsibilities.

Taking Offense at Offenders

Crime has risen to the top of the issues heap to become a major political hot potato in the past two years. This is not surprising. Government statistics show that crime rates have risen by more than 500% in the past two decades.[2] Our research prior to President Clinton's election and subsequent public discussions about crime showed that not only do people believe crime is getting more prolific, but also that the fear of becoming a victim of crime changes people's daily activities and habits.[3]

How are people reacting to the lawlessness that fills our streets? Nearly half of all adults (47%) said they would like the death penalty to be mandatory for anyone who commits premeditated murder. Twenty percent preferred mandating lengthy prison terms with no possibility of parole. The remaining one-quarter said the decision should be left to the jury. One unexpected result was that evangelicals were the group most likely to propose leaving the penalty in the hands of the jury: 43% preferred that approach, nearly double the national average.

The Right to Die

The issue of euthanasia has hit headlines sporadically over the last few years, thanks to the efforts of Dr. Jack Kevorkian (known by some as "Dr. Death"), who has assisted a number of people in expediting their death. As with abortion, this is an issue on which people have weakly held opinions.

A plurality of adults sided with Dr. Kevorkian: 30% said they felt a doctor should be allowed to painlessly end a patient's life if the person has an incurable disease and requests such assistance. Not quite as many (23%) said the doctor should be given such a license only if the patient and the patient's immediate family concur that a "mercy killing" is appropriate. A similar proportion (22%) felt that there are no circumstances under which a person should be allowed to end his or her life, regardless of the situation. One out of every six adults (17%) took the opposite extreme and said people should be permitted to end their lives at their own discretion, by any means they desire.

Evangelicals were more than twice as likely as other adults to contend that people should never be allowed to end their lives; born-again Christians were twice as likely as nonbelievers to select this as the most viable option.

Place Your Bets

Gambling has been a public issue for years. The recent softening of regulations pertaining to the establishment of casinos in various parts of the nation has raised the issue to a higher profile. In total, 36% of the public would like to see the continued expansion of gambling opportunities by making the establishment of casinos legal in all parts of the country. A similar proportion (39%) believe enough casinos are already in existence. They believe that the existing casinos should be allowed to remain, but no new casinos permitted to open. A small percentage of adults (14%) would like to see all gambling, including the existing casinos, outlawed. This latter philosophy is supported by half of all evangelicals but just 5% of all Catholics.

Table 8.1
How People Feel About Potential Legislation
(N=601)

Description of legislation	Favor	Oppose	Don't Know
Prayer would be allowed in public schools on a voluntary basis	87	11	3
Businesses would be prohibited from selling or distributing any information about you or the products you buy without having your permission to do so	68	28	4
Adults could choose to end their lives through the use of special drugs if they are suffering or physically impaired	58	33	9
Households would be fined if they did not recycle all recyclable materials	48	49	4
Magazines and movies that contain sexually explicit or pornographic pictures would be illegal to distribute	44	51	5
Taxes on businesses would be raised to help lower the federal budget deficit	44	49	7
Married couples could get divorced without going through the courts by filing notarized papers to show their desire to do so	42	51	8
Homosexual adults would be able to get married to each other	29	62	10
Doctors who perform an abortion would be sentenced to prison for murder	26	68	6

Table 8.2
Policy Choices that People Favor
(N=602)

Policy alternatives	Support
Abortions would be:	
legal only under certain circumstances	49%
legal under any circumstances	29%
illegal under all circumstances	17%
Public schools should:	
teach sex education, make birth control devices available	28%
teach sex education, promote abstinence	28%
teach sex education, mention abstinence as an option	19%
leave sex education to parents, not make any birth control devices available	18%
Children under 18 who want to live apart from their parents should:	
be allowed to only if neglect or abuse can be proven	68%
not be allowed under any circumstances	12%
be allowed to, under any circumstances	10%
For those who commit premeditated murder, the government should:	
make the death penalty mandatory	47%
leave the penalty up to the jury	25%
make long sentences without parole mandatory	20%
For people with incurable, life-ending diseases: doctors should be allowed to end the person's life if the patient requests it	30%
doctors should be allowed to end the person's life if the patient and family request it	23%
under no circumstances should the person's life be ended	22%
the person should be allowed to end their life by any means they choose	17%

Legalized gambling, in casinos, should:

be legal where they already exist, but no new casinos allowed	39%
be legal in all parts of the United States	36%
be made illegal, even in places where they currently exist	14%

Notes

1. George Barna, *The Barna Report, Absolute Confusion* (Ventura, CA: Regal Books, 1993).
2. William Bennett, *The Index of Leading Cultural Indicators* (New York: Simon & Schuster, 1994).
3. George Barna, *The Barna Report, America Renews Its Search for God* (Ventura, CA: Regal Books, 1992).

Section III

What It Means

So far, we have explored how we live these days and the thought processes behind those lifestyles. Now, as a wrap-up to our journey, let's pursue two final paths of study: some of the implications and the insights we may derive from these patterns of thought and deed, and what we might anticipate happening in the future.

These reflections are of paramount significance because they should move us beyond mere understanding to a point of confident and effective response to our current conditions. As a minister of God's Word, whatever form that ministry may take, yours should be an intelligent and strategic response to the challenges and opportunities that await your influence. Just as each of us is called to be a good steward of the financial resources God has entrusted to us, so must we be superb stewards of the information resources we have been given in order to maximize our influence for God's glory.

Perhaps your analysis of some of the data and conditions described in the preceding pages will differ from the perspective you will read in the pages that follow. That is not only feasible, but it is also both valuable and to be expected. Only you can know how to interpret such information, considering the unique context for ministry in which you operate. I encourage you to reflect on the data in this book carefully, to pray incessantly and then to respond with courage and creativity in light of how God has prepared you to serve Him and His people at this moment in history.

What We Can Expect in the Future

I'm not big on prognostication. During my company's decade of serving churches, parachurches and other organizations by conducting research and drawing conclusions regarding strategic decision making, we have shied away from long-term predictions and forecasts because we know that most measures of people's future behavior are unreliable indicators of what is coming. The predictions we have made, in books or reports, have generally come to pass; but part of the reason is that we made relatively few predictions, and have restricted those to the areas about which we knew the most and, thus, felt comfortable hypothesizing future scenarios.

Given the breadth of research we conduct every year, and the depth of information we have analyzed over the last decade, we have developed a sense of where things may be heading. Anticipating the future, rather than simply being steamrollered by it, is one of the trademarks of successful and influential organizations. Because the pace of life is moving quickly and life has become so complex, preparing for various conditions is a key strategic approach to having influence. This philosophy has proven to be vital for every kind of organization, whether they are for profit or not for profit.

In the desire to facilitate some strategic decision making among those who wish to be leading the nation, rather than frantically chasing it, let me propose the following short list of likely future behaviors and outcomes. But let me precede this brief list with two caveats.

Caveat number one is that you can never really *know* the future, you can only estimate what may happen. Such predictions are based on an unscientific mixture of current conditions and facts, assumptions, historical patterns and instinct. As such, developing predictions is always an art, not a science. Over the long run, although a handful of predictions may hit the bull's-eye, most of them will reflect a mixture of accuracy and inaccuracy. At best, predictions about the future should act as general guidelines that need to be monitored carefully. Predictions are best used as directional guides rather than detailed notions of coming history.

The second caveat is that the mere fact of predicting the future may have the effect of changing people's lives in ways that thereby alter the veracity of the predictions. Paradoxical as it may seem, it is this reality that explains my motivation for taking a risk and offering a few predictions for your consideration.

Personally, I am both distraught and enraged by the direction our nation is moving. If you are alarmed by what seems to be unfolding, you may either lie down and accept it as unavoidable, or you may rise up and devote yourself to influencing the direction of our culture. If you wish to do the latter, it is my desire to prime your pump with a few notions of what might be most likely to happen unless you and others step in and redirect the path of our nation.

Here, then, are some of the things I anticipate happening between now and the end of the century in the areas of personal relationships, morality and perspectives, cultural development, and spirituality and religious behavior.

Relationships

1. Before the end of the decade, America will experience another spate of racial-tinged riots, predominantly in major urban centers such as Los Angeles, Miami, New York, Chicago, Seattle and San Francisco.
2. People will become increasingly lonely and isolated as technology develops, as the movement to have people work from their homes expands, as businesses downsize and more people work on their own or for minicompanies, as fear of crime restructures the nature of people's interactions with others, as communication skills deteriorate, and as families become more fluid and less per-

manent. Among the effects will be a higher suicide rate among adults, increased physical assaults, a series of short-lived fads geared to facilitating relationships, increased numbers of divorced people remarrying, heightened acceptance of cohabitation, the birth of resentment toward technology and a greater emphasis within churches on building community.

Morals and Truth

1. America's moral decline will continue, amidst feeble attempts to legislate acceptable behavior. Busters and boomers will lead the charge, as political correctness evolves into a spiritual and moral correctness movement. Busters, in particular, will be frustrated over the lack of predictable and consistent values embraced by their generation.
2. The big game in the middle and late '90s will be "passing the blame," in which people will seek the ultimate culprit who can be blamed for the moral decadence that nobody seems to want, but everybody seems to accept.
3. More and more discussion will ensue regarding the meaning of life and purpose for living. However, without the recognition of basic biblical principles as nonnegotiable truth, people will experience a "dead end" in their quest to discover substantive answers.

Cultural Integrity

1. The values and beliefs that have been the underpinning of American culture will cease to be transmitted effectively by the written word, but will instead become part of the new communications strategy—a video tradition, rather than an oral or written tradition. As functional literacy declines, you will see schools, government, business and other institutions relying more heavily upon interactive media and traditional video media (e.g., TV, videocassettes, laser disks) to convey the crux of our culture to

young people. Expect much to get lost in the translation.

2. The Hispanic population, in particular, will go through huge upheavals in the battle for cultural identity. Hispanic adults, teens and adolescents will go through a major period of experimentation, exploring a variety of faiths, lifestyles and values as they strive to clarify their identity in America.

3. Inconsistencies in thoughts and actions will abound. Among them: proclaimed reverence for the family in spite of continued divorce, cohabitation, adultery and births outside of marriage; despair over the pace of life and the diminished joy it brings, in spite of the acceptance of and reliance upon technology as the means to "success" and "happiness"; continued interest in religion, despite declining involvement in church life and personal ministry.

4. Levels of confidence in major social institutions will regularly shift, depending on the performance of those institutions. Rather than having confidence in the people and values of these entities, adults will place their confidence in those organizations that have recently proven to be worthy of such confidence. There will be little trust, however, in the character of these organizations, only in their ability or inability to perform prescribed duties in a given manner.

5. Our educational system will remain in confusion as we become increasing inundated by factual data and infatuated with passing along trivia to students. Consequently, we will operate with greater knowledge but transmit less wisdom.

Religion

1. The groups responsible for the most rapid growth in new Christians, among adults, will be the Hispanic and the Catholic communities.

2. Closer ties and cooperation will develop between Protestant and Catholic churches as denominationalism dies, busters become a larger part of the adult population, the Catholic church experiences an exodus of Hispanics and increasing numbers of Catholics become evangelical.

3. The aggregate proportion of adults who are born-again Christians will slowly decrease.

4. Baby busters will be the generation least likely to accept Christ as their Savior.

5. Donations to churches will decline, although charitable donations, in general, will increase.

6. Involvement in church-based small groups (i.e., 10 or fewer people meeting regularly, not including Sunday School classes, for some form of intentional spiritual development) will rebound somewhat, though not reaching the lofty attendance levels of the late '80s and early '90s.

7. Evangelicals will become increasingly isolated and disenfranchised from the mainstream culture because of their adherence to absolutes, the intensity with which they maintain attitudes commonly rejected by the rest of society and their image as being judgmental.

8. Hispanic adults will divide in one of three ways religiously: Some will retain their traditional tie to the Catholic Church, some will transition to Protestant churches and some will abandon organized religion altogether. The biggest loser will be the Catholic Church; the biggest winner will be agnosticism.

9. America's search for God will continue at full speed. This will result in a restructuring of the American Protestant Church, as a new form of church growth (based on basic marketing principles) emerges to try to reach people with an uncompromised gospel presented in a contextualized manner.

10. New strategies for evangelism will be developed that reflect an understanding of the idiosyncrasies of various people groups. However, fewer Christians will be actively involved in sharing the fundamentals of their faith with nonbelievers—a result of society's promotion of privacy in matters of religious faith, along with the inability of increasing numbers of Christians to adequately explain or defend the foundations of their faith.

The Big Picture

By themselves, the thousands of bits of data, and the tens of thousands of individual answers we have reflected upon thus far may seem disjointed. Unless we step back and seek a view of the big picture—that is, the portrait of our cultural landscape that is created when all of these tiny fragments are properly positioned and pieced together—conducting such research may seem like an exercise in data collection for its own sake. To be faithful stewards of our time and resources, we must devote ourselves to scrutinizing not just the individual, detailed fragments of our collective behavior and perspective, but also to evaluating the aggregate condition of our society in order to strategically affect it for God's glory.

When Absolutes Are Absent

One of the clear insights that emerges from this study is that Americans are continuing to adjust their thinking and their behavioral patterns to foster the creation of a new pattern of criteria for judging value in life. Our lives are shaped by the truths, values and principles we adopt, which then serve as the filter through which critical life decisions are made. Our filter helps us determine right from wrong, success from failure, good fortune from bad, excitement from boredom, meaning from fluff. Whenever the components of the filter are altered or restructured, so is our view of the world and our reactions to ideas and circumstances.

The survey data suggest that Americans are still exploring the value of new concepts and principles that might yet be encompassed in our evolving criteria for determining meaning, purpose and value in our lives. This search is still in place—and will continue for some time to come—because the majority have either lost or never really grasped a satisfying answer to the reason for living, and have never truly understood God's view of purpose and futility. This enduring quest for a solid, workable, productive values system and life philosophy will undoubtedly remain alive well into the opening years of the next century.

One of the cornerstones of the current perspective embraced by most people—a core criterion—is that no one has the right to impose their standards upon anyone else. When you determine a standard that fits your life, it is useful to you; but it is not considered a transferable or universal standard to which everyone else must also measure up.

Let me make three observations regarding the standards and perspectives we embrace.

First, we expect more of others than we allow them to demand of us. We set our expectations of others quite high, and see no inconsistency in relaxing the level for ourselves.

Second, we respond to opportunities in life on the basis of what works best for us, at the moment, without reference to the impact of our decision upon others or upon our own long-term future.

Third, the future we are striving to attain has no real parameters and no nonnegotiable elements. Because we have no absolute standards we feel we must conform to, achieving satisfaction in life will be easier to reach. But satisfaction in life will never be felt as intensely as might have been experienced if our expectations were more deeply anchored and tied to a comprehensive and heartfelt sense of life purpose.

What does a life journey based on relativism look like in practice?

- What a person does, or how an assigned task is performed, whether on the job or in a relationship, is immune to the judgment of others because nobody else has the definitive understanding of the person's momentary goals, standards and motivations.
- When a person lodges complaints about others, that person cannot be satisfied until his or her viewpoint is wholly accepted. Those who receive the wrath of the person can never have a viable defense, because the complainer is, in his or her own view, the sole dictator of what is acceptable and what is not. The complainer is the only one who can grasp what was expected and why the efforts of others fell short.

- Few can accurately and consistently predict how the public will respond to a given product, service or experience because nobody can consistently and precisely understand the ever-changing swirl of emotions, perspectives and needs that reshape public sentiment from moment to moment.
- Employers cannot win in discussions over employee performance and conduct because the employee works for different reasons and operates with disparate expectations. Employees will remain impervious to both complaints and commendations.
- A wife, for instance, has no grounds for complaints about her husband's indulgences in adultery or emotional abandonment because she is unable to see things from her mate's point of view, or to understand the depth of emotion that caused such actions. As a result, society will stand by its man, asserting that the woman is unjustified in rebuking her husband for behavior she would describe as immoral, disloyal, unjustified, selfish, hurtful or irreparable.
- When religious leaders castigate people for sinful behavior, such challenges are considered intellectually interesting, but considered personally irrelevant, because both parties are operating from different planes of perspective, values, circumstances and meaning. For the church to indicate that a person has sinned, becomes viewed as an abridgement of that person's rights, rather than a reasonable performance of the purpose and mandate of the body of faith.

It Ain't Me, Babe

Isn't it fascinating that most adults are willing to point the finger at American society and decry its moral decay, the insufferable perversion of the family, the immobilizing isolation of people from each other, and the distancing of people from a relational God and others who hold common beliefs and desires? In various ways, our culture has created the opportunity for people to remove themselves from the madness, excoriate others for their wicked and inappropriate behavior, and continue on with their own pathologies and corruptness, unaffected by the blatant hypocrisy of their response.

But I believe something deeper is also happening here. It is not just that we have become a nation of self-absorbed, willful, unmanageable creatures who are beyond hope. We are all that—and more! What has happened is that we have created a world that has so many alluring diversions, captivating opportunities and irresistible challenges that we have lost our focus. Because most people are not leaders, and we are a nation bereft of strong, godly leadership, we have taken to mimicking the thoughts and actions of people who hold positions of leadership but are not truly leaders.[1]

God's Standards Are Being Abandoned

If we are, to borrow a biblical analogy, sheep waiting to be shepherded, why have we experienced such a rapid and monumental fall? Because too few of the shepherds in place today have been called by God to that role, and so many who are seeking to lead have not been willing to make God's standards their standards. This is not simply a reference to the disintegration of the Church, but to our society in general. Political leaders, educational leaders, sociological leaders, business leaders, medical leaders, scientific leaders—many of these people in leadership positions have allowed themselves to be sidetracked, their foci diverted to interesting but unrighteous ends, their values corrupted by persuasive but ungodly perspectives. They have led the sheep into a deep ravine from which there may be no return.

To sedate ourselves into feeling at peace with our aberrant pursuits, we have simply redefined both our standards and our basic perceptions about reality. Divorce has become permissible, morally as well as emotionally, because family now means "all those people who I care about deeply or who deeply care about me."[2] The "traditional" definition of family is generally dismissed as anachronistic, a relic of the past called upon by those who are neither suave enough nor sufficiently in touch to possess a refined and enlightened view of the world.

Lapses of integrity are defended because lying, cheating, stealing and physical assault are simply the ways people must behave these days to get by. Personal survival is recast as a higher value than the corporate good; whatever it takes to make it through the day is justifiable. The conventional wisdom reminds us that rules, after all, are made to be broken, and structures exist to facilitate personal development and achievement. When these parameters get in the way of personal progress, those structures must simply be changed.

Involvement with a faith community, in the hope of becoming spiritually connected to God and consequently more righteous on earth, is not rejected so much as it is abandoned in light of higher, more tangible and immediately beneficial priorities. Having never truly experienced the full awesomeness of God, nor having understood how His principles could shape our lives and enhance our earthly experience, we instead substitute our own decisions for His, our own fluid standards for His permanent dictates, our own dreams and desires for His vision and plan.

Americans Are Skin Deep

In this age, we find that Americans have been seduced by breadth rather than depth, by quantity rather than quality, by style rather than substance.

It is the rare person who reads publications that require reflection; instead, the likes of *People, Sports Illustrated* and *TV Guide* dominate the newsstands. Harlequin novels and pop psychology reign at the bookstore.

Conversations about the weather and the Super Bowl are more common and more intense than those about values and meaning in life. The political "wanna-bes" who prevail are most often those who offer superficial solutions to complex social problems, those who are the most photogenic or silver tongued, and those whose background is innocuous enough that the media cannot dredge up a scandal or otherwise assassinate their character.

Partakers of All, Masters of Nothing

Besieged by offers to spend our time and mental energy in a myriad of different activities, we seek to maximize our pleasure by hurriedly experiencing as many of those alternatives as possible. We become the partakers of all, the masters of nothing. We are more impressed by a church of 4,000 people who have no clue about God's character and His expectations, than by a church of 100 deeply committed saints who are serving humankind in quiet but significant ways. Our heroes are sports figures and entertainment celebrities who have big salaries, bigger egos and often live in ways that reflect spiritual and emotional depravity and futility.

Such superficiality is made possible by the rejection of moral absolutes, the reduction of Christianity to a series of simplistic do's and don'ts, the embrace of alluring actions without consideration of the long-term consequences and the ability to formulate public policy decisions through innovative uses of technology, the media and political clout.

Without a worldview based on God's immutable and perfect laws, the chance of people developing a culture that reaches God's intended outcomes is very predictable: none. Without a permanent, growing, personal commitment to the pursuit of absolute truths and moral purity, we devolve into a morass of self-serving, unreliable isolates, to whom acquisition and achievement are more important than community, service, compassion, justice and obedience to God.

What We Need

It seems that our nation desperately needs several elements if it is to cease its moral and spiritual decline and return to vitality and health.

Leadership. Both inside and outside of the Church, America needs strong, focused, godly leaders who will model righteousness, hold the people accountable to viable standards of behavior and challenge the nation to reach higher, rather than guide it as it sinks lower. We must identify and support those people who have a righteous vision for the future, one that will not be compromised by the pressures and pleasures of the world. We need people who will sacrifice the comforts and conveniences that their abilities could provide them, in favor of experiencing the suffering, the frustrations and the injustices that come with effective, godly leadership.

Are we willing to allow God's chosen servants to take us on a journey that departs radically from the path currently being pursued by our nation and, to a considerable extent, by the Church?

Prophets. In every culture, God raises up people who provide a context for understanding the elements of decay and collapse that are in force. Because these people typically offer views that challenge the prevailing point of view, they generate hostility and receive wrath rather than gratitude. We are moving beyond the biblical reminder that a prophet has no honor in his own country, to a society in which the prophet is censored and controlled by those whose views prevail.

Who are the prophets in our society today, calling the culture to task for its decadence and foolishness? Are we esteeming them for the gift of "tough love" they bring, or do we dismiss them as part of the lunatic fringe, the out-of-touch losers or the fanatical traditionalists? Do we address the substance of their analysis, or do we dismiss them as cranks, preferring the popular analysis of modern lifestyles and thought served up in homogeneous, bite-sized pieces for us by the mass media?

The Church. No other organism is capable of restoring the soul of America to a place of life and health. But is the Church poised to attack the perversions that undermine people and organizations, and prepared to handle the overwhelming body of personal and corporate needs that exists in America today?

Probably not. But with insightful, visionary, committed pastoral leadership, working in conjunction with a cadre of zealous, purposeful, loyal laity, a revolution of the heart is conceivable. God wants to work through His people to restore all humans to true life. Unless the Church undertakes a spiritual reawakening as its primary mandate for the time remaining, we may expect to see America dissipate in the throes of societal anarchy, an agonizing national collapse unlike that of any previously witnessed on this earth.

A Church that passionately and intensively pursues the development of values, character, spirituality and godly lifestyles may yet prompt God to perform one of His greatest miracles. In that process, we may play a useful role as well. To create a society that not only recognizes God to be the King that He is, but also seeks to serve Him with purity of purpose and the fullness of joy that is reserved for His servants, we must establish firm spiritual foundations on which we may build for future growth. Without the development of such sturdy underpinnings, all the talk and programs in the world will be the same as building a house on a foundation of sand. We must restore the people to the depth of spiritual and moral character that will enable them to respond to life's challenges in ways that reflect hearts that are turned toward heaven.

Notes
1. For a discussion of how this has influenced the organized Church these days, see *Today's Pastors,* George Barna (Ventura, CA: Regal Books, 1993); *The Body,* Chuck Colson and Ellen Vaughn (Dallas, TX: WORD Inc., 1993); and *The Heart of a Great Pastor,* H. B. London Jr. and Neil B. Wiseman (Ventura, CA: Regal Books, 1994).
2. See chapter 2 of *The Future of the American Family,* George Barna (Chicago, IL: Moody Press, 1993).

Appendices

1. Definitions and Survey Methodology
2. Data Tables Directory
        July 1993 Survey Tables
        January 1994 Survey Tables
3. About the Barna Research Group, Ltd.
4. Index

Appendix I

Definitions and Survey Methodology

Definitions

As you review some of the subgroup labels used in tables and charts throughout this book, or as you examine the data tables in the final pages of this volume, you will encounter a variety of descriptions. Here is an explanation of what those labels mean.

Total Responding: The entire population of adults interviewed in the survey. They were all 18 or older. As a random sample, their responses are projectable to the aggregate national population of 192 million adults who are 18 or older.

Gender: All respondents were classified as either male or female.

Age Group: Four generations were represented in these age breaks. Those 18 to 28 are the baby busters, 29 to 47 are the baby boomers, 48 to 66 are the builders, 67 or older are seniors. For more detail on these generations, refer to the introduction.

Married: Adults currently married were in the "yes" category; those who were never married, currently divorced, currently separated or widowed were in the "no" category.

Kids Under 18: Parents of children 17 years of age or younger were included in the "yes" category. Other adults were placed in the "no" ranks.

Household Income: This was based on self-reported annual, household income before taxes were removed. We divided respondents into three general categories: those from households earning less than $25,000, those from households with incomes of $25,000 to less than $50,000, and those from households bringing in $50,000 or more.

Region: We divided the nation into 10 regions, then collapsed those into the 4 primary regions used by the Census Bureau in their demographic studies. Those regions, and the states included within each, were as follows:

Northeast: ME, VT, NH, MA, RI, CT, NY, NJ, PA, DE, MD
South: VA, WV, KY, TN, NC, SC, GA, FL, AL, LA, MS, AR, OK, TX
Midwest: OH, MI, IN, IL, IA, WI, ND, SD, MO, KS, NE, MN
West: AZ, NM, UT, CO, ID, WY, MT, NV, CA, OR, WA

Education: We used three categories: those who have gone as far as graduating from high school, those who attended college but did not graduate from college, and those who attended college and graduated. Those who attended or graduated from graduate studies are included in the "college graduate" category.

Ethnicity: By self-report, people placed themselves in one of several categories. The dominant ones were "white," "black," "Hispanic" and "Asian." Although Asians and Hispanics might technically be "white," they generally placed themselves in the category reflecting their national heritage, rather than their skin color.

Voter Registration: People who were not currently registered to vote, based on their present residence, were in the "not registered" category. Those who were registered were asked with what party they were registered—Democratic, Republican or no party (listed as "Independent").

Denominational Affiliation: Based on the denomination of the church the respondent claimed to attend most often, we placed them in either the Protestant or Catholic category.

Faith Perspective: Evangelicals, born-again Christians and non-Christians were based on responses to as many as eight questions regarding the person's religious beliefs. Nobody was categorized according to how they described their faith perspective. Evangelicals were people who said religion is important in their lives; they had made a personal commitment to Jesus Christ that is still important in their lives today; they believed that when they die they will go to heaven because they have confessed their sins and accepted Jesus Christ as their Savior; they believed that God is the all-powerful, all-knowing Creator of the universe who rules the world today; they rejected the notion that if a person is good enough, or does enough good things during life, they will earn a place in heaven; they believed that the Bible is accurate in all that it teaches; they rejected the notion that Satan is a symbol of evil rather than a living force; and they acknowledged that they, personally, have a responsibility to tell other people their religious beliefs.

Born-again Christians are people who meet two of the criteria described for evangelicals: They have made a personal commitment to Christ that is still important in their lives today, and they believe that when they die they will go to heaven because they have confessed their sins and accepted Jesus Christ as their Savior. (By this classification strategy an evangelical is always a born-again Christian, but a born-again Christian is not always an evangelical.) Non-Christians were people who did not meet the born-again criteria.

Data Collection

The data in this book are from one of two nationwide surveys conducted by the Barna Research Group, Ltd. The first survey included 1,205 adults in July 1993. The second survey involved 1,206 people in January 1994. The sample was a random-digit dial (RDD) sample of households provided by Maritz, Inc. The response rates to these surveys were 62% and 67%, respectively. The interviews lasted an average of 23 and 28 minutes, respectively. Note that each survey incorporated a split sample technique, in which roughly half of the sample was asked certain questions, while the other half was not. Thus, some of the survey questions were asked of approximately 600 adults, rather than the entire sample of 1,200.

All of the interviews were conducted from the central Barna Research Group facility in Glendale, California, and were conducted between 5:00 and 9:00 P.M., per time zone, on week nights; between 10:00 A.M. and 6:00 P.M. on Saturdays; and from noon to 9:00 P.M. on Sundays. Geographic quotas were employed to ensure that the sample would reflect the true geographic distribution of the population. Statistical weighting was also utilized to further ensure that the survey samples reflected an accurate balance of people according to ethnic character and gender. The result is a pair of samples that are very similar to the distribution of the population on key attributes, as shown in the accompanying table.

Category	Adult Population	July Sample	January Sample
Male	49%	49%	48%
Female	51%	51%	52%
18-28	18%	20%	21%
29-47	42%	40%	44%
48-66	22%	26%	24%
67 or older	18%	13%	10%
White	74%	74%	72%
Black	13%	13%	13%
Hispanic	9%	9%	9%
Asian	3%	3%	4%

Parameters for Analyzing Survey Data

Every survey of people's attitudes and experiences that is based upon a sample of the population is a representation of the attitudes and experiences of the people who comprise the aggregate population.

Error

If the sample is selected properly—that is, survey respondents are chosen in accordance with the principles of probability sampling—then it is possible to estimate the potential amount of error attributable to sampling inaccuracies in the survey data. The only way to fully eliminate that potential error is to conduct a census rather than a sample.

Statisticians have developed means of identifying how much error could be in survey measurements due to sampling inaccuracies, assuming that random sampling procedures are conscientiously applied. The Sampling Accuracy Table at the end of appendix 1 outlines such estimates of how much error might be found in surveys, based upon the sample size and the response levels to survey questions.

All of the figures shown assume that we are working at the 95% confidence interval, meaning that we would expect these statistics to be accurate in 95 out of 100 cases. This is the standard confidence level used in most survey research.

In general, the following conditions are true:

- The larger the sample size, the more reliable are the survey data. However, there is not a simple one-to-one relationship between sample size and sampling error reduction.
- The larger the difference in opinion evident through the response distribution related to the question, the less likely it is that the survey statistics are erroneous due to sampling.

Response Levels and Accuracy

The data in the Sampling Accuracy Table shown below indicate how accurate the data are at specific response levels and at different sample sizes. For instance, in a survey of 1,000 people, if the answers were about evenly divided (i.e., 50% said "yes," 50% said "no"), those responses are probably accurate to within plus or minus three percentage points of what the survey actually found. Thus, you could say that the most likely response to the question was 50% saying "yes," with a 3-point margin of error at the 95% confidence interval. And that means that in this situation, the true population response would be somewhere between 47% and 53% in 95 out of 100 cases.

Here is another example. Let's say you ask the question regarding whether or not people have attended a church worship service in the past year. You find that 71% say they have, and 29% say they have not. Assume that the question was asked of 380 adults.

To determine the approximate level of sampling error associated with this finding you would look under the 30%/70% column (since the 71%-29% outcome is closest to the 30%-70% distribution). You would use the figures on the row representing the sample size of 400 people. The intersection point of that row with the 30%/70% column indicates a maximum sampling error of four percentage points.

You might say that 71% of all adults have attended a church worship service in the past year; this information is accurate to within plus or minus four percentage points at the 95% confidence level.

In some cases, the sample size or response distributions you use might vary markedly from the parameters shown in this table. You can either extrapolate from the figures shown to arrive at a closer interpretation of the error statistic or consult a good statistics book that might have a more detailed table. If you really want to test your patience and mental acuity, you might use the statistical formula for determining the error figures and calculate the number from scratch. That formula is provided in most decent statistics textbooks.

Sampling Accuracy Table

Sample Size	.05 Confidence Interval Response Distribution				
	50/50	40/60	30/70	20/80	10/90
2,000	2	2	2	2	2
1,500	3	3	2	2	2
1,200	3	3	3	2	2
1,000	3	3	3	2	2
800	3	3	3	3	2
600	4	4	4	3	2
400	5	5	4	4	3
200	7	7	6	5	4
100	10	10	9	8	6
50	14	14	13	12	8

Reading the Data Tables

Many people look at a page filled with data—percentages, raw scores, indexes, frequencies or whatever—and break out in a cold sweat. Let me emphasize that you can get a multitude of insights out of this book without having to look at the data tables in the appendix. The statistics on which the survey commentary is based are provided for those hearty souls who can make sense out of the data, and who may wish to do some of their own data interpretation.

If you want to examine the data tables, here are a few clues to help you through the process. The sample data table below is coded to help you understand what each of the elements on the page represents.

A

Do you you agree strongly, agree somewhat, disagree somewhat, or disagree strongly with the statement: "One person cannot make a difference in the world"?

B

D   **C**

E

		N	Agree Strongly	Agree Somewhat	Disagree Somewhat	Disagree Strongly	Don't Know
Total Responding		1060	11%	11%	25%	51%	1%
Gender:	Male	510	14	8	25	52	1
	Female	549	9	13	26	51	1
Age:	18 to 26	226	13	9	33	45	1
	27-45	476	10	11	26	53	1
	46-64	234	10	10	23	56	0
	65 Plus	115	18	12	16	50	4
Education:	High School or Less	480	16	13	25	44	2
	Some College	289	7	8	28	57	0
	College Graduate	286	8	9	25	58	0
Ethnicity:	White	778	9	9	26	55	1
	Black	131	25	15	14	46	0
	Hispanic	90	18	9	34	36	3
Marital:	Married	575	10	10	26	54	0
	Single	311	13	10	27	50	0
	Divorced/Separated	100	8	14	26	48	4
	Widowed	70	19	15	19	43	3
Kids Under 18:	Yes	453	10	11	28	52	0
	No	607	13	11	24	51	2

A This is similar wording of the questions asked in the survey.

B Each of these columns represents one of the answers that respondents might have given. Also remember that each of the figures in any of the columns is a percentage, not the total number of respondents who gave that particular answer.

C This is the total number (not a percentage) of survey respondents who are described by the label in the far left column of the row, and who answered this question. For the question on the sample page, 1,060 adults were asked the question. The second row, which is the results among males, shows the responses of the 510 people in that age group who were interviewed for the survey.

D The "total responding" row presents the aggregate survey data. Among all of the people involved in the survey who answered the question, their answers are always shown in the top row.

E The rest of the population segments listed on the page represent the other people groups who were interviewed, and how they responded. In this table, for instance, six independent variables were measured: gender, age, education, ethnicity, marital status, and having kids under 18. The statistics across from the male respondents tell us that 14% agreed strongly with the statement "one person cannot make a difference in the world," 8% agreed somewhat, 25% disagreed somewhat, 52% disagreed strongly, and 1% volunteered that they did not know (which is what DK stands for). The data in the row labeled "total responding" and beneath the column label "male" tells us that 510 men answered this question. The next row of data shows the responses of the female respondents. Among them, 9% agreed strongly with the statement, 13% agreed somewhat, 26% disagreed somewhat, 51% disagreed strongly, and 1% did not know. The subgroup size was 549 women. Notice that for any row of data shown in the table, the answers will add up to 100%. If the numbers are off by one or two percentage points, it is due to the rounding off of the figures.

Data Tables Directory

July 1993 Survey Tables

I. How's Life?

1. In the last seven days, attended a meeting of a recovery group or 12-step program?

2. In the last seven days, watched an R-rated movie, at a movie theater, at home, on a VCR or cable TV?

3. Satisfaction with life these days

4. Satisfaction now compared to five years ago

5. Satisfaction with life five years from now

II. Conditions That May Be Desirable in the Future

6. Having a close relationship with God

7. Having good health

8. Having a high-paying job

9. Being part of a local church

10. Influencing other people's lives

11. Owning a large home

12. Living close to family and relatives
13. Achieving fame or public recognition
14. Having a comfortable lifestyle
15. Living to an old age
16. Having close, personal friendships
17. Having an active sex life
18. Having a clear purpose for living

III. Conditions Now Compared to 5 and 10 Years Ago

19. America now compared to five years ago
20. Moral values compared to 10 years ago
21. People's spiritual commitment
22. Honesty and integrity
23. Personal financial responsibility
24. Showing compassion for the needy
25. Job productivity
26. Involvement in community matters
27. People's ability to read and write
28. People's selfishness
29. Political awareness
30. Tolerance toward people who are different from ourselves
31. Views about the family

IV. Our Performance Rating of Other People's Areas of Responsibility

32. Parents
33. National political leaders
34. The clergy
35. Public school teachers
36. Journalists
37. Military leaders
38. Doctors and medical professionals
39. College professors
40. Business leaders

V. Who Would Get Ahead Easier Financially in Our Society?

41. Man or woman
42. Single person or married person
43. Christian or non-Christian
44. White adult or black adult

45. Someone with a college degree or someone with a high school diploma

46. White adult or Asian adult

47. A person who has children or a person who has no children

48. Black adult or Hispanic adult

49. A person active in a church or a person not active in a church

VI. How Well Do the Following Institutions Serve the Needs of People?

50. Cable TV companies

51. Hospitals

52. Local government officials

53. Representatives in Congress

54. Local churches

55. Local police

56. Local public schools

57. Public libraries

VII. The Importance of Issues Close to Our Hearts

58. Being a member of a church

59. Having a bright future to look forward to

60. Regarding morals and ethics: absolute standards apply to everybody in all situations

61. Ease in making lasting friendships

62. A satisfying leisure versus a satisfying job or career

63. Playing it safe rather than taking risks in life

64. The majority is almost always right

65. Most churches are more interested in raising money than in helping people

66. The main purpose in life is enjoyment and personal fulfillment

67. Political representatives reflect the best interests of the people

VIII. Political Leaders' Ideas Becoming Legal

68. Homosexual marriages

69. Divorces without courts; only notarized papers

70. Prayer in public schools on a voluntary basis

71. Taxes raised on businesses to lower the federal budget

72. Household fines for not recycling recyclable materials

73. Adults ending own life with special drugs if physically impaired or suffering

74. Businesses selling or distributing information about us or products we buy without our permission

75. Abortion doctors imprisoned for murder

76. Pornographic magazines and movies illegal to distribute

IX. The Importance of Issues in Our Lives Today

77. Relevance of the Christian faith

78. Relevance of Christian churches in our area

79. The United States is the most powerful nation on the earth

80. To survive, sometimes we have to bend the rules for our own benefit

81. A clear philosophy about life that constantly influences our decisions

82. Following traditional ways rather than pursuing personal dreams

83. Possibility of being a moral person

84. Importance of doing things for other people compared to a personal belief about Jesus Christ

85. How American businesses rank in the world marketplace

86. How the government's involvement in the marketplace affects public life

X. Nonprofit Organizations and Charities in America

87. Trustworthiness of leaders

88. Requesting financial statement before donating money

XI. The Importance of Religion

89. Church attendance in a typical month

90. Bible ownership

91. Number of Bibles owned

92. Versions of Bibles most read

January 1994 Survey Tables

XII. Our Activities in the Last Seven Days
93. Ordered a product or service by calling 800 number
94. Ordered a product advertised on TV home shopping channel
95. Borrowed something from public library
96. Read a book for pleasure, other than the Bible
97. Volunteered time in a church
98. Volunteered time in a nonprofit organization, other than a church

XIII. Amount of Time We Spent on Various Activities Compared to a Year Ago
99. Being home with family
100. Watching television
101. Spending time with friends
102. Working at a job
103. Active in a church
104. Volunteering time
105. Gaining additional formal education
106. Exercising
107. Reading for pleasure
108. Listening to the radio
109. Discussing meaning and challenges of life with family and others

XIV. Dealing with Life's Daily Issues
110. Serious needs and problems faced in life today: financial, job, time/stress, family, education, health, spiritual
111. Belief and definition of absolute truth
112. Relationships: quality time or quantity time
113. Movies and TV programs' reflection of real life
114. Main purpose in life: enjoyment and personal fulfillment?
115. News media: fair and objective?
116. God's care in time of personal crisis
117. Is life too complex these days?
118. Is life worth living?
119. Responsibility to share with poor and struggling
120. Legalization of abortions

121. Public schools' handling of birth control and sex education
122. Children under 18 living apart from parents
123. Penalties for premeditated murder
124. Doctors' rights in handling a patient's incurable disease
125. Ideas regarding legalizing gambling

XV. Money Matters: Donating to Nonprofit Organizations

126. In last 30 days: charitable organization, including a church or synagogue
127. During the past year: colleges or other educational organizations
128. Churches, synagogues or other houses of worship
129. Religious organizations, other than churches
130. Political parties or advocacy organizations
131. Health-care or medical-research organizations
132. Wildlife or environmental organizations
133. Community-development organizations
134. Music, art or cultural organizations

XVI. Religion's Importance: Activities in the Last Seven Days

135. Affiliated with Protestant, Catholic, Jewish or other religious faith
136. Attendance at a church or synagogue
137. Read from the Bible
138. Attended a Sunday School class
139. Attendance in a small group
140. Watched a church service on television
141. Listened to Christian preaching or teaching on a radio program
142. Read a book about the Bible or Christian principles
143. Listened to Christian music on a Christian radio station
144. Read a Christian magazine

XVII. Our Beliefs About Religious Issues

145. The Bible's accuracy in its teachings
146. Telling others about personal religious beliefs
147. Importance of religion in personal life
148. Belief in the devil as a living being, or a symbol of evil
149. Belief in being good, or doing enough good things for others, to earn a place in heaven
150. Did Jesus Christ make mistakes?

XVIII. What We Believe About God

151. Personal beliefs about God

152. A personal commitment to Jesus Christ that is still important today

153. Beliefs about what happens to us after death

154. Feeling the presence of God

155. How often feel the presence of God

156. The last time felt God's presence

157. Experiencing God's presence at church

XIX. How We Describe Our Worship Services

158. Boring

159. Challenging

160. Refreshing

161. Spirit-filled

162. Outdated

163. Life-transforming

164. Embarrassing

165. Participatory

166. Disappointing

167. Traditional

168. Modern or contemporary

169. Inspiring

170. Just a performance

171. Overall satisfaction with ability to worship God at church

Tables

July 1993
Survey Tables

TABLE 1

In the last seven days, did you attend a meeting of a recovery group or a 12-step program?

		N	Yes	No	Don't Know
Total Responding		1205	4%	95%	0%
Gender:	Male	589	6	94	0
	Female	616	3	96	0
Age:	18 to 28	243	5	94	1
	29 to 47	485	5	95	0
	48 to 66	310	4	96	0
	67 to 98	151	4	96	0
Married:	Yes	678	3	97	0
	No	527	6	93	1
Have Kids Under 18:	Yes	458	4	96	0
	No	745	5	95	0
Household Income:	Under $25,000	384	4	96	0
	$25,000 to $50,000	453	5	94	0
	Over $50,000	216	2	98	0
Region:	Northeast	260	3	96	0
	South	405	2	97	0
	Midwest	272	6	94	0
	West	268	7	92	0
Education:	High School or Less	668	4	95	0
	Some College	285	4	95	1
	College Graduate	251	5	95	0
Ethnicity:	White	888	4	96	0
	Black	155	4	96	0
	Hispanic	107	5	95	0
Voter Registration:	Not Registered	261	6	94	0
	Democrat	414	3	97	0
	Republican	253	6	94	0
	Independent	212	5	94	1
Church Type:	Protestant	510	5	94	0
	Catholic	222	6	93	0
Faith Perspective:	Evangelical	115	5	95	0
	Born Again	463	5	94	0
	Non-Christian	742	4	96	0

TABLE 2

In the last seven days, did you watch an R-rated movie, either at a movie theater or at home on a VCR or cable TV?

		N	Yes	No	Don't Know
Total Responding		1205	34%	64%	2%
Gender:	Male	589	42	56	2
	Female	616	25	72	2
Age:	18 to 28	243	54	45	1
	29 to 47	485	38	60	2
	48 to 66	310	20	76	4
	67 to 98	151	17	81	2
Married:	Yes	678	28	70	3
	No	527	41	57	1
Have Kids Under 18:	Yes	458	40	58	2
	No	745	29	68	3
Household Income:	Under $25,000	384	33	64	3
	$25,000 to $50,000	453	37	62	1
	Over $50,000	216	33	65	2
Region:	Northeast	260	35	63	2
	South	405	33	65	2
	Midwest	272	38	60	3
	West	268	29	69	3
Education:	High School or Less	668	31	66	3
	Some College	285	40	58	2
	College Graduate	251	32	66	2
Ethnicity:	White	888	30	67	3
	Black	155	46	51	2
	Hispanic	107	50	50	0
Voter Registration:	Not Registered	261	39	60	2
	Democrat	414	35	62	3
	Republican	253	25	72	3
	Independent	212	39	59	1
Church Type:	Protestant	510	26	72	2
	Catholic	222	37	61	2
Faith Perspective:	Evangelical	115	15	83	2
	Born Again	463	26	72	2
	Non-Christian	742	38	60	2

Table 3

Overall, how satisfied are you with your life these days?

		N	Very	Somewhat	Not Too	Not At All	Don't Know
Total Responding		690	59%	32%	7%	2%	1%
Gender:	Male	333	58	32	7	3	1
	Female	357	60	31	7	2	1
Age:	18 to 28	129	63	34	2	1	0
	29 to 47	291	58	34	7	1	0
	48 to 66	183	60	28	7	4	1
	67 to 98	81	57	25	14	4	0
Married:	Yes	383	65	27	5	3	0
	No	308	51	37	10	2	1
Have Kids Under 18:	Yes	266	60	36	3	1	1
	No	424	58	29	10	3	0
Household Income:	Under $25,000	227	47	38	12	3	0
	$25,000 to $50,000	245	59	36	4	1	0
	Over $50,000	132	74	23	1	1	1
Region:	Northeast	160	50	36	8	5	1
	South	211	64	25	8	3	0
	Midwest	177	54	39	5	1	0
	West	142	66	28	6	0	1
Education:	High School or Less	386	56	30	11	3	1
	Some College	167	64	33	2	1	0
	College Graduate	137	61	35	3	1	1
Ethnicity:	White	512	60	31	6	2	0
	Black	91	39	44	13	4	0
	Hispanic	57	83	12	6	0	0
Voter Registration:	Not Registered	141	57	30	10	2	1
	Democrat	231	57	32	9	2	0
	Republican	147	73	23	2	2	0
	Independent	141	51	39	6	3	1
Church Type:	Protestant	287	62	29	6	2	1
	Catholic	134	60	34	2	4	1
Faith Perspective:	Evangelical	51	79	16	4	1	0
	Born Again	275	63	28	6	2	0
	Non-Christian	416	56	34	7	2	1

TABLE 4

Think about your life today compared to your life five years ago. Would you say that, overall, you are more satisfied with your life today, less satisfied with your life today, or about equally satisfied today as you were five years ago?

		N	More	Equally	Less	Don't Know
Total Responding		690	52%	36%	12%	1%
Gender:	Male	333	54	33	13	0
	Female	357	50	38	11	1
Age:	18 to 28	129	69	26	5	0
	29 to 47	291	59	28	13	1
	48 to 66	183	42	43	14	0
	67 to 98	81	26	60	10	3
Married:	Yes	383	53	39	8	0
	No	308	51	32	16	1
Have Kids Under 18:	Yes	266	58	32	9	0
	No	424	48	38	13	1
Household Income:	Under $25,000	227	39	44	16	0
	$25,000 to $50,000	245	60	31	9	0
	Over $50,000	132	62	34	4	0
Region:	Northeast	160	46	37	16	1
	South	211	54	35	11	0
	Midwest	177	52	37	9	2
	West	142	56	33	11	0
Education:	High School or Less	386	45	40	14	1
	Some College	167	65	26	8	0
	College Graduate	137	57	34	7	2
Ethnicity:	White	512	52	37	10	1
	Black	91	39	42	18	1
	Hispanic	57	72	16	12	0
Voter Registration:	Not Registered	141	58	27	14	1
	Democrat	231	45	42	12	1
	Republican	147	59	31	9	0
	Independent	141	51	38	10	1
Church Type:	Protestant	287	50	37	12	1
	Catholic	134	51	38	10	0
Faith Perspective:	Evangelical	51	55	33	12	0
	Born Again	275	51	39	10	0
	Non-Christian	416	53	33	13	1

TABLE 5

Five years from now, in 1998, do you expect that your life will be more satisfying than it is today, less satisfying, or about equally satisfying as your life is today?

		N	More	Equally	Less	Don't Know
Total Responding		690	57%	24%	6%	13%
Gender:	Male	333	65	21	5	9
	Female	357	51	26	6	17
Age:	18 to 28	129	85	11	2	2
	29 to 47	291	65	22	4	9
	48 to 66	183	46	31	7	16
	67 to 98	81	13	35	17	36
Married:	Yes	383	53	28	7	13
	No	308	63	19	5	13
Have Kids Under 18:	Yes	266	66	23	4	8
	No	424	52	25	7	16
Household Income:	Under $25,000	227	56	20	7	16
	$25,000 to $50,000	245	64	26	5	4
	Over $50,000	132	62	26	2	10
Region:	Northeast	160	53	27	7	13
	South	211	59	15	6	21
	Midwest	177	55	32	6	7
	West	142	63	23	5	9
Education:	High School or Less	386	51	24	7	18
	Some College	167	64	25	4	7
	College Graduate	137	66	24	5	5
Ethnicity:	White	512	54	26	7	13
	Black	91	62	20	1	17
	Hispanic	57	72	17	0	10
Voter Registration:	Not Registered	141	67	12	4	16
	Democrat	231	50	25	6	19
	Republican	147	58	27	7	7
	Independent	141	58	30	6	6
Church Type:	Protestant	287	52	24	8	17
	Catholic	134	62	26	7	5
Faith Perspective:	Evangelical	51	46	22	10	22
	Born Again	275	53	23	9	15
	Non-Christian	416	60	24	4	12

TABLE 6

I'm going to read some conditions that you could possibly have in your life in the future. How desirable would it be for you to have a close relationship with God?

		N	Very	Somewhat	Not Too	Not At All	Don't Know
Total Responding		690	74%	18%	2%	4%	2%
Gender:	Male	333	66	24	3	6	1
	Female	357	82	12	2	1	2
Age:	18 to 28	129	66	26	4	2	2
	29 to 47	291	71	19	4	5	1
	48 to 66	183	83	15	0	2	1
	67 to 98	81	78	10	0	6	6
Married:	Yes	383	79	13	3	3	2
	No	308	68	24	2	4	1
Have Kids Under 18:	Yes	266	74	19	3	2	2
	No	424	74	18	2	4	2
Household Income:	Under $25,000	227	76	17	1	6	0
	$25,000 to $50,000	245	71	21	2	4	3
	Over $50,000	132	70	22	4	2	2
Region:	Northeast	160	71	21	1	3	3
	South	211	88	10	1	1	0
	Midwest	177	70	21	3	3	3
	West	142	63	22	4	8	2
Education:	High School or Less	386	75	16	2	5	2
	Some College	167	76	19	2	1	2
	College Graduate	137	69	21	3	4	2
Ethnicity:	White	512	72	19	3	3	2
	Black	91	90	10	0	0	0
	Hispanic	57	78	10	0	12	0
Voter Registration:	Not Registered	141	70	21	1	6	2
	Democrat	231	79	14	2	4	1
	Republican	147	78	16	3	3	1
	Independent	141	69	23	3	3	2
Church Type:	Protestant	287	91	8	0	0	1
	Catholic	134	80	18	0	0	1
Faith Perspective:	Evangelical	51	100	0	0	0	0
	Born Again	275	94	5	0	0	1
	Non-Christian	416	61	26	4	6	3

TABLE 7

How desirable would it be for you to have good health?

		N	Very	Somewhat	Not Too	Not At All	Don't Know
Total Responding		690	92%	7%	1%	0%	0%
Gender:	Male	333	88	10	1	0	0
	Female	357	95	4	0	0	1
Age:	18 to 28	129	86	12	2	0	0
	29 to 47	291	93	7	0	0	0
	48 to 66	183	95	4	1	0	0
	67 to 98	81	91	4	1	1	3
Married:	Yes	383	92	7	0	0	0
	No	308	92	6	1	0	1
Have Kids Under 18:	Yes	266	94	6	0	0	0
	No	424	90	7	1	0	1
Household Income:	Under $25,000	227	92	6	2	0	0
	$25,000 to $50,000	245	90	10	0	0	0
	Over $50,000	132	94	4	1	0	1
Region:	Northeast	160	92	7	1	0	0
	South	211	96	3	1	0	0
	Midwest	177	91	7	2	0	1
	West	142	87	12	0	0	1
Education:	High School or Less	386	89	9	1	0	1
	Some College	167	94	5	1	0	0
	College Graduate	137	97	2	0	0	1
Ethnicity:	White	512	94	5	1	0	1
	Black	91	86	12	2	0	0
	Hispanic	57	79	21	0	0	0
Voter Registration:	Not Registered	141	94	5	1	0	0
	Democrat	231	93	5	1	0	0
	Republican	147	85	11	2	0	2
	Independent	141	92	8	0	0	0
Church Type:	Protestant	287	93	6	1	0	1
	Catholic	134	91	7	1	0	1
Faith Perspective:	Evangelical	51	97	1	2	0	0
	Born Again	275	92	6	1	0	1
	Non-Christian	416	91	7	1	0	0

TABLE 8

How desirable would it be for you to have a high-paying job?

		N	Very	Somewhat	Not Too	Not At All	Don't Know
Total Responding		690	43%	31%	11%	12%	2%
Gender:	Male	333	44	36	8	10	1
	Female	357	42	26	14	15	3
Age:	18 to 28	129	59	36	4	1	1
	29 to 47	291	47	38	9	5	0
	48 to 66	183	35	27	16	15	5
	67 to 98	81	27	5	17	48	4
Married:	Yes	383	37	34	13	14	2
	No	308	51	28	8	10	3
Have Kids Under 18:	Yes	266	52	32	11	5	0
	No	424	38	31	11	17	4
Household Income:	Under $25,000	227	47	24	12	15	2
	$25,000 to $50,000	245	40	39	10	8	2
	Over $50,000	132	44	38	10	5	3
Region:	Northeast	160	39	30	14	16	1
	South	211	57	18	12	10	4
	Midwest	177	33	43	8	14	2
	West	142	41	38	11	10	1
Education:	High School or Less	386	45	27	9	16	3
	Some College	167	43	33	13	10	1
	College Graduate	137	40	40	13	5	2
Ethnicity:	White	512	40	32	12	14	2
	Black	91	64	15	7	9	5
	Hispanic	57	37	47	11	6	0
Voter Registration:	Not Registered	141	49	30	9	8	4
	Democrat	231	45	26	12	14	2
	Republican	147	35	38	11	15	1
	Independent	141	42	33	10	12	2
Church Type:	Protestant	287	43	26	15	14	2
	Catholic	134	45	40	8	5	1
Faith Perspective:	Evangelical	51	36	27	13	24	0
	Born Again	275	42	33	10	14	1
	Non-Christian	416	44	30	11	11	3

TABLE 9

How desirable would it be for you to be part of a local church?

		N	Very	Somewhat	Not Too	Not At All	Don't Know
Total Responding		690	49%	29%	10%	9%	2%
Gender:	Male	333	39	32	14	11	3
	Female	357	59	27	7	6	1
Age:	18 to 28	129	48	34	12	6	0
	29 to 47	291	44	31	12	9	3
	48 to 66	183	55	28	10	7	1
	67 to 98	81	57	21	4	12	5
Married:	Yes	383	55	24	10	8	3
	No	308	43	36	11	9	1
Have Kids Under 18:	Yes	266	49	30	11	7	4
	No	424	50	29	10	10	1
Household Income:	Under $25,000	227	52	30	8	10	0
	$25,000 to $50,000	245	51	30	11	6	2
	Over $50,000	132	48	32	14	7	0
Region:	Northeast	160	41	36	12	11	1
	South	211	64	22	6	3	5
	Midwest	177	46	32	13	7	2
	West	142	42	31	12	16	0
Education:	High School or Less	386	49	32	7	8	4
	Some College	167	53	25	14	8	1
	College Graduate	137	47	27	14	11	1
Ethnicity:	White	512	49	29	11	9	1
	Black	91	56	37	5	2	0
	Hispanic	57	45	22	11	6	16
Voter Registration:	Not Registered	141	39	36	12	6	8
	Democrat	231	56	26	11	7	1
	Republican	147	57	27	8	7	1
	Independent	141	46	31	10	13	0
Church Type:	Protestant	287	75	24	0	1	0
	Catholic	134	59	28	3	2	8
Faith Perspective:	Evangelical	51	89	5	0	5	0
	Born Again	275	73	21	2	4	0
	Non-Christian	416	34	35	16	11	4

TABLE 10

How desirable would it be for you to influence other people's lives?

		N	Very	Somewhat	Not Too	Not At All	Don't Know
Total Responding		690	39%	40%	9%	8%	3%
Gender:	Male	333	34	44	9	10	4
	Female	357	44	36	10	7	3
Age:	18 to 28	129	47	44	2	7	0
	29 to 47	291	36	43	11	6	4
	48 to 66	183	34	42	11	8	6
	67 to 98	81	51	16	12	17	3
Married:	Yes	383	37	40	12	6	5
	No	308	42	40	7	11	1
Have Kids Under 18:	Yes	266	43	38	10	5	4
	No	424	37	41	9	10	3
Household Income:	Under $25,000	227	41	36	10	10	3
	$25,000 to $50,000	245	42	41	10	4	3
	Over $50,000	132	35	50	7	7	1
Region:	Northeast	160	37	39	10	10	4
	South	211	44	35	9	5	7
	Midwest	177	37	49	8	6	1
	West	142	37	37	11	14	0
Education:	High School or Less	386	39	39	7	10	6
	Some College	167	38	44	12	6	0
	College Graduate	137	42	37	13	6	2
Ethnicity:	White	512	39	42	9	7	2
	Black	91	54	30	6	6	4
	Hispanic	57	19	38	6	22	16
Voter Registration:	Not Registered	141	31	43	9	10	6
	Democrat	231	47	34	5	9	4
	Republican	147	39	40	12	7	2
	Independent	141	34	43	14	7	2
Church Type:	Protestant	287	48	37	8	5	3
	Catholic	134	39	40	6	6	8
Faith Perspective:	Evangelical	51	71	23	0	2	4
	Born Again	275	48	39	5	5	3
	Non-Christian	416	33	40	12	10	4

TABLE 11

How desirable would it be for you to own a large home?

		N	Very	Somewhat	Not Too	Not At All	Don't Know
Total Responding		690	30%	32%	20%	17%	1%
Gender:	Male	333	30	36	18	16	1
	Female	357	29	28	23	18	1
Age:	18 to 28	129	41	43	9	7	0
	29 to 47	291	31	34	23	11	0
	48 to 66	183	25	27	24	23	1
	67 to 98	81	15	18	23	40	4
Married:	Yes	383	28	31	24	15	1
	No	308	32	33	16	19	1
Have Kids Under 18:	Yes	266	36	35	20	10	0
	No	424	25	31	21	22	1
Household Income:	Under $25,000	227	33	27	16	23	0
	$25,000 to $50,000	245	29	37	19	13	1
	Over $50,000	132	32	37	24	7	1
Region:	Northeast	160	24	24	23	28	2
	South	211	33	30	22	15	0
	Midwest	177	28	39	19	13	1
	West	142	33	35	17	14	1
Education:	High School or Less	386	28	29	21	22	1
	Some College	167	36	33	16	13	2
	College Graduate	137	26	40	26	8	0
Ethnicity:	White	512	27	31	22	18	1
	Black	91	45	30	9	16	0
	Hispanic	57	27	38	23	12	0
Voter Registration:	Not Registered	141	32	31	20	17	0
	Democrat	231	35	25	22	17	1
	Republican	147	22	39	17	19	2
	Independent	141	29	37	20	13	1
Church Type:	Protestant	287	30	35	15	19	1
	Catholic	134	27	37	29	4	2
Faith Perspective:	Evangelical	51	31	26	27	16	0
	Born Again	275	25	39	20	16	0
	Non-Christian	416	32	28	21	18	1

TABLE 12

How desirable would it be for you to live close to family and relatives?

		N	Very	Somewhat	Not Too	Not At All	Don't Know
Total Responding		690	63%	27%	5%	3%	2%
Gender:	Male	333	54	33	5	6	2
	Female	357	71	22	4	0	3
Age:	18 to 28	129	53	39	4	3	1
	29 to 47	291	57	31	7	4	1
	48 to 66	183	73	18	3	2	3
	67 to 98	81	77	13	0	3	7
Married:	Yes	383	62	27	5	4	2
	No	308	64	27	4	2	3
Have Kids Under 18:	Yes	266	59	29	7	4	1
	No	424	65	26	3	3	3
Household Income:	Under $25,000	227	67	18	7	4	4
	$25,000 to $50,000	245	62	33	3	1	1
	Over $50,000	132	56	37	5	1	2
Region:	Northeast	160	69	22	3	5	2
	South	211	69	22	4	5	1
	Midwest	177	59	34	5	1	3
	West	142	53	33	7	2	5
Education:	High School or Less	386	68	21	4	5	3
	Some College	167	56	37	5	1	2
	College Graduate	137	58	33	6	1	2
Ethnicity:	White	512	64	27	4	2	2
	Black	91	71	18	3	2	6
	Hispanic	57	48	26	10	16	0
Voter Registration:	Not Registered	141	60	21	6	8	4
	Democrat	231	71	23	4	0	1
	Republican	147	60	33	2	4	1
	Independent	141	57	31	7	2	2
Church Type:	Protestant	287	69	27	2	1	1
	Catholic	134	59	25	5	7	4
Faith Perspective:	Evangelical	51	74	22	2	2	0
	Born Again	275	63	30	3	1	4
	Non-Christian	416	63	25	5	5	1

TABLE 13

How desirable would it be for you to achieve fame or public recognition?

		N	Very	Somewhat	Not Too	Not At All	Don't Know
Total Responding		690	10%	26%	30%	33%	2%
Gender:	Male	333	8	30	29	32	1
	Female	357	11	22	31	33	3
Age:	18 to 28	129	14	34	28	22	2
	29 to 47	291	5	27	37	30	1
	48 to 66	183	14	22	23	38	3
	67 to 98	81	8	16	22	46	8
Married:	Yes	383	6	24	32	37	1
	No	308	14	28	27	27	4
Have Kids Under 18:	Yes	266	9	27	31	33	1
	No	424	10	25	29	33	3
Household Income:	Under $25,000	227	12	27	30	30	1
	$25,000 to $50,000	245	11	24	33	29	2
	Over $50,000	132	7	30	30	32	1
Region:	Northeast	160	9	24	30	35	3
	South	211	16	27	24	32	0
	Midwest	177	7	23	32	33	4
	West	142	5	29	35	29	2
Education:	High School or Less	386	11	24	27	34	3
	Some College	167	8	27	31	32	2
	College Graduate	137	7	28	36	29	0
Ethnicity:	White	512	8	25	29	36	3
	Black	91	27	33	21	19	0
	Hispanic	57	0	27	36	37	0
Voter Registration:	Not Registered	141	10	34	25	29	2
	Democrat	231	14	24	30	30	2
	Republican	147	5	24	30	36	5
	Independent	141	8	23	29	38	1
Church Type:	Protestant	287	13	24	29	31	3
	Catholic	134	7	27	32	32	3
Faith Perspective:	Evangelical	51	9	22	29	41	0
	Born Again	275	13	28	29	28	2
	Non-Christian	416	7	24	30	36	2

TABLE 14

How desirable would it be for you to have a comfortable lifestyle?

		N	Very	Somewhat	Not Too	Not At All	Don't Know
Total Responding		690	72%	22%	4%	1%	1%
Gender:	Male	333	69	23	7	1	0
	Female	357	75	22	1	0	1
Age:	18 to 28	129	79	13	8	0	0
	29 to 47	291	65	30	5	0	0
	48 to 66	183	76	23	1	1	0
	67 to 98	81	83	9	0	3	5
Married:	Yes	383	66	27	6	1	1
	No	308	80	17	2	0	1
Have Kids Under 18:	Yes	266	65	30	5	0	0
	No	424	77	18	3	1	1
Household Income:	Under $25,000	227	77	20	2	1	0
	$25,000 to $50,000	245	67	27	5	0	1
	Over $50,000	132	78	21	1	0	0
Region:	Northeast	160	74	21	2	2	1
	South	211	75	21	5	0	0
	Midwest	177	71	26	2	0	1
	West	142	69	24	7	1	0
Education:	High School or Less	386	72	21	6	1	1
	Some College	167	77	22	1	0	0
	College Graduate	137	69	28	2	0	0
Ethnicity:	White	512	74	23	1	1	1
	Black	91	83	14	2	0	0
	Hispanic	57	42	27	31	0	0
Voter Registration:	Not Registered	141	64	27	6	1	1
	Democrat	231	79	18	2	0	1
	Republican	147	70	20	8	2	0
	Independent	141	73	26	1	0	0
Church Type:	Protestant	287	74	21	5	0	0
	Catholic	134	67	23	9	0	1
Faith Perspective:	Evangelical	51	67	30	2	0	0
	Born Again	275	74	22	4	0	0
	Non-Christian	416	72	23	4	1	1

TABLE 15

How desirable would it be for you to live to an old age?

		N	Very	Somewhat	Not Too	Not At All	Don't Know
Total Responding		690	57%	31%	7%	3%	3%
Gender:	Male	333	56	32	7	3	3
	Female	357	57	30	7	3	2
Age:	18 to 28	129	58	36	3	2	1
	29 to 47	291	55	34	6	3	2
	48 to 66	183	56	27	9	4	3
	67 to 98	81	67	15	11	1	6
Married:	Yes	383	53	35	6	3	3
	No	308	61	26	7	3	3
Have Kids Under 18:	Yes	266	53	35	5	3	3
	No	424	59	28	8	3	3
Household Income:	Under $25,000	227	58	25	10	5	2
	$25,000 to $50,000	245	53	37	6	2	3
	Over $50,000	132	59	35	4	2	1
Region:	Northeast	160	46	37	6	5	5
	South	211	75	18	5	0	2
	Midwest	177	49	38	7	4	2
	West	142	52	33	9	4	2
Education:	High School or Less	386	56	28	7	4	4
	Some College	167	60	32	5	2	2
	College Graduate	137	54	36	8	1	1
Ethnicity:	White	512	55	32	6	3	3
	Black	91	71	27	0	2	0
	Hispanic	57	54	21	15	6	4
Voter Registration:	Not Registered	141	63	24	5	6	2
	Democrat	231	62	24	9	2	3
	Republican	147	51	39	5	2	3
	Independent	141	48	38	8	4	2
Church Type:	Protestant	287	59	32	5	3	1
	Catholic	134	58	27	12	1	2
Faith Perspective:	Evangelical	51	59	33	2	5	2
	Born Again	275	60	31	5	3	1
	Non-Christian	416	54	30	8	3	4

TABLE 16

How desirable would it be for you to have close, personal friendships?

		N	Very	Somewhat	Not Too	Not At All	Don't Know
Total Responding		690	79%	15%	3%	2%	2%
Gender:	Male	333	79	17	2	1	0
	Female	357	78	13	3	3	3
Age:	18 to 28	129	82	16	1	1	0
	29 to 47	291	81	14	2	2	1
	48 to 66	183	76	15	4	1	3
	67 to 98	81	75	12	0	8	6
Married:	Yes	383	81	14	2	1	1
	No	308	76	15	4	3	2
Have Kids Under 18:	Yes	266	81	14	3	2	1
	No	424	78	15	3	2	3
Household Income:	Under $25,000	227	80	14	2	3	1
	$25,000 to $50,000	245	77	17	3	2	1
	Over $50,000	132	82	15	3	0	0
Region:	Northeast	160	80	11	4	2	2
	South	211	80	15	1	3	2
	Midwest	177	77	15	3	2	3
	West	142	78	17	4	1	0
Education:	High School or Less	386	75	17	3	3	3
	Some College	167	83	12	3	1	1
	College Graduate	137	84	12	2	1	1
Ethnicity:	White	512	82	13	2	2	1
	Black	91	66	22	3	3	6
	Hispanic	57	82	18	0	0	0
Voter Registration:	Not Registered	141	71	19	3	4	2
	Democrat	231	82	12	1	1	3
	Republican	147	79	14	3	3	0
	Independent	141	78	16	3	1	1
Church Type:	Protestant	287	80	13	2	4	2
	Catholic	134	78	17	1	0	3
Faith Perspective:	Evangelical	51	81	14	0	5	0
	Born Again	275	81	15	1	2	1
	Non-Christian	416	78	14	4	2	3

TABLE 17

How desirable would it be for you to have an active sex life?

		N	Very	Somewhat	Not Too	Not At All	Don't Know
Total Responding		690	51%	31%	5%	10%	3%
Gender:	Male	333	61	33	2	3	1
	Female	357	41	30	8	16	5
Age:	18 to 28	129	56	39	3	1	1
	29 to 47	291	64	29	3	3	2
	48 to 66	183	43	30	10	12	4
	67 to 98	81	15	26	7	43	9
Married:	Yes	383	53	33	5	7	2
	No	308	48	29	6	13	5
Have Kids Under 18:	Yes	266	62	30	4	2	2
	No	424	43	32	6	15	4
Household Income:	Under $25,000	227	44	29	9	13	4
	$25,000 to $50,000	245	58	33	3	5	1
	Over $50,000	132	55	40	3	1	1
Region:	Northeast	160	51	30	7	10	1
	South	211	50	27	6	12	4
	Midwest	177	52	29	5	9	5
	West	142	50	41	1	6	3
Education:	High School or Less	386	49	27	7	14	4
	Some College	167	49	39	2	6	4
	College Graduate	137	58	34	4	2	2
Ethnicity:	White	512	49	31	6	10	3
	Black	91	55	26	2	11	6
	Hispanic	57	66	25	4	4	0
Voter Registration:	Not Registered	141	49	32	4	8	7
	Democrat	231	50	25	7	15	3
	Republican	147	49	37	4	8	3
	Independent	141	52	36	5	5	2
Church Type:	Protestant	287	47	34	5	13	2
	Catholic	134	49	31	11	7	2
Faith Perspective:	Evangelical	51	50	36	4	8	2
	Born Again	275	45	35	6	11	3
	Non-Christian	416	55	28	5	8	4

TABLE 18

How desirable would it be for you to have a clear purpose for living?

		N	Very	Somewhat	Not Too	Not At All	Don't Know
Total Responding		690	80%	14%	2%	1%	3%
Gender:	Male	333	77	17	2	1	3
	Female	357	84	11	1	1	2
Age:	18 to 28	129	88	11	1	0	1
	29 to 47	291	77	20	0	0	3
	48 to 66	183	82	10	4	3	1
	67 to 98	81	79	11	3	1	6
Married:	Yes	383	81	14	1	1	3
	No	308	80	15	2	1	2
Have Kids Under 18:	Yes	266	80	15	0	0	4
	No	424	81	14	3	1	2
Household Income:	Under $25,000	227	84	14	0	2	0
	$25,000 to $50,000	245	82	13	2	1	2
	Over $50,000	132	84	15	0	0	0
Region:	Northeast	160	78	17	2	0	3
	South	211	83	9	2	2	4
	Midwest	177	78	17	2	1	2
	West	142	82	16	0	1	1
Education:	High School or Less	386	76	16	2	1	4
	Some College	167	89	10	0	0	1
	College Graduate	137	82	14	2	1	2
Ethnicity:	White	512	83	14	1	1	1
	Black	91	77	14	4	4	0
	Hispanic	57	68	16	0	0	16
Voter Registration:	Not Registered	141	73	15	1	1	9
	Democrat	231	80	14	3	2	1
	Republican	147	91	6	2	0	1
	Independent	141	77	22	0	1	0
Church Type:	Protestant	287	84	12	2	2	1
	Catholic	134	81	10	1	0	9
Faith Perspective:	Evangelical	51	97	3	0	0	0
	Born Again	275	89	8	1	1	0
	Non-Christian	416	75	18	2	1	4

TABLE 19

All things considered, do you think America is doing better, doing worse, or doing about the same as it was five years ago?

		N	Better	Same	Worse	Don't Know
Total Responding		691	8%	36%	53%	3%
Gender:	Male	345	7	40	50	3
	Female	346	8	32	55	4
Age:	18 to 28	146	7	40	49	4
	29 to 47	261	10	39	48	3
	48 to 66	175	5	36	56	3
	67 to 98	99	6	27	63	5
Married:	Yes	390	8	34	55	3
	No	302	7	39	50	4
Have Kids Under 18:	Yes	255	8	43	47	3
	No	434	8	33	56	4
Household Income:	Under $25,000	209	6	34	56	3
	$25,000 to $50,000	272	8	40	50	2
	Over $50,000	123	9	38	51	2
Region:	Northeast	178	7	41	50	3
	South	204	5	32	60	3
	Midwest	177	12	41	44	3
	West	132	6	29	58	6
Education:	High School or Less	378	4	35	58	3
	Some College	165	10	36	52	2
	College Graduate	146	15	40	40	5
Ethnicity:	White	515	8	39	50	3
	Black	85	6	27	65	2
	Hispanic	56	10	30	52	8
Voter Registration:	Not Registered	146	7	33	52	8
	Democrat	233	11	36	51	2
	Republican	145	3	32	63	2
	Independent	124	8	45	45	3
Church Type:	Protestant	294	5	33	58	4
	Catholic	127	13	41	45	1
Faith Perspective:	Evangelical	75	1	27	69	3
	Born Again	254	6	34	58	2
	Non-Christian	437	9	38	50	4

TABLE 20

When it comes to moral values, do you think things have gotten better, gotten worse, or stayed about the same compared to 10 years ago?

		N	Better	Same	Worse	Don't Know
Total Responding		691	9%	65%	22%	4%
Gender:	Male	345	10	58	26	5
	Female	346	8	72	18	2
Age:	18 to 28	146	10	60	25	6
	29 to 47	261	11	60	26	3
	48 to 66	175	8	71	18	3
	67 to 98	99	5	76	14	5
Married:	Yes	390	11	67	20	2
	No	302	6	63	24	6
Have Kids Under 18:	Yes	255	8	66	24	2
	No	434	10	65	21	5
Household Income:	Under $25,000	209	10	67	18	6
	$25,000 to $50,000	272	9	63	25	3
	Over $50,000	123	11	66	22	1
Region:	Northeast	178	14	59	21	6
	South	204	8	67	23	2
	Midwest	177	7	65	25	2
	West	132	6	70	18	6
Education:	High School or Less	378	9	66	21	4
	Some College	165	11	66	21	3
	College Graduate	146	7	63	26	5
Ethnicity:	White	515	8	67	23	2
	Black	85	12	63	23	2
	Hispanic	56	12	67	15	6
Voter Registration:	Not Registered	146	6	66	17	10
	Democrat	233	12	61	25	2
	Republican	145	5	77	15	3
	Independent	124	9	58	31	2
Church Type:	Protestant	294	9	69	20	2
	Catholic	127	15	56	24	5
Faith Perspective:	Evangelical	75	2	87	10	1
	Born Again	254	10	75	14	1
	Non-Christian	437	9	60	27	5

TABLE 21

When it comes to people's spiritual commitment, do you think things have gotten better, gotten worse, or stayed about the same compared to 10 years ago?

		N	Better	Same	Worse	Don't Know
Total Responding		691	21%	37%	36%	6%
Gender:	Male	345	18	38	38	5
	Female	346	23	36	34	7
Age:	18 to 28	146	18	44	36	2
	29 to 47	261	19	36	42	3
	48 to 66	175	26	33	31	9
	67 to 98	99	17	34	33	16
Married:	Yes	390	22	36	37	5
	No	302	19	38	35	8
Have Kids Under 18:	Yes	255	18	37	43	2
	No	434	22	37	32	9
Household Income:	Under $25,000	209	21	38	34	7
	$25,000 to $50,000	272	22	36	37	5
	Over $50,000	123	19	35	41	5
Region:	Northeast	178	12	38	45	5
	South	204	25	35	35	5
	Midwest	177	22	34	36	8
	West	132	23	42	27	7
Education:	High School or Less	378	21	37	37	5
	Some College	165	22	38	31	9
	College Graduate	146	18	36	40	6
Ethnicity:	White	515	16	38	39	6
	Black	85	37	40	17	7
	Hispanic	56	26	43	30	0
Voter Registration:	Not Registered	146	23	37	34	7
	Democrat	233	23	34	36	6
	Republican	145	14	46	36	4
	Independent	124	21	30	44	5
Church Type:	Protestant	294	24	41	32	3
	Catholic	127	24	26	47	3
Faith Perspective:	Evangelical	75	19	63	17	1
	Born Again	254	24	41	31	3
	Non-Christian	437	19	34	39	8

TABLE 22

When it comes to honesty and integrity, do you think things have gotten better, gotten worse, or stayed about the same compared to 10 years ago?

		N	Better	Same	Worse	Don't Know
Total Responding		691	9%	53%	35%	2%
Gender:	Male	345	11	51	37	1
	Female	346	7	56	34	3
Age:	18 to 28	146	9	53	37	1
	29 to 47	261	12	52	35	1
	48 to 66	175	7	56	34	3
	67 to 98	99	6	54	35	5
Married:	Yes	390	10	54	34	2
	No	302	8	53	36	2
Have Kids Under 18:	Yes	255	10	52	36	2
	No	434	9	54	34	2
Household Income:	Under $25,000	209	9	58	30	3
	$25,000 to $50,000	272	12	51	36	0
	Over $50,000	123	8	51	39	2
Region:	Northeast	178	8	50	40	2
	South	204	11	55	32	2
	Midwest	177	9	49	40	2
	West	132	9	61	28	1
Education:	High School or Less	378	9	55	34	3
	Some College	165	13	52	35	1
	College Graduate	146	7	52	40	1
Ethnicity:	White	515	8	52	38	2
	Black	85	12	69	17	2
	Hispanic	56	16	51	32	2
Voter Registration:	Not Registered	146	13	51	32	3
	Democrat	233	11	49	38	2
	Republican	145	3	63	31	2
	Independent	124	10	51	37	2
Church Type:	Protestant	294	7	58	33	2
	Catholic	127	18	43	38	2
Faith Perspective:	Evangelical	75	3	80	17	0
	Born Again	254	10	60	28	1
	Non-Christian	437	9	49	39	3

TABLE 23

When it comes to personal financial responsibility, do you think things have gotten better, gotten worse, or stayed about the same compared to 10 years ago?

		N	Better	Same	Worse	Don't Know
Total Responding		691	19%	42%	34%	5%
Gender:	Male	345	22	43	32	2
	Female	346	16	42	35	7
Age:	18 to 28	146	33	39	25	3
	29 to 47	261	18	44	36	2
	48 to 66	175	15	40	37	8
	67 to 98	99	13	44	34	9
Married:	Yes	390	18	45	34	3
	No	302	21	39	33	7
Have Kids Under 18:	Yes	255	16	46	36	2
	No	434	21	40	32	6
Household Income:	Under $25,000	209	14	45	36	6
	$25,000 to $50,000	272	21	41	37	1
	Over $50,000	123	27	43	26	4
Region:	Northeast	178	18	44	33	5
	South	204	22	44	31	4
	Midwest	177	23	34	36	7
	West	132	12	48	37	3
Education:	High School or Less	378	15	43	37	5
	Some College	165	28	40	26	6
	College Graduate	146	20	43	34	3
Ethnicity:	White	515	17	43	35	5
	Black	85	27	39	34	0
	Hispanic	56	27	40	26	6
Voter Registration:	Not Registered	146	25	36	30	10
	Republican	233	21	40	37	2
	Democrat	145	13	49	31	6
	Independent	124	17	43	37	3
Church Type:	Protestant	294	16	49	30	5
	Catholic	127	23	39	35	3
Faith Perspective:	Evangelical	75	14	52	28	5
	Born Again	254	18	44	34	4
	Non-Christian	437	20	41	33	5

TABLE 24

When it comes to showing compassion for the needy, do you think things have gotten better, gotten worse, or stayed about the same compared to 10 years ago?

		N	Better	Same	Worse	Don't Know
Total Responding		691	45%	18%	34%	3%
Gender:	Male	345	41	18	38	3
	Female	346	48	19	29	4
Age:	18 to 28	146	46	24	30	1
	29 to 47	261	43	20	35	2
	48 to 66	175	44	14	36	6
	67 to 98	99	46	15	33	6
Married:	Yes	390	47	18	32	3
	No	302	41	19	36	4
Have Kids Under 18:	Yes	255	44	20	34	2
	No	434	45	17	34	4
Household Income:	Under $25,000	209	43	19	34	3
	$25,000 to $50,000	272	48	18	32	2
	Over $50,000	123	47	15	33	5
Region:	Northeast	178	43	18	34	5
	South	204	48	19	31	2
	Midwest	177	48	14	35	3
	West	132	37	23	36	4
Education:	High School or Less	378	45	20	31	4
	Some College	165	50	13	34	2
	College Graduate	146	38	20	39	3
Ethnicity:	White	515	42	17	37	3
	Black	85	55	23	17	5
	Hispanic	56	47	30	21	2
Voter Registration:	Not Registered	146	40	25	30	4
	Democrat	233	51	16	29	4
	Republican	145	38	20	39	2
	Independent	124	44	16	36	4
Church Type:	Protestant	294	44	21	33	2
	Catholic	127	55	10	30	5
Faith Perspective:	Evangelical	75	45	33	21	1
	Born Again	254	46	20	34	0
	Non-Christian	437	44	17	34	5

TABLE 25

When it comes to job productivity, do you think things have gotten better, gotten worse, or stayed about the same compared to 10 years ago?

		N	Better	Same	Worse	Don't Know
Total Responding		691	21%	40%	34%	5%
Gender:	Male	345	26	35	36	3
	Female	346	16	44	33	8
Age:	18 to 28	146	23	38	37	2
	29 to 47	261	21	38	37	3
	48 to 66	175	26	37	31	6
	67 to 98	99	10	50	27	13
Married:	Yes	390	21	38	37	4
	No	302	21	41	31	6
Have Kids Under 18:	Yes	255	19	37	40	4
	No	434	22	41	31	6
Household Income:	Under $25,000	209	13	48	31	7
	$25,000 to $50,000	272	26	36	34	3
	Over $50,000	123	30	33	34	3
Region:	Northeast	178	16	44	34	6
	South	204	20	40	34	5
	Midwest	177	22	37	36	6
	West	132	28	36	33	4
Education:	High School or Less	378	16	42	36	6
	Some College	165	27	37	30	6
	College Graduate	146	26	36	34	4
Ethnicity:	White	515	22	39	34	5
	Black	85	17	45	27	12
	Hispanic	56	24	30	45	0
Voter Registration:	Not Registered	146	18	39	41	3
	Democrat	233	25	36	31	8
	Republican	145	13	45	37	5
	Independent	124	24	40	34	2
Church Type:	Protestant	294	18	42	34	6
	Catholic	127	26	35	37	3
Faith Perspective:	Evangelical	75	20	41	33	6
	Born Again	254	19	38	37	6
	Non-Christian	437	22	40	33	5

TABLE 26

When it comes to involvement in community matters, do you think things have gotten better, gotten worse, or stayed about the same compared to 10 years ago?

		N	Better	Same	Worse	Don't Know
Total Responding		691	33%	22%	39%	6%
Gender:	Male	345	34	23	40	4
	Female	346	33	21	37	8
Age:	18 to 28	146	37	27	30	6
	29 to 47	261	35	22	38	5
	48 to 66	175	32	18	42	8
	67 to 98	99	26	20	46	8
Married:	Yes	390	33	23	39	5
	No	302	34	21	38	7
Have Kids Under 18:	Yes	255	33	25	36	6
	No	434	34	20	40	6
Household Income:	Under $25,000	209	33	23	38	6
	$25,000 to $50,000	272	37	21	37	5
	Over $50,000	123	37	21	40	2
Region:	Northeast	178	36	23	36	5
	South	204	36	25	34	5
	Midwest	177	27	20	47	5
	West	132	36	19	36	9
Education:	High School or Less	378	31	24	39	7
	Some College	165	34	19	42	4
	College Graduate	146	39	21	34	6
Ethnicity:	White	515	29	24	43	4
	Black	85	40	22	28	10
	Hispanic	56	55	15	24	6
Voter Registration:	Not Registered	146	34	21	34	11
	Democrat	233	37	22	38	3
	Republican	145	26	29	41	4
	Independent	124	30	17	44	9
Church Type:	Protestant	294	33	26	34	7
	Catholic	127	45	16	38	2
Faith Perspective:	Evangelical	75	31	35	26	8
	Born Again	254	36	25	34	4
	Non-Christian	437	32	20	41	7

Table 27

When it comes to people's ability to read and write, do you think things have gotten better, gotten worse, or stayed about the same compared to 10 years ago?

		N	Better	Same	Worse	Don't Know
Total Responding		691	37%	29%	28%	6%
Gender:	Male	345	33	34	27	5
	Female	346	40	24	30	6
Age:	18 to 28	146	44	31	23	2
	29 to 47	261	35	30	29	5
	48 to 66	175	29	28	33	10
	67 to 98	99	43	26	26	5
Married:	Yes	390	37	26	31	6
	No	302	36	33	25	6
Have Kids Under 18:	Yes	255	35	29	31	5
	No	434	37	29	27	6
Household Income:	Under $25,000	209	42	29	24	5
	$25,000 to $50,000	272	32	29	32	7
	Over $50,000	123	36	29	32	3
Region:	Northeast	178	35	24	33	8
	South	204	42	30	23	5
	Midwest	177	39	27	31	3
	West	132	27	38	29	7
Education:	High School or Less	378	40	27	27	6
	Some College	165	39	28	29	5
	College Graduate	146	24	37	32	7
Ethnicity:	White	515	35	30	30	5
	Black	85	41	33	22	4
	Hispanic	56	46	28	21	6
Voter Registration:	Not Registered	146	43	29	24	4
	Democrat	233	40	26	29	5
	Republican	145	26	36	30	7
	Independent	124	38	28	27	7
Church Type:	Protestant	294	36	27	31	6
	Catholic	127	49	24	22	5
Faith Perspective:	Evangelical	75	34	34	25	7
	Born Again	254	40	26	28	5
	Non-Christian	437	34	31	29	6

TABLE 28

When it comes to people's selfishness, do you think things have gotten better, gotten worse, or stayed about the same compared to 10 years ago?

		N	Better	Same	Worse	Don't Know
Total Responding		691	9%	52%	35%	4%
Gender:	Male	345	8	49	38	4
	Female	346	10	55	31	4
Age:	18 to 28	146	13	46	37	4
	29 to 47	261	10	50	38	2
	48 to 66	175	7	59	31	3
	67 to 98	99	4	53	32	11
Married:	Yes	390	11	53	34	3
	No	302	7	51	36	6
Have Kids Under 18:	Yes	255	9	50	39	2
	No	434	9	53	33	5
Household Income:	Under $25,000	209	9	54	31	6
	$25,000 to $50,000	272	9	54	35	2
	Over $50,000	123	13	42	43	2
Region:	Northeast	178	7	53	38	2
	South	204	10	58	29	3
	Midwest	177	10	45	40	5
	West	132	10	52	32	6
Education:	High School or Less	378	7	58	30	5
	Some College	165	12	47	38	3
	College Graduate	146	11	43	44	3
Ethnicity:	White	515	9	50	36	5
	Black	85	10	67	20	2
	Hispanic	56	0	47	53	0
Voter Registration:	Not Registered	146	10	53	32	4
	Democrat	233	8	52	38	2
	Republican	145	7	57	30	6
	Independent	124	8	46	39	6
Church Type:	Protestant	294	9	62	26	3
	Catholic	127	11	37	50	3
Faith Perspective:	Evangelical	75	2	84	14	0
	Born Again	254	11	59	27	3
	Non-Christian	437	8	48	39	5

TABLE 29

When it comes to people's political awareness, do you think things have gotten better, gotten worse, or stayed about the same compared to 10 years ago?

		N	Better	Same	Worse	Don't Know
Total Responding		691	50%	17%	30%	3%
Gender:	Male	345	52	18	28	2
	Female	346	48	16	32	4
Age:	18 to 28	146	56	17	27	0
	29 to 47	261	52	18	29	2
	48 to 66	175	57	10	30	4
	67 to 98	99	25	26	39	9
Married:	Yes	390	54	15	28	2
	No	302	45	18	33	4
Have Kids Under 18:	Yes	255	52	17	30	2
	No	434	50	17	30	4
Household Income:	Under $25,000	209	43	21	34	2
	$25,000 to $50,000	272	55	15	28	2
	Over $50,000	123	55	11	31	3
Region:	Northeast	178	53	14	30	2
	South	204	47	18	33	3
	Midwest	177	52	16	30	2
	West	132	49	19	27	5
Education:	High School or Less	378	45	20	31	4
	Some College	165	59	9	31	0
	College Graduate	146	53	16	29	3
Ethnicity:	White	515	48	17	31	3
	Black	85	44	21	33	2
	Hispanic	56	80	9	9	2
Voter Registration:	Not Registered	146	60	16	21	3
	Democrat	233	45	15	38	2
	Republican	145	43	23	30	4
	Independent	124	55	12	30	3
Church Type:	Protestant	294	45	17	35	2
	Catholic	127	65	10	22	3
Faith Perspective:	Evangelical	75	50	22	27	1
	Born Again	254	51	15	33	2
	Non-Christian	437	50	17	29	4

TABLE 30

When it comes to our tolerance toward people who are different from ourselves, do you think things have gotten better, gotten worse, or stayed about the same compared to 10 years ago?

		N	Better	Same	Worse	Don't Know
Total Responding		691	33%	31%	31%	5%
Gender:	Male	345	30	32	36	3
	Female	346	36	31	26	8
Age:	18 to 28	146	36	29	32	2
	29 to 47	261	35	31	31	2
	48 to 66	175	33	32	29	6
	67 to 98	99	25	33	29	14
Married:	Yes	390	31	29	35	5
	No	302	35	34	26	5
Have Kids Under 18:	Yes	255	31	29	36	3
	No	434	34	32	28	6
Household Income:	Under $25,000	209	29	36	25	10
	$25,000 to $50,000	272	37	32	30	1
	Over $50,000	123	32	22	44	2
Region:	Northeast	178	31	29	34	7
	South	204	29	36	29	6
	Midwest	177	44	19	32	5
	West	132	28	43	27	2
Education:	High School or Less	378	31	32	29	7
	Some College	165	40	27	29	4
	College Graduate	146	29	34	37	0
Ethnicity:	White	515	35	29	33	4
	Black	85	25	48	18	9
	Hispanic	56	24	38	39	0
Voter Registration:	Not Registered	146	30	33	32	5
	Democrat	233	32	34	31	3
	Republican	145	32	28	32	8
	Independent	124	39	31	30	1
Church Type:	Protestant	294	32	34	32	3
	Catholic	127	42	23	32	2
Faith Perspective:	Evangelical	75	20	35	45	0
	Born Again	254	35	28	33	4
	Non-Christian	437	32	33	29	6

TABLE 31

When it comes to views about the family, do you think things have gotten better, gotten worse, or stayed about the same compared to 10 years ago?

		N	Better	Same	Worse	Don't Know
Total Responding		691	21%	47%	28%	5%
Gender:	Male	345	21	42	31	6
	Female	346	20	52	25	3
Age:	18 to 28	146	25	40	28	7
	29 to 47	261	24	45	27	4
	48 to 66	175	18	48	29	4
	67 to 98	99	13	54	29	4
Married:	Yes	390	21	49	26	3
	No	302	20	43	30	7
Have Kids Under 18:	Yes	255	26	46	25	3
	No	434	18	47	30	6
Household Income:	Under $25,000	209	19	48	29	4
	$25,000 to $50,000	272	24	44	27	5
	Over $50,000	123	25	42	31	2
Region:	Northeast	178	23	45	28	3
	South	204	19	51	24	6
	Midwest	177	22	44	31	3
	West	132	18	45	29	8
Education:	High School or Less	378	19	50	26	5
	Some College	165	26	39	31	5
	College Graduate	146	18	48	30	4
Ethnicity:	White	515	20	47	30	4
	Black	85	33	58	9	0
	Hispanic	56	9	44	39	8
Voter Registration:	Not Registered	146	17	53	22	8
	Democrat	233	24	44	29	3
	Republican	145	17	58	23	2
	Independent	124	23	35	35	7
Church Type:	Protestant	294	21	50	25	4
	Catholic	127	23	39	34	4
Faith Perspective:	Evangelical	75	9	66	19	6
	Born Again	254	22	53	22	3
	Non-Christian	437	20	43	31	6

TABLE 32

How about the performance of various people within their areas of responsibility? Based on your own experience and observations, how would you rate the job being done by parents?

		N	Excellent	Good	Not Too Good	Poor	Don't Know
Total Responding		691	6%	41%	36%	15%	2%
Gender:	Male	345	8	39	34	17	2
	Female	346	4	42	38	13	3
Age:	18 to 28	146	8	60	22	9	0
	29 to 47	261	6	47	35	10	2
	48 to 66	175	3	28	44	21	4
	67 to 98	99	8	16	47	23	6
Married:	Yes	390	6	38	41	14	1
	No	302	6	44	30	16	4
Have Kids Under 18:	Yes	255	8	47	33	10	2
	No	434	5	36	38	18	3
Household Income:	Under $25,000	209	11	35	34	17	3
	$25,000 to $50,000	272	5	45	34	14	1
	Over $50,000	123	1	45	42	11	1
Region:	Northeast	178	4	45	35	13	3
	South	204	8	33	40	18	1
	Midwest	177	6	39	38	14	2
	West	132	6	47	28	14	4
Education:	High School or Less	378	7	35	39	16	3
	Some College	165	4	48	30	16	1
	College Graduate	146	4	48	35	11	2
Ethnicity:	White	515	3	40	38	16	3
	Black	85	13	33	36	19	0
	Hispanic	56	19	46	31	3	0
Voter Registration:	Not Registered	146	10	54	25	9	2
	Democrat	233	8	33	41	17	1
	Republican	145	3	30	44	19	3
	Independent	124	2	53	33	11	2
Church Type:	Protestant	294	5	34	45	14	1
	Catholic	127	9	49	30	8	3
Faith Perspective:	Evangelical	75	3	27	50	19	1
	Born Again	254	5	37	40	17	1
	Non-Christian	437	6	43	34	14	3

TABLE 33

Based on your own experience and observations, how would you rate the job being done by our national political leaders?

		N	Excellent	Good	Not Too Good	Poor	Don't Know
Total Responding		691	2%	30%	37%	27%	3%
Gender:	Male	345	3	26	35	34	1
	Female	346	1	34	39	21	6
Age:	18 to 28	146	3	39	32	24	1
	29 to 47	261	2	25	47	23	3
	48 to 66	175	1	33	28	33	4
	67 to 98	99	1	29	33	31	7
Married:	Yes	390	2	29	38	28	3
	No	302	2	32	35	27	3
Have Kids Under 18:	Yes	255	2	31	40	24	3
	No	434	2	30	35	30	4
Household Income:	Under $25,000	209	2	31	39	25	3
	$25,000 to $50,000	272	3	29	35	31	2
	Over $50,000	123	2	28	44	26	1
Region:	Northeast	178	0	28	40	30	2
	South	204	2	28	36	28	6
	Midwest	177	5	32	43	16	3
	West	132	0	35	27	37	2
Education:	High School or Less	378	2	33	33	27	5
	Some College	165	2	26	41	28	3
	College Graduate	146	1	30	43	26	1
Ethnicity:	White	515	1	27	38	31	3
	Black	85	4	47	34	10	5
	Hispanic	56	6	46	20	29	0
Voter Registration:	Not Registered	146	6	30	36	21	6
	Democrat	233	1	41	37	19	1
	Republican	145	0	16	35	46	3
	Independent	124	1	28	44	26	1
Church Type:	Protestant	294	1	29	40	26	3
	Catholic	127	6	37	36	20	1
Faith Perspective:	Evangelical	75	0	15	43	40	2
	Born Again	254	2	24	43	26	4
	Non-Christian	437	2	34	34	28	3

TABLE 34

Based on your own experience and observations, how would you rate the job being done by the clergy?

		N	Excellent	Good	Not Too Good	Poor	Don't Know
Total Responding		691	9%	58%	15%	7%	11%
Gender:	Male	345	7	53	18	9	13
	Female	346	10	63	13	4	10
Age:	18 to 28	146	10	62	12	6	10
	29 to 47	261	5	62	14	8	11
	48 to 66	175	10	59	9	8	14
	67 to 98	99	12	41	33	1	13
Married:	Yes	390	9	62	14	7	9
	No	302	9	53	17	7	15
Have Kids Under 18:	Yes	255	9	67	12	6	7
	No	434	9	53	17	7	14
Household Income:	Under $25,000	209	10	49	21	9	11
	$25,000 to $50,000	272	8	64	12	4	11
	Over $50,000	123	7	63	15	9	6
Region:	Northeast	178	10	59	15	9	7
	South	204	11	55	18	4	12
	Midwest	177	8	64	13	5	10
	West	132	3	53	15	9	19
Education:	High School or Less	378	9	56	14	8	12
	Some College	165	8	59	17	4	12
	College Graduate	146	7	61	16	7	8
Ethnicity:	White	515	7	61	15	6	12
	Black	85	24	41	23	5	6
	Hispanic	56	10	69	12	8	0
Voter Registration:	Not Registered	146	8	54	15	6	17
	Democrat	233	12	52	16	9	11
	Republican	145	8	62	20	3	6
	Independent	124	7	70	10	7	6
Church Type:	Protestant	294	11	60	17	3	9
	Catholic	127	11	63	12	5	8
Faith Perspective:	Evangelical	75	10	53	30	5	3
	Born Again	254	10	59	20	3	9
	Non-Christian	437	8	57	13	9	13

TABLE 35

Based on your own experience and observations, how would you rate the job being done by public school teachers?

		N	Excellent	Good	Not Too Good	Poor	Don't Know
Total Responding		691	9%	52%	22%	10%	7%
Gender:	Male	345	7	50	21	14	7
	Female	346	10	53	23	6	7
Age:	18 to 28	146	10	53	22	7	8
	29 to 47	261	9	55	24	9	4
	48 to 66	175	7	51	20	14	8
	67 to 98	99	11	43	23	10	13
Married:	Yes	390	8	56	21	11	4
	No	302	9	46	24	10	11
Have Kids Under 18:	Yes	255	11	53	25	8	3
	No	434	8	51	20	12	10
Household Income:	Under $25,000	209	11	46	21	12	10
	$25,000 to $50,000	272	9	55	20	11	5
	Over $50,000	123	7	55	24	10	3
Region:	Northeast	178	8	49	22	13	8
	South	204	8	52	22	12	7
	Midwest	177	9	48	30	8	4
	West	132	10	58	13	7	12
Education:	High School or Less	378	10	49	22	13	6
	Some College	165	7	50	26	10	7
	College Graduate	146	7	60	18	5	11
Ethnicity:	White	515	8	53	22	11	7
	Black	85	20	40	23	15	2
	Hispanic	56	6	82	5	0	8
Voter Registration:	Not Registered	146	11	45	27	6	11
	Democrat	233	9	56	17	13	5
	Republican	145	3	48	28	13	7
	Independent	124	13	58	15	7	7
Church Type:	Protestant	294	7	51	27	9	5
	Catholic	127	13	50	22	8	7
Faith Perspective:	Evangelical	75	5	51	27	9	7
	Born Again	254	6	52	27	9	6
	Non-Christian	437	10	51	19	11	8

TABLE 36

Based on your own experience and observations, how would you rate the job being done by journalists?

		N	Excellent	Good	Not Too Good	Poor	Don't Know
Total Responding		691	4%	47%	29%	16%	5%
Gender:	Male	345	2	47	26	21	3
	Female	346	5	47	31	10	7
Age:	18 to 28	146	5	62	19	11	3
	29 to 47	261	3	47	31	13	6
	48 to 66	175	2	44	30	19	5
	67 to 98	99	6	34	31	22	6
Married:	Yes	390	2	44	31	18	6
	No	302	6	51	26	13	4
Have Kids Under 18:	Yes	255	3	51	26	14	7
	No	434	4	45	30	17	4
Household Income:	Under $25,000	209	7	48	21	13	10
	$25,000 to $50,000	272	2	52	28	15	3
	Over $50,000	123	1	40	34	24	0
Region:	Northeast	178	5	46	28	15	5
	South	204	4	43	30	15	7
	Midwest	177	2	52	27	15	4
	West	132	2	49	29	19	2
Education:	High School or Less	378	4	46	27	15	7
	Some College	165	5	49	30	14	2
	College Graduate	146	1	48	29	20	1
Ethnicity:	White	515	3	44	30	18	4
	Black	85	6	46	24	15	8
	Hispanic	56	0	74	14	6	6
Voter Registration:	Not Registered	146	3	55	24	8	10
	Democrat	233	5	54	24	13	4
	Republican	145	2	32	36	29	1
	Independent	124	3	48	32	14	3
Church Type:	Protestant	294	5	40	33	17	6
	Catholic	127	2	52	30	11	5
Faith Perspective:	Evangelical	75	2	30	40	24	4
	Born Again	254	2	42	33	17	5
	Non-Christian	437	4	50	26	15	5

TABLE 37

Based on your own experience and observations, how would you rate the job being done by our military leaders?

		N	Excellent	Good	Not Too Good	Poor	Don't Know
Total Responding		691	14%	61%	13%	5%	7%
Gender:	Male	345	17	61	8	8	6
	Female	346	12	61	18	2	7
Age:	18 to 28	146	17	58	7	9	10
	29 to 47	261	13	64	13	5	4
	48 to 66	175	17	56	16	3	8
	67 to 98	99	12	66	14	1	7
Married:	Yes	390	14	63	14	4	6
	No	302	15	59	12	7	7
Have Kids Under 18:	Yes	255	14	67	9	3	7
	No	434	15	57	15	6	7
Household Income:	Under $25,000	209	12	55	15	11	7
	$25,000 to $50,000	272	15	67	11	2	5
	Over $50,000	123	19	62	10	5	5
Region:	Northeast	178	16	59	10	9	7
	South	204	14	59	17	4	6
	Midwest	177	16	63	12	2	6
	West	132	11	65	10	8	7
Education:	High School or Less	378	14	59	15	5	7
	Some College	165	16	60	9	6	9
	College Graduate	146	14	67	11	6	2
Ethnicity:	White	515	14	64	12	5	6
	Black	85	18	37	30	8	8
	Hispanic	56	12	80	0	2	6
Voter Registration:	Not Registered	146	16	58	11	6	11
	Democrat	233	13	58	17	7	6
	Republican	145	16	67	9	2	6
	Independent	124	15	62	9	8	5
Church Type:	Protestant	294	12	61	15	3	9
	Catholic	127	18	63	10	6	3
Faith Perspective:	Evangelical	75	15	60	8	9	8
	Born Again	254	17	58	15	4	6
	Non-Christian	437	13	63	12	6	7

TABLE 38

Based on your own experience and observations, how would you rate the job being done by doctors and medical professionals?

		N	Excellent	Good	Not Too Good	Poor	Don't Know
Total Responding		691	11%	62%	17%	7%	3%
Gender:	Male	345	10	62	19	7	2
	Female	346	13	62	16	6	3
Age:	18 to 28	146	14	63	13	7	3
	29 to 47	261	6	67	21	5	1
	48 to 66	175	12	58	15	9	5
	67 to 98	99	20	54	17	5	4
Married:	Yes	390	10	65	17	6	2
	No	302	13	58	18	7	4
Have Kids Under 18:	Yes	255	9	68	17	5	1
	No	434	13	59	17	7	4
Household Income:	Under $25,000	209	13	55	20	9	4
	$25,000 to $50,000	272	12	62	17	7	2
	Over $50,000	123	10	68	15	5	1
Region:	Northeast	178	10	59	19	8	4
	South	204	12	62	15	8	2
	Midwest	177	13	65	15	4	3
	West	132	10	62	20	6	2
Education:	High School or Less	378	10	65	15	6	4
	Some College	165	12	56	23	7	3
	College Graduate	146	15	61	17	7	0
Ethnicity:	White	515	10	66	16	6	2
	Black	85	16	52	25	2	6
	Hispanic	56	8	67	20	6	0
Voter Registration:	Not Registered	146	12	58	18	9	3
	Democrat	233	14	58	20	5	3
	Republican	145	9	71	14	4	2
	Independent	124	9	65	17	6	2
Church Type:	Protestant	294	9	64	20	4	3
	Catholic	127	16	61	15	6	3
Faith Perspective:	Evangelical	75	8	68	19	4	1
	Born Again	254	9	66	18	5	1
	Non-Christian	437	13	60	17	8	4

TABLE 39

Based on your own experience and observations, how would you rate the job being done by college professors?

		N	Excellent	Good	Not Too Good	Poor	Don't Know
Total Responding		691	5%	53%	15%	7%	19%
Gender:	Male	345	6	50	17	10	18
	Female	346	4	57	13	4	21
Age:	18 to 28	146	8	65	11	4	12
	29 to 47	261	5	62	14	5	14
	48 to 66	175	5	42	18	9	26
	67 to 98	99	1	33	23	13	29
Married:	Yes	390	5	53	15	8	18
	No	302	5	53	15	6	20
Have Kids Under 18:	Yes	255	7	61	10	4	18
	No	434	4	49	19	9	20
Household Income:	Under $25,000	209	8	49	13	9	20
	$25,000 to $50,000	272	4	58	14	6	18
	Over $50,000	123	2	54	24	9	11
Region:	Northeast	178	4	50	15	10	22
	South	204	6	59	14	7	15
	Midwest	177	5	56	19	4	16
	West	132	5	46	14	8	26
Education:	High School or Less	378	6	50	12	8	25
	Some College	165	3	57	19	4	16
	College Graduate	146	5	59	19	8	9
Ethnicity:	White	515	3	51	17	8	21
	Black	85	8	53	11	9	19
	Hispanic	56	14	72	4	0	9
Voter Registration:	Not Registered	146	9	54	10	4	23
	Democrat	233	5	54	16	7	19
	Republican	145	3	50	20	9	18
	Independent	124	4	61	14	9	12
Church Type:	Protestant	294	3	52	19	8	19
	Catholic	127	9	60	14	6	12
Faith Perspective:	Evangelical	75	3	45	23	9	20
	Born Again	254	4	50	20	8	18
	Non-Christian	437	6	55	13	7	20

TABLE 40

Based on your own experience and observations, how would you rate the job being done by business leaders?

		N	Excellent	Good	Not Too Good	Poor	Don't Know
Total Responding		691	3%	49%	31%	12%	5%
Gender:	Male	345	3	48	33	13	3
	Female	346	2	51	30	10	7
Age:	18 to 28	146	3	60	23	10	4
	29 to 47	261	3	48	34	14	1
	48 to 66	175	0	47	36	11	6
	67 to 98	99	8	41	27	11	12
Married:	Yes	390	2	50	33	12	3
	No	302	4	49	29	11	7
Have Kids Under 18:	Yes	255	1	57	31	8	3
	No	434	4	45	31	14	5
Household Income:	Under $25,000	209	5	45	29	16	4
	$25,000 to $50,000	272	2	49	35	9	5
	Over $50,000	123	4	57	30	9	0
Region:	Northeast	178	4	40	39	15	3
	South	204	3	49	32	13	3
	Midwest	177	3	59	25	6	6
	West	132	1	51	28	12	8
Education:	High School or Less	378	3	48	30	13	7
	Some College	165	4	49	35	9	2
	College Graduate	146	1	55	31	11	2
Ethnicity:	White	515	2	51	31	11	4
	Black	85	9	35	34	13	9
	Hispanic	56	6	60	30	3	0
Voter Registration:	Not Registered	146	3	52	26	10	9
	Democrat	233	4	47	33	11	5
	Republican	145	2	46	34	15	3
	Independent	124	3	54	30	12	1
Church Type:	Protestant	294	2	48	33	9	6
	Catholic	127	3	53	33	9	2
Faith Perspective:	Evangelical	75	2	40	41	13	5
	Born Again	254	3	49	31	12	5
	Non-Christian	437	3	50	32	11	4

TABLE 41

Who would probably have an easier time getting ahead financially in our society today: a man or a woman?

		N	Man	Woman	No Difference	Don't Know
Total Responding		604	65%	13%	20%	1%
Gender:	Male	291	66	14	19	2
	Female	313	65	13	21	1
Age:	18 to 28	111	75	13	11	1
	29 to 47	258	65	12	22	1
	48 to 66	160	61	12	27	0
	67 to 98	70	60	23	11	6
Married:	Yes	333	69	12	18	1
	No	271	61	15	21	2
Have Kids Under 18:	Yes	237	67	11	20	2
	No	366	64	15	19	1
Household Income:	Under $25,000	200	51	22	25	3
	$25,000 to $50,000	216	76	8	17	0
	Over $50,000	112	71	9	18	1
Region:	Northeast	122	71	17	12	0
	South	207	58	13	28	2
	Midwest	133	68	16	14	1
	West	141	69	9	20	2
Education:	High School or Less	335	59	17	22	2
	Some College	148	74	9	17	1
	College Graduate	122	74	9	17	0
Ethnicity:	White	443	68	10	21	1
	Black	79	44	36	20	0
	Hispanic	54	72	11	11	6
Voter Registration:	Not Registered	127	55	17	22	6
	Democrat	201	66	18	17	0
	Republican	132	75	9	16	0
	Independent	117	67	8	24	1
Church Type:	Protestant	260	67	13	20	1
	Catholic	107	73	9	18	0
Faith Perspective:	Evangelical	47	69	10	21	0
	Born Again	244	62	15	22	1
	Non-Christian	360	68	12	18	2

TABLE 42

Who would probably have an easier time getting ahead financially in our society today: a single person or a married person?

		N	Single Person	Married Person	No Difference	Don't Know
Total Responding		604	35%	40%	23%	2%
Gender:	Male	291	36	44	19	1
	Female	313	33	37	26	3
Age:	18 to 28	111	51	32	17	1
	29 to 47	258	35	41	22	2
	48 to 66	160	23	46	29	2
	67 to 98	70	36	39	22	3
Married:	Yes	333	36	41	21	2
	No	271	33	40	25	2
Have Kids Under 18:	Yes	237	37	42	19	2
	No	366	33	40	25	2
Household Income:	Under $25,000	200	36	38	25	1
	$25,000 to $50,000	216	44	34	21	2
	Over $50,000	112	26	52	22	1
Region:	Northeast	122	37	37	26	1
	South	207	37	39	21	3
	Midwest	133	40	36	23	2
	West	141	26	49	23	1
Education:	High School or Less	335	36	41	19	3
	Some College	148	35	37	27	0
	College Graduate	122	30	41	28	1
Ethnicity:	White	443	35	39	24	3
	Black	79	40	39	21	0
	Hispanic	54	34	55	11	0
Voter Registration:	Not Registered	127	31	40	26	3
	Democrat	201	34	47	17	2
	Republican	132	37	35	27	1
	Independent	117	41	38	18	2
Church Type:	Protestant	260	38	37	23	2
	Catholic	107	30	48	21	1
Faith Perspective:	Evangelical	47	34	43	22	1
	Born Again	244	38	37	23	3
	Non-Christian	360	33	43	23	1

TABLE 43

Who would probably have an easier time getting ahead financially in our society today: a Christian or a non-Christian?

		N	Christian	Non-Christian	No Difference	Don't Know
Total Responding		1206	41%	12%	42%	5%
Gender:	Male	589	40	10	46	4
	Female	616	42	13	39	6
Age:	18 to 28	243	27	10	58	4
	29 to 47	485	38	12	46	4
	48 to 66	310	47	13	35	5
	67 to 98	151	60	8	23	9
Married:	Yes	678	43	13	40	4
	No	527	38	10	45	6
Have Kids Under 18:	Yes	458	39	11	45	4
	No	745	42	12	41	6
Household Income:	Under $25,000	384	49	12	34	6
	$25,000 to $50,000	453	39	14	42	5
	Over $50,000	216	29	9	58	3
Region:	Northeast	260	32	8	54	6
	South	405	54	13	29	4
	Midwest	272	35	13	46	6
	West	268	35	12	47	5
Education:	High School or Less	668	48	11	36	5
	Some College	285	35	14	45	7
	College Graduate	251	30	10	56	4
Ethnicity:	White	888	39	12	43	5
	Black	155	46	10	39	5
	Hispanic	107	57	14	29	0
Voter Registration:	Not Registered	261	44	7	45	4
	Democrat	414	47	11	37	6
	Republican	253	36	21	39	4
	Independent	212	38	7	51	4
Church Type:	Protestant	510	47	17	31	5
	Catholic	222	47	4	47	2
Faith Perspective:	Evangelical	115	38	38	23	0
	Born Again	463	45	20	31	4
	Non-Christian	742	38	7	49	6

TABLE 44

Who would probably have an easier time getting ahead financially in our society today: a white adult or a black adult?

		N	White Adult	Black Adult	No Difference	Don't Know
Total Responding		604	60%	5%	32%	4%
Gender:	Male	291	67	6	24	2
	Female	313	54	3	38	5
Age:	18 to 28	111	58	5	34	3
	29 to 47	258	62	4	31	3
	48 to 66	160	62	5	30	3
	67 to 98	70	54	7	30	9
Married:	Yes	333	62	4	28	5
	No	271	57	5	36	2
Have Kids Under 18:	Yes	237	60	4	33	3
	No	366	60	5	31	4
Household Income:	Under $25,000	200	48	5	42	5
	$25,000 to $50,000	216	71	3	23	3
	Over $50,000	112	71	8	20	1
Region:	Northeast	122	69	6	24	1
	South	207	53	3	40	4
	Midwest	133	60	8	25	7
	West	141	62	3	33	2
Education:	High School or Less	335	52	5	38	5
	Some College	148	67	2	29	2
	College Graduate	122	74	7	18	1
Ethnicity:	White	443	56	6	34	5
	Black	79	66	4	30	0
	Hispanic	54	84	0	16	0
Voter Registration:	Not Registered	127	51	7	39	3
	Democrat	201	66	2	29	3
	Republican	132	62	8	28	1
	Independent	117	63	3	29	5
Church Type:	Protestant	260	60	6	31	3
	Catholic	107	69	1	28	1
Faith Perspective:	Evangelical	47	53	14	31	2
	Born Again	244	57	6	33	4
	Non-Christian	360	63	4	31	3

TABLE 45

Who would probably have an easier time getting ahead financially in our society today: someone with a college degree, or someone with a high school diploma?

		N	College Degree	High School Diploma	No Difference	Don't Know
Total Responding		604	82%	3%	14%	2%
Gender:	Male	291	87	3	9	1
	Female	313	77	3	18	2
Age:	18 to 28	111	88	1	11	0
	29 to 47	258	82	2	14	2
	48 to 66	160	79	3	17	2
	67 to 98	70	80	6	10	4
Married:	Yes	333	84	3	12	2
	No	271	80	2	16	2
Have Kids Under 18:	Yes	237	83	2	13	2
	No	366	81	3	14	1
Household Income:	Under $25,000	200	77	2	18	3
	$25,000 to $50,000	216	85	3	11	0
	Over $50,000	112	88	3	8	0
Region:	Northeast	122	82	5	14	0
	South	207	79	1	20	0
	Midwest	133	80	4	11	5
	West	141	89	1	7	3
Education:	High School or Less	335	77	4	16	3
	Some College	148	86	1	12	1
	College Graduate	122	90	0	10	0
Ethnicity:	White	443	82	4	13	1
	Black	79	72	0	26	2
	Hispanic	54	94	0	0	6
Voter Registration:	Not Registered	127	74	1	20	6
	Democrat	201	81	3	16	0
	Republican	132	87	3	10	0
	Independent	117	89	3	8	1
Church Type:	Protestant	260	82	4	14	1
	Catholic	107	85	1	14	0
Faith Perspective:	Evangelical	47	83	11	6	0
	Born Again	244	82	3	14	2
	Non-Christian	360	82	2	14	2

TABLE 46

Who would probably have an easier time getting ahead financially in our society today: a white adult or an Asian adult?

		N	White Adult	Asian Adult	No Difference	Don't Know
Total Responding		604	57%	15%	23%	6%
Gender:	Male	298	56	15	26	3
	Female	303	58	15	19	8
Age:	18 to 28	132	63	6	25	6
	29 to 47	227	51	20	24	5
	48 to 66	150	56	18	19	6
	67 to 98	81	58	11	24	6
Married:	Yes	344	55	18	22	5
	No	257	59	11	23	7
Have Kids Under 18:	Yes	220	56	14	24	6
	No	379	57	15	22	6
Household Income:	Under $25,000	184	56	14	23	7
	$25,000 to $50,000	237	58	18	20	4
	Over $50,000	104	60	13	25	2
Region:	Northeast	137	60	12	22	6
	South	198	55	21	19	5
	Midwest	139	65	10	21	4
	West	127	46	15	31	8
Education:	High School or Less	333	51	17	25	7
	Some College	137	63	13	19	5
	College Graduate	130	64	12	22	2
Ethnicity:	White	445	51	17	25	7
	Black	76	83	11	6	0
	Hispanic	53	67	6	26	0
Voter Registration:	Not Registered	133	59	13	21	7
	Democrat	214	60	17	21	2
	Republican	121	53	11	28	7
	Independent	94	53	18	18	10
Church Type:	Protestant	250	55	18	21	6
	Catholic	115	65	15	19	2
Faith Perspective:	Evangelical	69	49	20	24	7
	Born Again	219	58	15	21	7
	Non-Christian	382	56	15	24	5

TABLE 47

Who would probably have an easier time getting ahead financially in our society today: a person who has children, or a person who does not have children?

		N	With Children	Without Children	No Difference	Don't Know
Total Responding		604	18%	65%	15%	3%
Gender:	Male	298	21	61	15	3
	Female	303	14	68	14	3
Age:	18 to 28	132	6	75	14	5
	29 to 47	227	17	68	13	1
	48 to 66	150	25	56	15	4
	67 to 98	81	23	57	16	4
Married:	Yes	344	21	61	17	2
	No	257	13	70	12	5
Have Kids Under 18:	Yes	220	15	72	13	1
	No	379	19	61	16	4
Household Income:	Under $25,000	184	19	65	13	3
	$25,000 to $50,000	237	21	64	13	2
	Over $50,000	104	12	73	14	1
Region:	Northeast	137	13	68	16	3
	South	198	25	62	12	1
	Midwest	139	14	66	18	2
	West	127	15	64	14	7
Education:	High School or Less	333	18	63	15	4
	Some College	137	19	68	10	3
	College Graduate	130	15	67	17	1
Ethnicity:	White	445	16	65	17	2
	Black	76	25	63	11	1
	Hispanic	53	22	72	0	6
Voter Registration:	Not Registered	133	19	68	8	6
	Democrat	214	14	69	15	3
	Republican	121	21	63	16	1
	Independent	94	16	67	17	1
Church Type:	Protestant	250	17	66	12	5
	Catholic	115	19	68	11	1
Faith Perspective:	Evangelical	69	12	69	18	1
	Born Again	219	16	62	17	4
	Non-Christian	382	18	66	13	2

TABLE 48

Who would probably have an easier time getting ahead financially in our society today: a black adult or a Hispanic adult?

		N	Black Adult	Hispanic Adult	No Difference	Don't Know
Total Responding		604	32%	20%	38%	10%
Gender:	Male	298	29	23	42	5
	Female	303	34	17	34	14
Age:	18 to 28	132	33	20	44	3
	29 to 47	227	32	21	41	6
	48 to 66	150	36	19	30	15
	67 to 98	81	22	23	38	18
Married:	Yes	344	31	20	39	10
	No	257	33	21	37	10
Have Kids Under 18:	Yes	220	35	13	44	8
	No	379	30	25	35	10
Household Income:	Under $25,000	184	32	25	36	7
	$25,000 to $50,000	237	35	18	39	9
	Over $50,000	104	37	19	40	4
Region:	Northeast	137	28	24	39	9
	South	198	34	23	31	11
	Midwest	139	35	17	39	9
	West	127	29	15	47	9
Education:	High School or Less	333	32	20	37	12
	Some College	137	31	19	41	9
	College Graduate	130	32	24	39	6
Ethnicity:	White	445	34	17	39	10
	Black	76	40	25	27	9
	Hispanic	53	15	36	49	0
Voter Registration:	Not Registered	133	26	25	38	10
	Democrat	214	37	24	31	8
	Republican	121	32	15	42	11
	Independent	94	29	17	44	10
Church Type:	Protestant	250	37	19	34	10
	Catholic	115	30	20	42	8
Faith Perspective:	Evangelical	69	40	8	38	14
	Born Again	219	39	13	40	8
	Non-Christian	382	28	25	37	10

TABLE 49

Who would probably have an easier time getting ahead financially in our society today: a person active in a church, or a person not active in a church?

		N	Active in a Church	Not Active in a Church	No Difference	Don't Know
Total Responding		604	43%	9%	42%	6%
Gender:	Male	298	43	7	45	5
	Female	303	43	10	39	7
Age:	18 to 28	132	30	7	59	3
	29 to 47	227	43	8	44	5
	48 to 66	150	50	9	32	9
	67 to 98	81	53	9	27	10
Married:	Yes	344	46	9	41	5
	No	257	39	8	44	8
Have Kids Under 18:	Yes	220	38	7	50	5
	No	379	46	9	38	7
Household Income:	Under $25,000	184	49	9	35	7
	$25,000 to $50,000	237	40	10	44	6
	Over $50,000	104	43	2	52	3
Region:	Northeast	137	28	5	53	13
	South	198	56	11	29	4
	Midwest	139	43	7	43	6
	West	127	37	11	49	3
Education:	High School or Less	333	48	9	36	7
	Some College	137	40	9	45	6
	College Graduate	130	32	8	56	5
Ethnicity:	White	445	42	9	43	6
	Black	76	49	6	40	4
	Hispanic	53	59	4	38	0
Voter Registration:	Not Registered	133	39	7	48	6
	Democrat	214	50	8	35	7
	Republican	121	47	12	38	3
	Independent	94	31	11	52	5
Church Type:	Protestant	250	50	12	32	6
	Catholic	115	49	5	42	4
Faith Perspective:	Evangelical	69	47	22	29	2
	Born Again	219	50	13	34	3
	Non-Christian	382	39	6	47	8

TABLE 50

Overall, do you think cable TV companies serve the needs of people very well, pretty well, only fairly, not too well, or poorly?

		N	Very Well	Pretty Well	Only Fairly	Not Too Well	Poorly	Don't Know
Total Responding		604	11%	22%	29%	14%	12%	12%
Gender:	Male	291	12	20	29	18	16	6
	Female	313	10	24	29	10	9	18
Age:	18 to 28	111	13	23	27	14	18	4
	29 to 47	258	10	24	26	16	9	14
	48 to 66	160	11	17	36	12	11	13
	67 to 98	70	8	26	22	10	18	17
Married:	Yes	333	11	19	30	15	13	12
	No	271	10	25	27	13	12	12
Have Kids Under 18:	Yes	237	11	20	30	16	10	13
	No	366	10	23	28	12	14	12
Household Income:	Under $25,000	200	13	18	34	11	12	11
	$25,000 to $50,000	216	10	24	27	15	15	10
	Over $50,000	112	11	25	34	15	7	8
Region:	Northeast	122	9	25	24	22	13	8
	South	207	15	19	33	10	10	13
	Midwest	133	4	27	28	16	10	16
	West	141	12	19	29	11	19	11
Education:	High School or Less	335	11	18	30	13	15	14
	Some College	148	8	27	28	17	13	8
	College Graduate	122	12	26	28	13	5	15
Ethnicity:	White	443	10	22	29	13	12	14
	Black	79	8	30	35	12	5	11
	Hispanic	54	18	7	17	22	29	8
Voter Registration:	Not Registered	127	11	27	26	15	8	13
	Democrat	201	8	20	31	18	10	14
	Republican	132	9	24	26	11	21	8
	Independent	117	16	17	31	8	13	14
Church Type:	Protestant	260	10	21	28	14	13	14
	Catholic	107	5	20	33	22	9	10
Faith Perspective:	Evangelical	47	16	21	22	19	9	12
	Born Again	244	8	26	29	12	12	14
	Non-Christian	360	12	19	29	15	13	11

TABLE 51

Overall, do you think hospitals serve the needs of people very well, pretty well, only fairly, not too well, or poorly?

		N	Very Well	Pretty Well	Only Fairly	Not Too Well	Poorly	Don't Know
Total Responding		604	26%	40%	20%	6%	6%	3%
Gender:	Male	291	27	37	23	5	8	1
	Female	313	25	42	17	6	5	4
Age:	18 to 28	111	22	46	23	5	3	1
	29 to 47	258	25	42	22	5	4	2
	48 to 66	160	28	34	19	5	9	4
	67 to 98	70	34	35	9	10	7	5
Married:	Yes	333	24	40	23	6	6	1
	No	271	29	40	16	5	6	4
Have Kids Under 18:	Yes	237	22	46	21	5	4	1
	No	366	29	36	18	6	8	3
Household Income:	Under $25,000	200	33	35	15	7	10	1
	$25,000 to $50,000	216	21	47	22	4	4	2
	Over $50,000	112	31	43	17	4	4	1
Region:	Northeast	122	35	34	13	8	7	2
	South	207	27	32	25	7	6	2
	Midwest	133	21	53	12	6	6	2
	West	141	22	42	25	2	5	4
Education:	High School or Less	335	25	36	21	7	9	2
	Some College	148	28	42	19	3	4	3
	College Graduate	122	26	47	18	5	2	4
Ethnicity:	White	443	28	41	17	6	6	2
	Black	79	26	44	13	8	5	5
	Hispanic	54	12	24	54	0	6	5
Voter Registration:	Not Registered	127	25	39	23	4	9	1
	Democrat	201	25	34	22	9	5	5
	Republican	132	28	41	17	6	7	2
	Independent	117	25	49	16	4	3	2
Church Type:	Protestant	260	28	40	20	7	3	3
	Catholic	107	26	37	29	5	3	0
Faith Perspective:	Evangelical	47	38	39	15	2	5	2
	Born Again	244	24	44	21	6	4	2
	Non-Christian	360	27	37	19	6	8	3

TABLE 52

Overall, do you think your local government officials serve the needs of people very well, pretty well, only fairly, not too well, or poorly?

		N	Very Well	Pretty Well	Only Fairly	Not Too Well	Poorly	Don't Know
Total Responding		604	8%	21%	32%	16%	18%	4%
Gender:	Male	291	8	18	31	15	24	4
	Female	313	7	25	33	17	13	5
Age:	18 to 28	111	6	27	25	15	19	8
	29 to 47	258	6	19	33	17	20	4
	48 to 66	160	10	20	33	16	20	1
	67 to 98	70	11	26	37	16	6	6
Married:	Yes	333	6	20	35	16	20	3
	No	271	10	23	28	16	17	6
Have Kids Under 18:	Yes	237	4	23	29	20	18	5
	No	366	10	20	34	14	18	4
Household Income:	Under $25,000	200	15	16	31	17	16	6
	$25,000 to $50,000	216	4	24	32	17	19	4
	Over $50,000	112	4	24	35	20	16	2
Region:	Northeast	122	9	23	32	24	10	3
	South	207	11	20	30	11	24	5
	Midwest	133	5	28	31	18	11	7
	West	141	5	16	36	16	25	3
Education:	High School or Less	335	9	20	30	17	22	4
	Some College	148	6	21	32	19	15	7
	College Graduate	122	6	27	38	13	13	3
Ethnicity:	White	443	6	24	35	16	15	4
	Black	79	21	16	24	18	22	0
	Hispanic	54	7	17	24	11	42	0
Voter Registration:	Not Registered	127	10	18	27	14	19	11
	Democrat	201	10	21	40	11	16	2
	Republican	132	6	24	25	21	22	3
	Independent	117	4	21	35	19	17	4
Church Type:	Protestant	260	7	26	28	19	17	4
	Catholic	107	7	24	35	11	18	4
Faith Perspective:	Evangelical	47	12	28	27	24	10	0
	Born Again	244	7	24	30	18	18	3
	Non-Christian	360	8	19	33	15	19	6

TABLE 53

Overall, do you think your representatives in Congress serve the needs of people very well, pretty well, only fairly, not too well, or poorly?

		N	Very Well	Pretty Well	Only Fairly	Not Too Well	Poorly	Don't Know
Total Responding		604	7%	20%	29%	19%	20%	4%
Gender:	Male	291	8	16	28	19	26	2
	Female	313	6	24	31	18	15	7
Age:	18 to 28	111	6	20	21	20	26	8
	29 to 47	258	6	19	30	22	19	4
	48 to 66	160	10	20	32	17	20	1
	67 to 98	70	4	28	38	10	12	9
Married:	Yes	333	6	19	31	18	23	3
	No	271	8	22	27	20	16	6
Have Kids Under 18:	Yes	237	4	19	29	23	21	5
	No	366	9	21	30	16	20	4
Household Income:	Under $25,000	200	8	18	29	24	14	7
	$25,000 to $50,000	216	4	22	30	20	20	3
	Over $50,000	112	6	18	36	17	23	1
Region:	Northeast	122	11	17	34	21	16	1
	South	207	9	20	26	15	22	9
	Midwest	133	5	28	28	20	15	5
	West	141	2	18	32	23	25	1
Education:	High School or Less	335	6	20	27	20	22	5
	Some College	148	9	18	31	20	19	4
	College Graduate	122	7	23	35	14	17	5
Ethnicity:	White	443	6	21	32	16	19	5
	Black	79	13	21	23	24	18	1
	Hispanic	54	7	17	17	22	37	0
Voter Registration:	Not Registered	127	6	20	28	15	18	13
	Democrat	201	11	20	32	19	16	2
	Republican	132	4	20	29	17	29	1
	Independent	117	4	22	27	25	19	3
Church Type:	Protestant	260	7	24	28	21	15	5
	Catholic	107	8	15	31	18	26	2
Faith Perspective:	Evangelical	47	9	18	25	37	9	2
	Born Again	244	7	24	28	19	18	3
	Non-Christian	360	7	18	30	18	21	5

TABLE 54

Overall, do you think local churches serve the needs of people very well, pretty well, only fairly, not too well, or poorly?

		N	Very Well	Pretty Well	Only Fairly	Not Too Well	Poorly	Don't Know
Total Responding		604	35%	35%	17%	2%	1%	9%
Gender:	Male	291	36	34	17	3	1	9
	Female	313	34	36	17	2	1	10
Age:	18 to 28	111	39	45	3	1	0	12
	29 to 47	258	34	32	19	3	1	11
	48 to 66	160	32	36	21	4	2	5
	67 to 98	70	37	31	22	1	1	7
Married:	Yes	333	36	35	18	3	1	7
	No	271	33	35	16	2	1	12
Have Kids Under 18:	Yes	237	37	33	17	2	1	9
	No	366	33	37	17	2	1	9
Household Income:	Under $25,000	200	36	35	17	3	1	9
	$25,000 to $50,000	216	32	38	16	2	2	11
	Over $50,000	112	32	35	23	4	1	5
Region:	Northeast	122	37	30	20	3	2	8
	South	207	46	31	15	2	0	7
	Midwest	133	31	41	13	3	2	9
	West	141	21	41	22	2	1	14
Education:	High School or Less	335	39	32	18	2	1	8
	Some College	148	31	41	15	2	2	9
	College Graduate	122	27	38	17	5	1	12
Ethnicity:	White	443	35	35	18	2	1	10
	Black	79	36	36	13	7	2	7
	Hispanic	54	45	40	4	0	0	11
Voter Registration:	Not Registered	127	36	29	19	2	2	12
	Democrat	201	35	32	18	5	1	10
	Republican	132	27	44	17	1	1	10
	Independent	117	39	38	14	0	2	7
Church Type:	Protestant	260	41	39	14	3	0	3
	Catholic	107	39	40	17	2	1	1
Faith Perspective:	Evangelical	47	41	33	19	6	2	0
	Born Again	244	37	41	16	3	1	3
	Non-Christian	360	33	32	18	2	1	14

TABLE 55

Overall, do you think your local police serve the needs of people very well, pretty well, only fairly, not too well, or poorly?

		N	Very Well	Pretty Well	Only Fairly	Not Too Well	Poorly	Don't Know
Total Responding		604	26%	40%	21%	3%	7%	4%
Gender:	Male	291	23	39	22	3	9	4
	Female	313	29	40	20	3	5	3
Age:	18 to 28	111	17	43	25	5	9	2
	29 to 47	258	24	41	23	3	5	5
	48 to 66	160	31	35	20	3	9	2
	67 to 98	70	40	44	3	0	6	7
Married:	Yes	333	26	40	20	4	6	4
	No	271	26	39	22	2	8	3
Have Kids Under 18:	Yes	237	22	43	22	4	4	6
	No	366	28	38	20	3	9	2
Household Income:	Under $25,000	200	31	37	19	2	10	1
	$25,000 to $50,000	216	23	38	27	3	6	2
	Over $50,000	112	28	48	17	5	2	0
Region:	Northeast	122	36	40	12	3	7	1
	South	207	24	35	21	3	10	7
	Midwest	133	23	49	15	5	5	3
	West	141	24	37	32	2	5	1
Education:	High School or Less	335	27	33	24	2	9	5
	Some College	148	24	47	20	3	5	1
	College Graduate	122	27	50	13	4	4	2
Ethnicity:	White	443	28	44	18	2	5	2
	Black	79	20	35	16	7	19	2
	Hispanic	54	21	13	43	0	7	17
Voter Registration:	Not Registered	127	26	28	22	3	10	11
	Democrat	201	27	37	22	2	8	2
	Republican	132	23	45	22	4	4	1
	Independent	117	28	50	14	3	4	2
Church Type:	Protestant	260	26	38	21	4	7	3
	Catholic	107	30	36	21	2	2	9
Faith Perspective:	Evangelical	47	35	37	19	9	0	0
	Born Again	244	23	41	22	5	6	2
	Non-Christian	360	28	39	20	1	8	5

TABLE 56

Overall, do you think your local public schools serve the needs of people very well, pretty well, only fairly, not too well, or poorly?

		N	Very Well	Pretty Well	Only Fairly	Not Too Well	Poorly	Don't Know
Total Responding		604	18%	32%	27%	8%	10%	5%
Gender:	Male	291	15	31	30	7	13	4
	Female	313	21	33	25	9	6	6
Age:	18 to 28	111	16	28	27	12	13	5
	29 to 47	258	17	36	28	6	9	6
	48 to 66	160	20	27	30	9	11	3
	67 to 98	70	25	38	17	7	6	7
Married:	Yes	333	15	35	31	5	12	2
	No	271	22	28	23	11	7	9
Have Kids Under 18:	Yes	237	17	34	32	7	9	2
	No	366	19	31	25	8	10	7
Household Income:	Under $25,000	200	27	30	24	9	6	4
	$25,000 to $50,000	216	12	36	26	7	15	3
	Over $50,000	112	17	31	34	8	7	4
Region:	Northeast	122	17	33	26	7	13	4
	South	207	23	23	28	11	8	7
	Midwest	133	18	40	23	7	8	4
	West	141	13	37	31	4	11	4
Education:	High School or Less	335	20	29	30	7	10	4
	Some College	148	16	35	28	7	9	5
	College Graduate	122	16	38	19	11	7	9
Ethnicity:	White	443	18	35	27	7	8	5
	Black	79	21	20	24	16	11	7
	Hispanic	54	17	23	40	0	20	0
Voter Registration:	Not Registered	127	20	27	33	5	3	11
	Democrat	201	21	28	27	11	9	5
	Republican	132	12	40	26	5	15	3
	Independent	117	18	37	24	6	13	2
Church Type:	Protestant	260	19	34	24	7	11	5
	Catholic	107	16	30	35	6	10	2
Faith Perspective:	Evangelical	47	11	35	31	7	13	3
	Born Again	244	19	29	30	8	11	3
	Non-Christian	360	18	34	26	7	9	6

TABLE 57

Overall, do you think public libraries in your area serve the needs of people very well, pretty well, only fairly, not too well, or poorly?

		N	Very Well	Pretty Well	Only Fairly	Not Too Well	Poorly	Don't Know
Total Responding		604	45%	36%	8%	2%	1%	8%
Gender:	Male	291	41	38	10	2	1	7
	Female	313	48	34	5	3	1	9
Age:	18 to 28	111	40	43	7	3	2	6
	29 to 47	258	39	42	8	4	1	6
	48 to 66	160	48	27	11	1	2	11
	67 to 98	70	67	17	2	0	0	14
Married:	Yes	333	47	36	8	2	1	6
	No	271	42	36	7	3	2	11
Have Kids Under 18:	Yes	237	45	39	6	3	2	5
	No	366	44	34	9	2	1	10
Household Income:	Under $25,000	200	47	34	6	4	1	8
	$25,000 to $50,000	216	43	38	8	1	2	8
	Over $50,000	112	39	40	13	3	1	3
Region:	Northeast	122	44	39	5	4	1	8
	South	207	47	28	8	2	1	14
	Midwest	133	50	38	5	1	3	4
	West	141	37	43	12	3	1	4
Education:	High School or Less	335	45	33	7	3	2	11
	Some College	148	44	42	9	1	1	4
	College Graduate	122	44	37	7	4	2	7
Ethnicity:	White	443	49	34	7	3	1	6
	Black	79	29	32	12	3	2	21
	Hispanic	54	45	44	6	0	0	5
Voter Registration:	Not Registered	127	45	35	9	2	0	10
	Democrat	201	39	36	9	2	2	12
	Republican	132	42	41	9	1	0	7
	Independent	117	53	32	4	5	4	2
Church Type:	Protestant	260	42	35	9	3	1	10
	Catholic	107	52	35	5	5	2	2
Faith Perspective:	Evangelical	47	47	26	12	6	0	9
	Born Again	244	44	36	7	3	1	8
	Non-Christian	360	45	35	8	2	1	8

TABLE 58

Do you agree or disagree that it is important to be a member of a church? Do you (agree/disagree) strongly or somewhat?

		N	Agree Strongly	Agree Somewhat	Disagree Somewhat	Disagree Strongly	Don't Know
Total Responding		604	50%	27%	13%	9%	1%
Gender:	Male	291	45	28	13	13	1
	Female	313	54	26	13	5	1
Age:	18 to 28	111	47	39	6	6	2
	29 to 47	258	41	30	18	11	1
	48 to 66	160	60	18	14	7	1
	67 to 98	70	66	16	8	7	4
Married:	Yes	333	54	23	14	8	0
	No	271	44	31	12	10	2
Have Kids Under 18:	Yes	237	45	30	15	9	1
	No	366	52	25	12	9	1
Household Income:	Under $25,000	200	55	25	9	11	0
	$25,000 to $50,000	216	48	29	15	7	1
	Over $50,000	112	38	32	20	10	1
Region:	Northeast	122	47	30	12	9	2
	South	207	63	22	10	6	0
	Midwest	133	43	32	13	10	2
	West	141	40	27	20	12	1
Education:	High School or Less	335	61	20	11	6	2
	Some College	148	36	37	16	11	0
	College Graduate	122	37	33	17	13	1
Ethnicity:	White	443	44	29	16	9	2
	Black	79	80	15	0	4	0
	Hispanic	54	61	15	11	13	0
Voter Registration:	Not Registered	127	45	32	10	9	4
	Democrat	201	58	24	10	8	0
	Republican	132	53	24	15	8	0
	Independent	117	44	28	16	11	1
Church Type:	Protestant	260	69	22	7	1	0
	Catholic	107	57	31	9	3	1
Faith Perspective:	Evangelical	47	85	7	8	0	0
	Born Again	244	67	25	6	2	0
	Non-Christian	360	38	29	18	14	2

TABLE 59

Do you agree or disagree that today's children have a bright future to look forward to?
Do you (agree/disagree) strongly or somewhat?

		N	Agree Strongly	Agree Somewhat	Disagree Somewhat	Disagree Strongly	Don't Know
Total Responding		604	16%	26%	33%	22%	3%
Gender:	Male	291	18	26	35	20	2
	Female	313	14	26	31	25	4
Age:	18 to 28	111	14	26	39	17	4
	29 to 47	258	17	28	35	18	1
	48 to 66	160	17	23	30	28	2
	67 to 98	70	14	23	19	33	12
Married:	Yes	333	19	26	34	19	2
	No	271	13	26	31	26	4
Have Kids Under 18:	Yes	237	18	27	32	21	1
	No	366	15	25	33	23	4
Household Income:	Under $25,000	200	20	20	34	24	2
	$25,000 to $50,000	216	10	31	34	23	2
	Over $50,000	112	14	30	36	17	2
Region:	Northeast	122	17	28	27	26	2
	South	207	25	20	28	22	5
	Midwest	133	5	35	34	22	4
	West	141	12	24	44	19	1
Education:	High School or Less	335	19	21	31	25	4
	Some College	148	9	30	38	23	1
	College Graduate	122	17	34	30	14	4
Ethnicity:	White	443	13	28	31	24	4
	Black	79	21	19	39	19	1
	Hispanic	54	40	11	32	17	0
Voter Registration:	Not Registered	127	25	21	32	17	5
	Democrat	201	15	22	35	23	4
	Republican	132	15	33	28	21	2
	Independent	117	11	27	34	28	0
Church Type:	Protestant	260	15	25	30	26	4
	Catholic	107	23	32	25	18	3
Faith Perspective:	Evangelical	47	11	13	32	39	4
	Born Again	244	13	23	35	25	4
	Non-Christian	360	18	28	32	20	2

Table 60

Do you agree or disagree that when it comes to morals and ethics, people must decide for themselves what is right and wrong; there are no absolute standards that apply to everybody in all situations? Do you (agree/disagree) strongly or somewhat?

		N	Agree Strongly	Agree Somewhat	Disagree Somewhat	Disagree Strongly	Don't Know
Total Responding		604	46%	25%	9%	15%	4%
Gender:	Male	291	44	28	10	14	4
	Female	313	49	23	9	16	3
Age:	18 to 28	111	44	36	7	12	1
	29 to 47	258	45	26	10	16	4
	48 to 66	160	53	18	12	16	2
	67 to 98	70	45	22	7	14	12
Married:	Yes	333	46	22	11	18	3
	No	271	47	30	7	12	4
Have Kids Under 18:	Yes	237	44	27	9	16	4
	No	366	48	25	9	15	3
Household Income:	Under $25,000	200	46	29	11	12	3
	$25,000 to $50,000	216	51	25	6	17	0
	Over $50,000	112	50	23	11	15	0
Region:	Northeast	122	45	33	8	14	0
	South	207	46	22	10	15	8
	Midwest	133	50	25	7	16	2
	West	141	45	24	12	16	2
Education:	High School or Less	335	48	25	7	13	6
	Some College	148	46	23	11	20	1
	College Graduate	122	42	29	12	16	0
Ethnicity:	White	443	47	25	10	16	2
	Black	79	53	30	2	12	2
	Hispanic	54	40	11	11	17	21
Voter Registration:	Not Registered	127	31	33	8	19	10
	Democrat	201	55	23	6	13	3
	Republican	132	41	22	10	25	2
	Independent	117	54	28	13	6	0
Church Type:	Protestant	260	45	22	8	23	2
	Catholic	107	46	24	12	8	9
Faith Perspective:	Evangelical	47	31	9	7	53	0
	Born Again	244	39	25	7	26	3
	Non-Christian	360	52	25	11	8	4

TABLE 61

Do you agree or disagree that it's getting harder and harder to make lasting friendships? Do you (agree/disagree) strongly or somewhat?

		N	Agree Strongly	Agree Somewhat	Disagree Somewhat	Disagree Strongly	Don't Know
Total Responding		604	25%	33%	25%	16%	1%
Gender:	Male	291	26	33	27	13	1
	Female	313	24	32	24	18	1
Age:	18 to 28	111	20	34	25	18	2
	29 to 47	258	25	32	28	14	1
	48 to 66	160	27	32	25	15	0
	67 to 98	70	26	36	20	16	3
Married:	Yes	333	24	38	25	12	2
	No	271	27	26	26	20	1
Have Kids Under 18:	Yes	237	23	31	28	16	1
	No	366	26	33	24	15	1
Household Income:	Under $25,000	200	29	32	27	12	1
	$25,000 to $50,000	216	23	27	31	19	1
	Over $50,000	112	14	49	24	12	0
Region:	Northeast	122	31	33	19	16	1
	South	207	31	30	23	14	2
	Midwest	133	21	32	32	13	1
	West	141	15	35	29	20	1
Education:	High School or Less	335	30	31	24	14	2
	Some College	148	24	33	32	11	0
	College Graduate	122	14	38	22	26	0
Ethnicity:	White	443	22	36	24	16	1
	Black	79	41	25	23	10	0
	Hispanic	54	27	19	34	20	0
Voter Registration:	Not Registered	127	30	34	23	11	2
	Democrat	201	34	27	23	15	1
	Republican	132	16	39	27	16	1
	Independent	117	16	36	27	21	1
Church Type:	Protestant	260	23	35	25	15	2
	Catholic	107	23	28	27	21	0
Faith Perspective:	Evangelical	47	25	48	23	4	0
	Born Again	244	25	37	25	12	2
	Non-Christian	360	25	30	26	18	1

TABLE 62

Do you agree or disagree that you'd rather have satisfying leisure than a satisfying job or career? Do you (agree/disagree) strongly or somewhat?

		N	Agree Strongly	Agree Somewhat	Disagree Somewhat	Disagree Strongly	Don't Know
Total Responding		604	15%	25%	29%	25%	6%
Gender:	Male	291	14	26	28	30	3
	Female	313	17	23	30	21	9
Age:	18 to 28	111	9	25	31	34	2
	29 to 47	258	15	27	30	23	4
	48 to 66	160	17	24	30	23	6
	67 to 98	70	25	19	12	25	20
Married:	Yes	333	15	28	30	23	4
	No	271	16	21	27	28	8
Have Kids Under 18:	Yes	237	12	27	30	27	4
	No	366	18	23	28	24	7
Household Income:	Under $25,000	200	13	26	28	24	8
	$25,000 to $50,000	216	13	27	28	29	3
	Over $50,000	112	11	28	34	24	2
Region:	Northeast	122	19	22	27	28	4
	South	207	19	23	26	26	7
	Midwest	133	13	29	26	24	8
	West	141	9	25	37	24	5
Education:	High School or Less	335	18	23	27	25	7
	Some College	148	13	24	31	27	5
	College Graduate	122	12	30	30	24	4
Ethnicity:	White	443	14	26	30	23	7
	Black	79	24	23	16	38	0
	Hispanic	54	17	18	26	34	5
Voter Registration:	Not Registered	127	12	32	29	19	9
	Democrat	201	21	22	24	27	5
	Republican	132	14	20	35	27	5
	Independent	117	13	26	30	25	7
Church Type:	Protestant	260	18	24	28	24	6
	Catholic	107	17	22	27	28	5
Faith Perspective:	Evangelical	47	18	29	27	21	5
	Born Again	244	15	25	28	25	6
	Non-Christian	360	15	24	29	25	6

TABLE 63

Do you agree or disagree that if you had to make a choice, you'd rather play it safe than take risks in life? Do you (agree/disagree) strongly or somewhat?

		N	Agree Strongly	Agree Somewhat	Disagree Somewhat	Disagree Strongly	Don't Know
Total Responding		604	40%	27%	20%	10%	2%
Gender:	Male	291	34	28	24	12	2
	Female	313	45	27	17	8	2
Age:	18 to 28	111	35	20	29	16	1
	29 to 47	258	31	33	21	13	2
	48 to 66	160	46	29	19	5	2
	67 to 98	70	66	16	7	4	7
Married:	Yes	333	38	31	23	7	1
	No	271	42	23	17	15	3
Have Kids Under 18:	Yes	237	37	31	21	10	1
	No	366	42	25	19	10	3
Household Income:	Under $25,000	200	50	23	16	8	4
	$25,000 to $50,000	216	30	33	22	14	1
	Over $50,000	112	28	33	26	12	1
Region:	Northeast	122	37	31	19	12	1
	South	207	51	20	20	7	2
	Midwest	133	32	34	18	11	4
	West	141	35	28	23	14	1
Education:	High School or Less	335	50	25	17	6	3
	Some College	148	31	28	25	14	1
	College Graduate	122	25	33	23	18	2
Ethnicity:	White	443	37	30	20	11	3
	Black	79	57	22	15	6	0
	Hispanic	54	34	19	39	9	0
Voter Registration:	Not Registered	127	49	22	18	7	4
	Democrat	201	49	24	16	9	1
	Republican	132	32	31	21	15	1
	Independent	117	26	30	29	13	3
Church Type:	Protestant	260	43	29	19	8	2
	Catholic	107	37	21	22	18	2
Faith Perspective:	Evangelical	47	47	31	15	7	0
	Born Again	244	41	30	20	7	1
	Non-Christian	360	40	25	20	12	3

TABLE 64

Do you agree or disagree that as it turns out, the majority is almost always right? Do you (agree/disagree) strongly or somewhat?

		N	Agree Strongly	Agree Somewhat	Disagree Somewhat	Disagree Strongly	Don't Know
Total Responding		604	9%	28%	35%	24%	4%
Gender:	Male	291	11	33	27	24	5
	Female	313	7	23	43	24	4
Age:	18 to 28	111	12	27	32	28	1
	29 to 47	258	7	26	40	23	5
	48 to 66	160	11	29	34	23	3
	67 to 98	70	11	32	22	23	12
Married:	Yes	333	8	30	32	26	5
	No	271	11	25	39	22	4
Have Kids Under 18:	Yes	237	10	27	37	22	5
	No	366	9	29	34	25	4
Household Income:	Under $25,000	200	12	26	37	22	4
	$25,000 to $50,000	216	7	30	32	30	1
	Over $50,000	112	6	34	39	20	1
Region:	Northeast	122	8	23	37	30	3
	South	207	12	26	35	21	7
	Midwest	133	4	32	35	26	2
	West	141	11	31	35	20	4
Education:	High School or Less	335	13	26	32	24	6
	Some College	148	5	30	41	23	2
	College Graduate	122	3	29	38	26	4
Ethnicity:	White	443	9	29	35	25	3
	Black	79	7	24	45	22	2
	Hispanic	54	18	19	15	26	21
Voter Registration:	Not Registered	127	15	33	26	15	11
	Democrat	201	8	22	39	28	4
	Republican	132	6	26	36	30	2
	Independent	117	8	34	36	20	1
Church Type:	Protestant	260	8	28	34	28	2
	Catholic	107	7	23	38	24	8
Faith Perspective:	Evangelical	47	11	11	29	45	4
	Born Again	244	5	31	34	29	2
	Non-Christian	360	12	26	36	21	6

TABLE 65

Do you agree or disagree that most churches are more interested in raising money than in helping people? Do you (agree/disagree) strongly or somewhat?

		N	Agree Strongly	Agree Somewhat	Disagree Somewhat	Disagree Strongly	Don't Know
Total Responding		604	23%	26%	27%	19%	5%
Gender:	Male	291	21	26	25	22	6
	Female	313	24	26	29	16	5
Age:	18 to 28	111	9	21	30	37	3
	29 to 47	258	18	33	30	14	5
	48 to 66	160	35	22	22	15	7
	67 to 98	70	36	20	19	19	6
Married:	Yes	333	22	26	28	20	4
	No	271	23	26	25	18	7
Have Kids Under 18:	Yes	237	18	28	31	19	4
	No	366	26	24	24	19	7
Household Income:	Under $25,000	200	32	24	26	13	4
	$25,000 to $50,000	216	15	27	29	25	4
	Over $50,000	112	13	28	34	18	7
Region:	Northeast	122	23	31	24	15	7
	South	207	33	23	23	18	3
	Midwest	133	20	26	35	15	5
	West	141	10	26	28	29	7
Education:	High School or Less	335	30	26	22	18	5
	Some College	148	16	30	33	17	4
	College Graduate	122	12	22	34	26	7
Ethnicity:	White	443	21	26	29	18	6
	Black	79	38	35	16	11	0
	Hispanic	54	27	11	21	40	0
Voter Registration:	Not Registered	127	27	26	27	12	8
	Democrat	201	25	23	29	17	6
	Republican	132	21	25	29	24	2
	Independent	117	18	32	21	24	5
Church Type:	Protestant	260	20	26	28	24	2
	Catholic	107	20	22	25	26	7
Faith Perspective:	Evangelical	47	16	25	29	31	0
	Born Again	244	19	28	25	25	3
	Non-Christian	360	25	24	28	15	7

TABLE 66

Do you agree or disagree that the main purpose in life is enjoyment and personal fulfillment? Do you (agree/disagree) strongly or somewhat?

		N	Agree Strongly	Agree Somewhat	Disagree Somewhat	Disagree Strongly	Don't Know
Total Responding		604	29%	30%	20%	17%	4%
Gender:	Male	291	25	33	19	18	5
	Female	313	32	28	21	17	2
Age:	18 to 28	111	34	28	17	20	1
	29 to 47	258	24	30	23	19	4
	48 to 66	160	26	33	21	16	5
	67 to 98	70	41	28	12	14	4
Married:	Yes	333	24	32	19	21	3
	No	271	34	28	21	13	4
Have Kids Under 18:	Yes	237	23	29	21	23	4
	No	366	32	31	19	14	3
Household Income:	Under $25,000	200	33	30	21	16	1
	$25,000 to $50,000	216	29	26	23	22	0
	Over $50,000	112	22	44	16	16	2
Region:	Northeast	122	29	38	17	15	0
	South	207	36	24	17	16	7
	Midwest	133	23	30	23	22	1
	West	141	23	33	23	17	4
Education:	High School or Less	335	35	27	15	17	6
	Some College	148	18	32	29	21	1
	College Graduate	122	25	36	23	16	1
Ethnicity:	White	443	28	32	22	17	2
	Black	79	42	28	14	11	5
	Hispanic	54	21	25	9	29	17
Voter Registration:	Not Registered	127	30	28	16	14	12
	Democrat	201	28	34	21	15	2
	Republican	132	22	30	19	29	0
	Independent	117	38	26	21	14	0
Church Type:	Protestant	260	26	28	20	24	1
	Catholic	107	19	35	23	15	8
Faith Perspective:	Evangelical	47	18	14	22	46	0
	Born Again	244	27	25	19	29	0
	Non-Christian	360	30	34	21	10	6

TABLE 67

Do you agree or disagree that our political representatives reflect the best interests of the people? Do you (agree/disagree) strongly or somewhat?

		N	Agree Strongly	Agree Somewhat	Disagree Somewhat	Disagree Strongly	Don't Know
Total Responding		604	5%	20%	37%	33%	5%
Gender:	Male	291	3	18	38	37	5
	Female	313	8	22	36	30	5
Age:	18 to 28	111	3	28	33	35	1
	29 to 47	258	3	14	49	30	4
	48 to 66	160	5	27	27	37	4
	67 to 98	70	21	12	21	33	13
Married:	Yes	333	5	18	35	36	5
	No	271	6	22	39	29	5
Have Kids Under 18:	Yes	237	4	19	43	31	4
	No	366	7	20	33	35	5
Household Income:	Under $25,000	200	10	21	35	31	3
	$25,000 to $50,000	216	2	21	38	37	2
	Over $50,000	112	3	21	42	33	0
Region:	Northeast	122	3	18	40	37	2
	South	207	9	17	31	34	10
	Midwest	133	2	27	45	25	2
	West	141	7	20	35	36	2
Education:	High School or Less	335	8	18	33	33	8
	Some College	148	3	16	43	37	1
	College Graduate	122	2	28	41	28	0
Ethnicity:	White	443	3	19	40	35	3
	Black	79	16	25	32	20	7
	Hispanic	54	11	13	18	41	17
Voter Registration:	Not Registered	127	7	24	37	19	12
	Democrat	201	8	24	36	27	5
	Republican	132	2	15	36	48	0
	Independent	117	4	17	34	45	1
Church Type:	Protestant	260	7	19	34	35	5
	Catholic	107	2	21	34	34	8
Faith Perspective:	Evangelical	47	4	7	26	59	4
	Born Again	244	7	18	39	34	3
	Non-Christian	360	5	21	36	33	6

TABLE 68

There are many ideas that have been discussed by political leaders. For each idea I describe, please tell me if you favor or oppose that idea becoming legal. Do you favor or oppose homosexual adults being able to get married becoming legal?

		N	Favor	Oppose	Don't Know
Total Responding		602	29%	62%	10%
Gender:	Male	298	23	68	9
	Female	303	34	56	10
Age:	18 to 28	132	42	50	9
	29 to 47	227	33	57	9
	48 to 66	150	20	68	12
	67 to 98	81	11	81	8
Married:	Yes	344	23	68	8
	No	257	35	53	12
Have Kids Under 18:	Yes	220	31	58	11
	No	379	27	64	9
Household Income:	Under $25,000	184	29	63	7
	$25,000 to $50,000	237	27	62	11
	Over $50,000	104	42	53	5
Region:	Northeast	137	38	49	13
	South	198	17	76	7
	Midwest	139	30	58	12
	West	127	34	57	9
Education:	High School or Less	333	25	65	10
	Some College	137	29	62	9
	College Graduate	130	38	53	9
Ethnicity:	White	445	29	62	10
	Black	76	31	65	4
	Hispanic	53	34	63	4
Voter Registration:	Not Registered	133	28	55	17
	Democrat	214	33	57	9
	Republican	121	13	85	2
	Independent	94	41	50	9
Church Type:	Protestant	250	21	71	8
	Catholic	115	30	57	13
Faith Perspective:	Evangelical	69	3	97	0
	Born Again	219	17	78	6
	Non-Christian	382	35	52	12

TABLE 69

Do you favor or oppose married couples being able to get a divorce without having to go through the courts? Instead they would file notarized papers to show their desire to dissolve their marriage.

		N	Don't Favor	Oppose	Know
Total Responding		602	42%	51%	8%
Gender:	Male	298	49	43	8
	Female	303	35	57	7
Age:	18 to 28	132	48	45	7
	29 to 47	227	48	46	6
	48 to 66	150	37	52	11
	67 to 98	81	26	66	8
Married:	Yes	344	38	53	8
	No	257	47	47	6
Have Kids Under 18:	Yes	220	48	47	5
	No	379	38	53	9
Household Income:	Under $25,000	184	38	57	5
	$25,000 to $50,000	237	44	50	7
	Over $50,000	104	52	43	4
Region:	Northeast	137	48	44	8
	South	198	36	56	9
	Midwest	139	36	58	6
	West	127	52	41	7
Education:	High School or Less	333	38	53	9
	Some College	137	39	55	6
	College Graduate	130	55	39	6
Ethnicity:	White	445	43	50	7
	Black	76	37	58	5
	Hispanic	53	30	64	6
Voter Registration:	Not Registered	133	39	47	14
	Democrat	214	50	46	4
	Republican	121	28	70	3
	Independent	94	47	44	9
Church Type:	Protestant	250	33	59	9
	Catholic	115	39	56	5
Faith Perspective:	Evangelical	69	16	78	6
	Born Again	219	30	64	6
	Non-Christian	382	48	43	8

TABLE 70

Do you favor or oppose prayer being allowed in public schools by students on a voluntary basis becoming legal?

		N	Favor	Oppose	Don't Know
Total Responding		602	87%	11%	3%
Gender:	Male	298	81	16	4
	Female	303	93	5	2
Age:	18 to 28	132	85	12	3
	29 to 47	227	84	14	2
	48 to 66	150	94	6	0
	67 to 98	81	87	5	8
Married:	Yes	344	89	10	1
	No	257	84	11	4
Have Kids Under 18:	Yes	220	91	8	1
	No	379	84	12	4
Household Income:	Under $25,000	184	85	11	3
	$25,000 to $50,000	237	90	10	0
	Over $50,000	104	85	15	0
Region:	Northeast	137	86	14	0
	South	198	93	6	1
	Midwest	139	83	11	5
	West	127	81	13	5
Education:	High School or Less	333	90	5	4
	Some College	137	85	14	1
	College Graduate	130	80	20	0
Ethnicity:	White	445	88	10	2
	Black	76	86	11	2
	Hispanic	53	84	9	6
Voter Registration:	Not Registered	133	85	12	3
	Democrat	214	87	12	1
	Republican	121	89	7	4
	Independent	94	85	12	2
Church Type:	Protestant	250	93	5	2
	Catholic	115	89	11	0
Faith Perspective:	Evangelical	69	96	4	0
	Born Again	219	94	4	1
	Non-Christian	382	83	14	3

TABLE 71

Do you favor or oppose taxes on businesses being raised to help lower the federal budget deficit becoming legal?

		N	Favor	Oppose	Don't Know
Total Responding		602	44%	49%	7%
Gender:	Male	298	41	55	5
	Female	303	47	44	9
Age:	18 to 28	132	48	50	2
	29 to 47	227	45	48	7
	48 to 66	150	44	46	10
	67 to 98	81	39	51	10
Married:	Yes	344	40	52	8
	No	257	49	45	5
Have Kids Under 18:	Yes	220	50	42	8
	No	379	41	53	6
Household Income:	Under $25,000	184	55	38	7
	$25,000 to $50,000	237	45	49	6
	Over $50,000	104	37	59	4
Region:	Northeast	137	50	40	10
	South	198	44	50	6
	Midwest	139	43	52	6
	West	127	40	55	6
Education:	High School or Less	333	49	45	6
	Some College	137	40	54	6
	College Graduate	130	36	56	9
Ethnicity:	White	445	42	51	7
	Black	76	54	44	2
	Hispanic	53	47	39	13
Voter Registration:	Not Registered	133	46	48	6
	Democrat	214	50	42	8
	Republican	121	28	65	7
	Independent	94	52	46	3
Church Type:	Protestant	250	43	49	7
	Catholic	115	43	43	14
Faith Perspective:	Evangelical	69	27	67	6
	Born Again	219	43	51	6
	Non-Christian	382	45	48	7

TABLE 72

Do you favor or oppose households being fined if they do not recycle all recyclable materials becoming legal?

		N	Favor	Oppose	Don't Know
Total Responding		602	48%	49%	4%
Gender:	Male	298	47	52	2
	Female	303	48	46	5
Age:	18 to 28	132	56	43	1
	29 to 47	227	49	48	3
	48 to 66	150	44	50	6
	67 to 98	81	35	60	6
Married:	Yes	344	47	48	5
	No	257	49	49	2
Have Kids Under 18:	Yes	220	47	49	4
	No	379	48	49	3
Household Income:	Under $25,000	184	52	46	2
	$25,000 to $50,000	237	50	49	1
	Over $50,000	104	49	48	3
Region:	Northeast	137	57	41	3
	South	198	47	48	5
	Midwest	139	48	46	6
	West	127	37	63	0
Education:	High School or Less	333	45	50	5
	Some College	137	57	41	2
	College Graduate	130	43	55	2
Ethnicity:	White	445	44	51	4
	Black	76	54	46	0
	Hispanic	53	56	44	0
Voter Registration:	Not Registered	133	44	52	4
	Democrat	214	54	42	4
	Republican	121	40	59	1
	Independent	94	52	44	3
Church Type:	Protestant	250	47	49	4
	Catholic	115	55	42	2
Faith Perspective:	Evangelical	69	47	52	2
	Born Again	219	50	46	4
	Non-Christian	382	46	51	3

TABLE 73

Do you favor or oppose adults being able to choose to end their lives through the use of special drugs if they are physically impaired or suffering becoming legal?

		N	Favor	Oppose	Don't Know
Total Responding		602	58%	33%	9%
Gender:	Male	298	61	28	10
	Female	303	55	38	7
Age:	18 to 28	132	62	29	9
	29 to 47	227	64	29	7
	48 to 66	150	50	41	9
	67 to 98	81	54	36	11
Married:	Yes	344	51	41	8
	No	257	67	23	10
Have Kids Under 18:	Yes	220	60	33	7
	No	379	57	33	10
Household Income:	Under $25,000	184	53	35	12
	$25,000 to $50,000	237	62	32	5
	Over $50,000	104	64	28	8
Region:	Northeast	137	69	22	8
	South	198	50	43	8
	Midwest	139	56	33	11
	West	127	61	30	9
Education:	High School or Less	333	57	34	9
	Some College	137	61	32	7
	College Graduate	130	57	33	10
Ethnicity:	White	445	61	30	9
	Black	76	39	55	6
	Hispanic	53	53	39	8
Voter Registration:	Not Registered	133	59	30	11
	Democrat	214	59	34	8
	Republican	121	51	40	9
	Independent	94	63	28	9
Church Type:	Protestant	250	48	46	7
	Catholic	115	53	38	9
Faith Perspective:	Evangelical	69	28	68	4
	Born Again	219	44	49	6
	Non-Christian	382	66	24	10

Table 74

Do you favor or oppose businesses being prohibited from selling or distributing any information about you or the products you buy, without your permission, becoming legal?

		N	Favor	Oppose	Don't Know
Total Responding		602	68%	28%	4%
Gender:	Male	298	66	30	4
	Female	303	71	25	4
Age:	18 to 28	132	64	28	7
	29 to 47	227	79	19	2
	48 to 66	150	69	27	4
	67 to 98	81	43	54	3
Married:	Yes	344	72	24	4
	No	257	64	32	4
Have Kids Under 18:	Yes	220	74	22	4
	No	379	65	31	4
Household Income:	Under $25,000	184	61	35	4
	$25,000 to $50,000	237	71	26	3
	Over $50,000	104	79	16	5
Region:	Northeast	137	71	25	4
	South	198	65	32	3
	Midwest	139	72	27	1
	West	127	68	25	8
Education:	High School or Less	333	60	34	5
	Some College	137	76	23	1
	College Graduate	130	81	16	2
Ethnicity:	White	445	72	25	3
	Black	76	54	41	5
	Hispanic	53	72	28	0
Voter Registration:	Not Registered	133	61	32	7
	Democrat	214	69	28	3
	Republican	121	70	27	2
	Independent	94	79	17	3
Church Type:	Protestant	250	66	28	6
	Catholic	115	74	22	4
Faith Perspective:	Evangelical	69	76	23	1
	Born Again	219	76	21	3
	Non-Christian	382	64	31	4

TABLE 75

Do you favor or oppose doctors who perform an abortion being sentenced to prison for murder becoming legal?

		N	Favor	Oppose	Don't Know
Total Responding		602	26%	68%	6%
Gender:	Male	298	25	70	4
	Female	303	26	66	8
Age:	18 to 28	132	26	72	2
	29 to 47	227	24	74	2
	48 to 66	150	31	56	13
	67 to 98	81	20	71	10
Married:	Yes	344	27	66	7
	No	257	25	71	5
Have Kids Under 18:	Yes	220	24	73	3
	No	379	27	65	8
Household Income:	Under $25,000	184	32	59	9
	$25,000 to $50,000	237	28	69	4
	Over $50,000	104	13	83	5
Region:	Northeast	137	17	78	4
	South	198	32	59	9
	Midwest	139	20	73	7
	West	127	31	67	2
Education:	High School or Less	333	31	62	7
	Some College	137	22	72	6
	College Graduate	130	16	81	3
Ethnicity:	White	445	21	72	7
	Black	76	37	56	7
	Hispanic	53	54	46	0
Voter Registration:	Not Registered	133	32	60	8
	Democrat	214	25	68	7
	Republican	121	28	68	3
	Independent	94	19	77	5
Church Type:	Protestant	250	33	62	6
	Catholic	115	36	56	9
Faith Perspective:	Evangelical	69	57	37	6
	Born Again	219	36	59	5
	Non-Christian	382	20	74	7

TABLE 76

Do you favor or oppose magazines and movies that contain sexually explicit or pornographic pictures being made illegal to distribute?

		N	Favor	Oppose	Don't Know
Total Responding		602	44%	51%	5%
Gender:	Male	298	38	56	6
	Female	303	49	45	5
Age:	18 to 28	132	38	54	8
	29 to 47	227	38	58	4
	48 to 66	150	63	32	5
	67 to 98	81	30	64	6
Married:	Yes	344	49	47	4
	No	257	37	56	6
Have Kids Under 18:	Yes	220	45	50	5
	No	379	43	51	5
Household Income:	Under $25,000	184	42	52	6
	$25,000 to $50,000	237	50	48	2
	Over $50,000	104	37	61	2
Region:	Northeast	137	47	50	2
	South	198	43	53	4
	Midwest	139	41	53	6
	West	127	45	46	9
Education:	High School or Less	333	46	47	7
	Some College	137	51	46	4
	College Graduate	130	32	66	2
Ethnicity:	White	445	42	53	5
	Black	76	44	46	9
	Hispanic	53	56	38	6
Voter Registration:	Not Registered	133	43	48	9
	Democrat	214	46	52	1
	Republican	121	42	54	4
	Independent	94	43	48	9
Church Type:	Protestant	250	50	46	5
	Catholic	115	46	52	2
Faith Perspective:	Evangelical	69	59	40	1
	Born Again	219	54	44	3
	Non-Christian	382	38	55	7

TABLE 77

Do you agree or disagree that the Christian faith is relevant to the way you live today? Do you (agree/disagree) strongly or somewhat?

		N	Agree Strongly	Agree Somewhat	Disagree Somewhat	Disagree Strongly	Don't Know
Total Responding		602	45%	34%	10%	8%	4%
Gender:	Male	298	41	33	13	11	1
	Female	303	48	34	7	4	7
Age:	18 to 28	132	36	37	13	12	2
	29 to 47	227	40	36	12	9	2
	48 to 66	150	50	30	7	5	7
	67 to 98	81	61	28	2	3	7
Married:	Yes	344	51	30	9	5	4
	No	257	36	38	11	11	4
Have Kids Under 18:	Yes	220	44	39	7	8	1
	No	379	45	30	11	8	6
Household Income:	Under $25,000	184	49	32	7	10	3
	$25,000 to $50,000	237	41	37	13	6	3
	Over $50,000	104	47	35	11	7	1
Region:	Northeast	137	38	36	8	11	7
	South	198	51	33	9	2	5
	Midwest	139	46	37	11	7	0
	West	127	41	29	12	14	3
Education:	High School or Less	333	40	35	10	9	5
	Some College	137	53	31	9	4	4
	College Graduate	130	47	32	10	10	1
Ethnicity:	White	445	47	31	11	6	4
	Black	76	32	46	4	11	7
	Hispanic	53	49	32	11	8	0
Voter Registration:	Not Registered	133	42	29	10	13	7
	Democrat	214	36	41	9	9	5
	Republican	121	69	22	4	2	2
	Independent	94	40	38	15	7	1
Church Type:	Protestant	250	56	32	5	4	4
	Catholic	115	48	30	12	3	7
Faith Perspective:	Evangelical	69	86	7	5	1	1
	Born Again	219	72	20	6	1	2
	Non-Christian	382	29	41	12	11	5

TABLE 78

Do you agree or disagree that the Christian churches in your area are relevant to the way you live today? Do you (agree/disagree) strongly or somewhat?

		N	Agree Strongly	Agree Somewhat	Disagree Somewhat	Disagree Strongly	Don't Know
Total Responding		602	33%	38%	14%	9%	5%
Gender:	Male	298	29	38	16	12	4
	Female	303	38	38	12	7	5
Age:	18 to 28	132	30	36	16	13	5
	29 to 47	227	25	43	18	10	4
	48 to 66	150	39	38	10	7	6
	67 to 98	81	49	28	9	8	6
Married:	Yes	344	36	44	12	5	3
	No	257	30	31	17	15	7
Have Kids Under 18:	Yes	220	29	44	14	10	3
	No	379	36	35	14	9	6
Household Income:	Under $25,000	184	38	28	15	12	7
	$25,000 to $50,000	237	34	41	15	8	2
	Over $50,000	104	28	49	11	9	3
Region:	Northeast	137	27	42	18	8	5
	South	198	45	33	10	6	6
	Midwest	139	31	44	14	10	1
	West	127	25	35	15	17	8
Education:	High School or Less	333	35	39	13	8	5
	Some College	137	33	39	14	11	3
	College Graduate	130	30	34	17	12	7
Ethnicity:	White	445	33	38	15	9	4
	Black	76	37	32	20	4	7
	Hispanic	53	38	41	0	21	0
Voter Registration:	Not Registered	133	34	31	14	10	11
	Democrat	214	30	39	17	11	3
	Republican	121	44	40	7	5	4
	Independent	94	25	47	14	12	2
Church Type:	Protestant	250	44	37	9	5	5
	Catholic	115	43	38	12	7	1
Faith Perspective:	Evangelical	69	56	31	4	8	1
	Born Again	219	48	36	7	5	4
	Non-Christian	382	25	40	18	12	6

TABLE 79

Do you agree or disagree that overall, the United States is the most powerful nation on the earth today? Do you (agree/disagree) strongly or somewhat?

		N	Agree Strongly	Agree Somewhat	Disagree Somewhat	Disagree Strongly	Don't Know
Total Responding		602	54%	26%	12%	5%	2%
Gender:	Male	298	61	22	9	5	2
	Female	303	48	30	15	5	2
Age:	18 to 28	132	54	25	10	7	3
	29 to 47	227	53	27	15	5	0
	48 to 66	150	55	25	14	3	3
	67 to 98	81	54	29	6	7	4
Married:	Yes	344	56	26	13	3	2
	No	257	52	27	11	8	3
Have Kids Under 18:	Yes	220	59	23	13	4	1
	No	379	52	28	12	5	3
Household Income:	Under $25,000	184	48	26	13	9	4
	$25,000 to $50,000	237	58	27	11	2	1
	Over $50,000	104	58	24	15	2	1
Region:	Northeast	137	53	32	8	5	2
	South	198	61	19	12	7	1
	Midwest	139	52	31	14	1	2
	West	127	50	25	16	5	4
Education:	High School or Less	333	56	23	12	7	3
	Some College	137	47	34	16	1	2
	College Graduate	130	58	28	10	3	1
Ethnicity:	White	445	52	29	13	3	2
	Black	76	62	20	6	7	4
	Hispanic	53	67	7	10	16	0
Voter Registration:	Not Registered	133	56	20	15	7	2
	Democrat	214	53	31	9	5	2
	Republican	121	59	24	11	3	4
	Independent	94	50	28	16	4	2
Church Type:	Protestant	250	58	25	14	1	2
	Catholic	115	56	30	5	8	1
Faith Perspective:	Evangelical	69	60	20	17	2	1
	Born Again	219	55	28	13	2	2
	Non-Christian	382	54	25	12	6	2

TABLE 80

Do you agree or disagree that to get by in life these days, sometimes you have to bend the rules for your own benefit? Do you (agree/disagree) strongly or somewhat?

		N	Agree Strongly	Agree Somewhat	Disagree Somewhat	Disagree Strongly	Don't Know
Total Responding		602	18%	29%	19%	32%	2%
Gender:	Male	298	19	32	20	27	2
	Female	303	18	26	17	36	3
Age:	18 to 28	132	31	35	11	18	4
	29 to 47	227	12	28	22	38	1
	48 to 66	150	14	26	19	39	2
	67 to 98	81	22	31	21	26	1
Married:	Yes	344	14	27	23	34	2
	No	257	24	32	13	28	3
Have Kids Under 18:	Yes	220	20	26	21	31	2
	No	379	17	31	17	32	3
Household Income:	Under $25,000	184	19	32	15	33	0
	$25,000 to $50,000	237	19	31	17	32	2
	Over $50,000	104	17	21	30	31	1
Region:	Northeast	137	17	41	10	27	5
	South	198	19	26	23	30	2
	Midwest	139	16	33	18	33	0
	West	127	20	17	21	38	3
Education:	High School or Less	333	23	29	15	29	4
	Some College	137	14	35	21	29	1
	College Graduate	130	11	22	26	40	0
Ethnicity:	White	445	13	29	23	34	2
	Black	76	39	32	7	22	0
	Hispanic	53	28	22	9	35	6
Voter Registration:	Not Registered	133	25	28	10	31	6
	Democrat	214	20	33	16	29	1
	Republican	121	18	20	22	37	3
	Independent	94	8	31	27	34	1
Church Type:	Protestant	250	13	26	21	38	3
	Catholic	115	19	26	21	31	4
Faith Perspective:	Evangelical	69	6	13	23	57	1
	Born Again	219	10	20	23	46	1
	Non-Christian	382	23	34	16	24	3

TABLE 81

Do you agree or disagree that you have developed a clear philosophy about life that consistently influences the decisions you make and the way you live? Do you (agree/disagree) strongly or somewhat?

		N	Agree Strongly	Agree Somewhat	Disagree Somewhat	Disagree Strongly	Don't Know
Total Responding		602	54%	29%	8%	2%	6%
Gender:	Male	298	50	34	10	2	4
	Female	303	58	25	7	3	7
Age:	18 to 28	132	48	34	10	3	5
	29 to 47	227	55	36	7	1	1
	48 to 66	150	57	19	9	4	11
	67 to 98	81	57	21	10	1	11
Married:	Yes	344	56	30	8	2	4
	No	257	52	28	9	3	8
Have Kids Under 18:	Yes	220	55	33	7	2	2
	No	379	54	27	9	2	8
Household Income:	Under $25,000	184	55	29	8	2	6
	$25,000 to $50,000	237	53	32	9	2	4
	Over $50,000	104	62	32	4	1	1
Region:	Northeast	137	52	36	9	0	3
	South	198	55	25	5	3	11
	Midwest	139	49	32	13	1	5
	West	127	59	26	7	5	2
Education:	High School or Less	333	47	32	10	3	9
	Some College	137	54	31	10	3	2
	College Graduate	130	72	23	3	0	2
Ethnicity:	White	445	56	32	6	2	4
	Black	76	48	25	12	5	10
	Hispanic	53	46	14	24	7	10
Voter Registration:	Not Registered	133	44	26	16	6	8
	Democrat	214	49	35	6	2	8
	Republican	121	71	20	4	1	4
	Independent	94	55	38	7	0	0
Church Type:	Protestant	250	54	30	5	5	7
	Catholic	115	51	32	13	0	3
Faith Perspective:	Evangelical	69	68	21	5	6	0
	Born Again	219	63	22	7	3	4
	Non-Christian	382	49	33	9	2	7

TABLE 82

Do you agree or disagree that it's better to devote yourself to following the traditional way than to pursue your dreams? Do you (agree/disagree) strongly or somewhat?

		N	Agree Strongly	Agree Somewhat	Disagree Somewhat	Disagree Strongly	Don't Know
Total Responding		602	16%	18%	31%	28%	7%
Gender:	Male	298	21	15	29	30	5
	Female	303	12	21	33	25	9
Age:	18 to 28	132	16	15	27	34	8
	29 to 47	227	12	17	37	31	3
	48 to 66	150	16	15	34	24	11
	67 to 98	81	30	26	16	16	13
Married:	Yes	344	13	19	35	24	8
	No	257	20	16	26	32	6
Have Kids Under 18:	Yes	220	11	19	35	29	5
	No	379	19	17	29	26	8
Household Income:	Under $25,000	184	19	20	25	29	7
	$25,000 to $50,000	237	20	14	35	27	5
	Over $50,000	104	13	16	40	29	2
Region:	Northeast	137	13	21	35	24	8
	South	198	19	15	27	32	8
	Midwest	139	12	21	41	22	4
	West	127	21	17	21	32	9
Education:	High School or Less	333	21	22	28	21	9
	Some College	137	10	14	38	32	5
	College Graduate	130	10	14	32	40	4
Ethnicity:	White	445	12	21	35	26	5
	Black	76	27	14	27	23	9
	Hispanic	53	28	4	8	55	6
Voter Registration:	Not Registered	133	16	14	20	35	14
	Democrat	214	18	18	34	26	4
	Republican	121	16	16	36	27	6
	Independent	94	18	20	34	22	6
Church Type:	Protestant	250	17	19	36	20	8
	Catholic	115	15	17	31	31	6
Faith Perspective:	Evangelical	69	25	12	29	27	6
	Born Again	219	17	16	37	22	7
	Non-Christian	382	16	19	27	31	7

TABLE 83

Do you agree or disagree that it's almost impossible to be a moral person these days? Do you (agree/disagree) strongly or somewhat?

		N	Agree Strongly	Agree Somewhat	Disagree Somewhat	Disagree Strongly	Don't Know
Total Responding		602	14%	17%	21%	47%	2%
Gender:	Male	298	14	16	21	47	1
	Female	303	13	18	21	46	2
Age:	18 to 28	132	11	24	20	44	1
	29 to 47	227	9	14	25	51	1
	48 to 66	150	16	15	20	47	2
	67 to 98	81	24	15	15	42	5
Married:	Yes	344	13	16	20	49	2
	No	257	14	19	23	43	2
Have Kids Under 18:	Yes	220	9	16	22	51	1
	No	379	16	17	20	44	2
Household Income:	Under $25,000	184	18	20	23	38	1
	$25,000 to $50,000	237	10	16	23	49	1
	Over $50,000	104	6	16	20	58	0
Region:	Northeast	137	18	21	22	38	1
	South	198	11	18	21	46	3
	Midwest	139	14	18	25	42	1
	West	127	13	10	16	61	1
Education:	High School or Less	333	19	21	19	38	3
	Some College	137	7	15	27	51	0
	College Graduate	130	6	9	21	65	0
Ethnicity:	White	445	14	16	19	49	2
	Black	76	14	25	32	29	0
	Hispanic	53	6	12	19	62	0
Voter Registration:	Not Registered	133	13	17	20	48	2
	Democrat	214	16	20	22	40	1
	Republican	121	14	11	21	52	2
	Independent	94	11	21	18	49	1
Church Type:	Protestant	250	14	18	23	44	1
	Catholic	115	11	15	19	52	3
Faith Perspective:	Evangelical	69	13	16	15	55	1
	Born Again	219	12	15	21	50	2
	Non-Christian	382	14	18	21	45	2

TABLE 84

Do you agree or disagree that what you do for other people is more important than what you believe about Jesus Christ? Do you (agree/disagree) strongly or somewhat?

		N	Agree Strongly	Agree Somewhat	Disagree Somewhat	Disagree Strongly	Don't Know
Total Responding		602	16%	15%	18%	38%	13%
Gender:	Male	298	22	17	17	32	13
	Female	303	11	12	19	44	14
Age:	18 to 28	132	14	17	21	38	10
	29 to 47	227	17	16	24	33	10
	48 to 66	150	17	13	14	44	13
	67 to 98	81	20	12	7	39	22
Married:	Yes	344	15	14	18	43	11
	No	257	19	16	19	30	16
Have Kids Under 18:	Yes	220	16	15	27	33	10
	No	379	17	14	13	41	15
Household Income:	Under $25,000	184	18	12	17	45	9
	$25,000 to $50,000	237	14	15	20	40	11
	Over $50,000	104	22	24	21	24	9
Region:	Northeast	137	18	21	18	29	14
	South	198	14	11	17	47	12
	Midwest	139	9	13	23	41	14
	West	127	27	15	17	28	13
Education:	High School or Less	333	15	15	18	40	12
	Some College	137	15	11	20	38	16
	College Graduate	130	20	19	17	31	13
Ethnicity:	White	445	16	16	19	37	13
	Black	76	16	12	14	45	12
	Hispanic	53	21	12	21	35	11
Voter Registration:	Not Registered	133	17	12	15	40	16
	Democrat	214	16	18	20	35	12
	Republican	121	12	12	17	42	16
	Independent	94	21	18	21	33	7
Church Type:	Protestant	250	12	13	16	48	12
	Catholic	115	12	17	24	31	16
Faith Perspective:	Evangelical	69	5	4	4	85	3
	Born Again	219	6	7	22	58	8
	Non-Christian	382	22	19	16	26	16

TABLE 85

Do you agree or disagree that American businesses are losing ground in the world marketplace? Do you (agree/disagree) strongly or somewhat?

		N	Agree Strongly	Agree Somewhat	Disagree Somewhat	Disagree Strongly	Don't Know
Total Responding		602	45%	36%	9%	4%	6%
Gender:	Male	298	55	30	9	5	2
	Female	303	36	42	9	4	9
Age:	18 to 28	132	46	37	8	4	5
	29 to 47	227	43	42	11	3	1
	48 to 66	150	51	30	10	3	6
	67 to 98	81	37	27	6	13	17
Married:	Yes	344	46	38	9	3	4
	No	257	44	33	9	6	8
Have Kids Under 18:	Yes	220	42	43	10	1	3
	No	379	46	32	9	6	7
Household Income:	Under $25,000	184	52	31	7	4	6
	$25,000 to $50,000	237	44	35	14	4	3
	Over $50,000	104	45	41	7	4	2
Region:	Northeast	137	45	37	10	6	3
	South	198	48	35	6	3	9
	Midwest	139	46	35	12	2	4
	West	127	40	37	10	8	5
Education:	High School or Less	333	46	33	7	5	8
	Some College	137	46	39	10	3	2
	College Graduate	130	41	40	13	4	2
Ethnicity:	White	445	44	37	11	4	5
	Black	76	41	31	6	5	16
	Hispanic	53	61	36	4	0	0
Voter Registration:	Not Registered	133	52	29	7	3	9
	Democrat	214	44	37	8	6	4
	Republican	121	44	32	11	5	8
	Independent	94	44	43	11	1	1
Church Type:	Protestant	250	45	35	9	3	7
	Catholic	115	46	39	8	5	2
Faith Perspective:	Evangelical	69	54	35	8	1	2
	Born Again	219	43	41	8	3	5
	Non-Christian	382	46	33	10	5	6

TABLE 86

Do you agree or disagree that the more involved the government gets in the marketplace, the better off the public is? Do you (agree/disagree) strongly or somewhat?

		N	Agree Strongly	Agree Somewhat	Disagree Somewhat	Disagree Strongly	Don't Know
Total Responding		602	11%	12%	27%	45%	5%
Gender:	Male	298	14	10	22	50	3
	Female	303	7	15	31	40	7
Age:	18 to 28	132	18	21	27	27	7
	29 to 47	227	8	10	33	48	1
	48 to 66	150	10	8	20	57	5
	67 to 98	81	6	12	21	50	12
Married:	Yes	344	11	11	26	50	3
	No	257	10	15	29	39	8
Have Kids Under 18:	Yes	220	13	10	31	44	2
	No	379	9	14	24	46	7
Household Income:	Under $25,000	184	11	14	27	43	4
	$25,000 to $50,000	237	14	11	27	46	2
	Over $50,000	104	8	11	33	47	2
Region:	Northeast	137	13	17	31	33	6
	South	198	11	9	23	51	5
	Midwest	139	10	16	29	41	4
	West	127	7	8	26	55	4
Education:	High School or Less	333	15	11	19	47	7
	Some College	137	6	14	37	42	1
	College Graduate	130	3	12	36	44	4
Ethnicity:	White	445	5	12	28	51	4
	Black	76	24	15	22	35	4
	Hispanic	53	36	6	26	26	6
Voter Registration:	Not Registered	133	17	13	20	41	8
	Democrat	214	13	11	32	39	5
	Republican	121	5	8	14	69	4
	Independent	94	3	17	36	42	2
Church Type:	Protestant	250	11	12	27	45	6
	Catholic	115	16	10	30	41	4
Faith Perspective:	Evangelical	69	3	5	36	54	1
	Born Again	219	11	6	32	47	4
	Non-Christian	382	11	16	24	44	5

TABLE 87

Overall, how trustworthy are the leaders of nonprofit organizations and charities in America? In general, do you feel you can trust them a lot, somewhat, not too much, or not at all?

		N	A Lot	Somewhat	Not Too Much	Not At All	Don't Know
Total Responding		1205	6%	59%	23%	9%	3%
Gender:	Male	589	8	58	21	10	3
	Female	616	5	60	24	8	3
Age:	18 to 28	243	6	69	16	5	4
	29 to 47	485	7	60	24	7	3
	48 to 66	310	5	53	29	12	1
	67 to 98	151	5	54	17	16	8
Married:	Yes	678	7	58	25	8	2
	No	527	5	59	20	10	5
Have Kids Under 18:	Yes	458	6	62	24	7	2
	No	745	6	57	22	10	4
Household Income:	Under $25,000	384	5	56	24	12	3
	$25,000 to $50,000	453	7	63	24	4	1
	Over $50,000	216	8	69	17	5	2
Region:	Northeast	260	5	61	20	9	4
	South	405	6	53	26	13	2
	Midwest	272	8	61	25	4	2
	West	268	5	63	20	8	5
Education:	High School or Less	668	5	55	24	12	4
	Some College	285	5	62	24	7	2
	College Graduate	251	10	65	19	4	2
Ethnicity:	White	888	6	62	21	7	3
	Black	155	4	46	32	17	1
	Hispanic	107	9	52	18	15	6
Voter Registration:	Not Registered	261	5	51	27	10	6
	Democrat	414	6	59	22	11	2
	Republican	253	7	63	22	6	2
	Independent	212	6	63	22	7	2
Church Type:	Protestant	510	6	62	22	8	2
	Catholic	222	11	57	20	9	3
Faith Perspective:	Evangelical	115	8	66	22	4	1
	Born Again	463	6	64	21	8	1
	Non-Christian	742	6	56	24	10	4

TABLE 88

In the past, have you ever asked for a financial statement from a nonprofit organization before sending them a contribution?

		N	Yes	No	Don't Know
Total Responding		1205	10%	89%	1%
Gender:	Male	589	11	88	1
	Female	616	9	90	1
Age:	18 to 28	243	11	87	1
	29 to 47	485	13	86	1
	48 to 66	310	7	93	0
	67 to 98	151	6	92	1
Married:	Yes	678	12	87	1
	No	527	8	91	1
Have Kids Under 18:	Yes	458	12	88	1
	No	745	9	90	1
Household Income:	Under $25,000	384	5	95	0
	$25,000 to $50,000	453	13	87	0
	Over $50,000	216	15	84	1
Region:	Northeast	260	12	87	1
	South	405	9	90	1
	Midwest	272	9	90	1
	West	268	11	88	2
Education:	High School or Less	668	7	92	1
	Some College	285	11	89	1
	College Graduate	251	18	81	1
Ethnicity:	White	888	11	89	1
	Black	155	6	94	0
	Hispanic	107	11	84	5
Voter Registration:	Not Registered	261	6	91	2
	Democrat	414	8	92	0
	Republican	253	16	82	1
	Independent	212	13	87	0
Church Type:	Protestant	510	13	86	1
	Catholic	222	9	90	0
Faith Perspective:	Evangelical	115	11	87	2
	Born Again	463	12	88	1
	Non-Christian	742	9	90	1

TABLE 89

In a typical month, how many times would you attend services at a church, synagogue, or other religious meeting place?

		N	Four or More	Three Times	Two Times	Once	Less Than Once	None	Don't Know
Total Responding		1205	39%	6%	10%	11%	3%	29%	3%
Gender:	Male	589	31	6	9	13	5	35	1
	Female	616	46	6	10	9	1	24	4
Age:	18 to 28	243	34	9	11	9	5	27	4
	29 to 47	485	33	7	11	15	2	31	2
	48 to 66	310	46	4	9	9	3	27	2
	67 to 98	151	46	4	6	7	3	31	3
Married:	Yes	678	44	6	8	12	2	25	2
	No	527	31	6	11	10	4	35	3
Have Kids Under 18:	Yes	458	36	9	12	13	3	26	2
	No	745	40	4	8	10	3	32	3
Household Income:	Under $25,000	384	37	6	9	8	4	32	4
	$25,000 to $50,000	453	41	6	12	12	2	26	0
	Over $50,000	216	38	6	8	16	2	29	0
Region:	Northeast	260	35	5	10	12	5	31	3
	South	405	48	6	10	10	1	20	4
	Midwest	272	34	10	10	14	3	27	1
	West	268	32	3	7	10	4	43	1
Education:	High School or Less	668	40	5	10	9	3	29	3
	Some College	285	36	6	7	16	2	30	3
	College Graduate	251	37	7	10	13	3	29	1
Ethnicity:	White	888	39	6	8	11	3	31	2
	Black	155	39	11	15	6	0	25	4
	Hispanic	107	36	0	16	23	0	23	3
Voter Registration:	Not Registered	261	28	3	10	12	3	38	6
	Democrat	414	42	7	9	11	2	27	1
	Republican	253	47	5	11	9	3	24	1
	Independent	212	35	9	10	13	3	29	1
Church Type:	Protestant	510	60	9	13	14	0	0	3
	Catholic	222	58	6	15	20	0	0	1
Faith Perspective:	Evangelical	115	88	1	2	2	0	6	0
	Born Again	463	60	8	7	8	2	14	2
	Non-Christian	742	25	5	11	13	4	39	3

TABLE 90

Does your household own a Bible?

		N	Yes	No	Don't Know
Total Responding		602	92%	7%	1%
Gender:	Male	298	91	8	1
	Female	303	93	6	1
Age:	18 to 28	132	90	9	1
	29 to 47	227	92	7	1
	48 to 66	150	96	4	0
	67 to 98	81	87	10	3
Married:	Yes	344	94	6	0
	No	257	89	9	2
Have Kids Under 18:	Yes	220	96	4	0
	No	379	89	9	2
Household Income:	Under $25,000	184	91	8	1
	$25,000 to $50,000	237	91	8	0
	Over $50,000	104	95	5	0
Region:	Northeast	137	85	15	1
	South	198	96	3	1
	Midwest	139	96	3	1
	West	127	88	11	1
Education:	High School or Less	333	93	7	1
	Some College	137	90	6	3
	College Graduate	130	91	9	0
Ethnicity:	White	445	92	7	1
	Black	76	95	5	0
	Hispanic	53	94	6	0
Voter Registration:	Not Registered	133	87	12	1
	Democrat	214	92	8	0
	Republican	121	96	3	1
	Independent	94	93	6	1
Church Type:	Protestant	250	98	1	0
	Catholic	115	90	9	1
Faith Perspective:	Evangelical	69	100	0	0
	Born Again	219	100	0	0
	Non-Christian	382	87	11	2

Table 91

How many Bibles, in total, does your household own? *(Base: people who own Bibles)*

		N	One	Two	Three to Four	Five to Six	Seven or More	Don't Know
Total Responding		551	17%	17%	32%	18%	13%	3%
Gender:	Male	270	20	18	30	15	13	5
	Female	281	14	16	34	20	13	2
Age:	18 to 28	118	21	21	27	14	12	6
	29 to 47	208	16	21	27	21	13	2
	48 to 66	144	15	12	36	21	14	3
	67 to 98	70	16	12	49	11	11	0
Married:	Yes	323	11	15	36	21	17	1
	No	228	25	20	28	14	8	6
Have Kids Under 18:	Yes	211	12	21	30	21	13	2
	No	338	19	15	34	16	13	3
Household Income:	Under $25,000	167	22	15	34	20	9	0
	$25,000 to $50,000	217	14	20	28	21	16	2
	Over $50,000	99	13	16	39	13	18	1
Region:	Northeast	116	24	19	34	14	6	2
	South	191	9	11	29	28	17	5
	Midwest	133	14	24	39	9	13	1
	West	112	25	16	28	14	14	3
Education:	High School or Less	309	17	15	32	22	11	4
	Some College	124	16	20	31	13	20	1
	College Graduate	117	17	19	35	14	13	2
Ethnicity:	White	409	16	15	36	17	14	2
	Black	72	13	20	24	29	13	0
	Hispanic	50	24	30	15	10	7	13
Voter Registration:	Not Registered	115	16	22	23	21	8	10
	Democrat	196	17	18	32	17	14	1
	Republican	116	9	12	42	16	20	1
	Independent	87	26	19	29	13	13	0
Church Type:	Protestant	246	6	11	31	27	23	3
	Catholic	104	34	18	31	9	6	2
Faith Perspective:	Evangelical	69	0	4	19	28	50	0
	Born Again	219	7	10	34	24	24	1
	Non-Christian	333	23	22	31	14	6	4

TABLE 92

Which version or translation of the Bible do you read most often? *(Base: people who own Bibles)*

		N	KJV	The Living Bible	NASB	NIV	NKJV	NRSV	RSV	Catholic	Other	None	Don't Know
Total Responding		551	38%	5%	2%	5%	3%	1%	1%	2%	7%	2%	34%
Gender:	Male	270	39	5	2	4	3	1	1	2	5	4	34
	Female	281	36	5	2	6	4	1	1	3	8	0	34
Age:	18 to 28	118	20	2	3	6	1	1	0	3	3	6	56
	29 to 47	208	43	4	3	6	7	0	1	1	7	2	27
	48 to 66	144	42	7	2	5	1	1	2	3	6	1	30
	67 to 98	70	45	4	1	1	2	2	5	5	5	0	29
Married:	Yes	323	40	6	3	6	4	1	2	2	7	2	28
	No	228	34	3	2	4	2	1	1	3	6	2	42
Have Kids Under 18:	Yes	211	34	3	2	8	4	1	0	1	9	3	35
	No	338	40	6	2	3	3	1	2	3	4	1	34
Household Income:	Under $25,000	167	41	5	1	2	5	1	2	2	8	2	31
	$25,000 to $50,000	217	37	5	2	8	3	1	1	1	4	2	35
	Over $50,000	99	42	5	7	5	2	0	1	3	6	1	28
Region:	Northeast	116	30	3	2	3	2	0	2	3	8	3	45
	South	191	44	7	1	4	5	1	2	2	5	0	27
	Midwest	133	37	4	2	7	1	1	1	3	8	4	32
	West	112	37	3	5	6	4	1	0	1	6	2	37
Education:	High School or Less	309	37	5	1	4	3	0	1	2	7	3	36
	Some College	124	43	6	3	5	2	2	1	4	6	1	28
	College Graduate	117	35	2	4	7	5	2	3	0	6	2	34
Ethnicity:	White	409	38	5	3	6	3	1	2	3	6	2	32
	Black	72	41	9	0	2	5	0	0	3	7	0	34
	Hispanic	50	37	0	0	4	0	0	0	0	12	0	48
Voter Registration:	Not Registered	115	32	1	3	4	2	0	0	0	5	5	49
	Republican	196	42	6	1	4	4	0	1	6	9	1	26
	Democrat	116	44	3	3	9	3	3	3	1	5	1	24
	Independent	87	30	6	4	6	4	1	0	0	5	2	41
Church Type:	Protestant	246	44	8	2	8	6	2	2	0	5	0	23
	Catholic	104	28	0	3	2	1	0	0	9	10	1	46
Faith Perspective:	Evangelical	69	47	7	4	21	9	1	0	0	1	0	8
	Born Again	219	46	6	3	10	6	1	1	2	4	0	20
	Non-Christian	333	32	4	2	1	1	1	1	2	8	3	44

January 1994
Survey Tables

TABLE 93

In the last seven days, did you order a product or service by calling a toll-free 800 number?

		N	Yes	No	Don't Know
Total Responding		1206	13%	87%	0%
Gender:	Male	584	11	89	0
	Female	622	15	85	0
Age:	18 to 28	252	9	91	0
	29 to 47	514	15	85	0
	48 to 66	291	15	85	0
	67 to 98	120	7	93	0
Married:	Yes	659	15	85	0
	No	547	10	89	0
Have Kids Under 18:	Yes	513	13	87	0
	No	687	13	87	0
Household Income:	Under $25,000	382	11	89	0
	$25,000 to $50,000	438	15	85	0
	Over $50,000	227	16	83	0
Region:	Northeast	265	15	84	0
	South	398	13	87	0
	Midwest	279	12	88	0
	West	264	13	87	0
Education:	High School or Less	625	13	87	0
	Some College	325	11	89	0
	College Graduate	249	16	84	0
Ethnicity:	White	867	14	86	0
	Black	162	9	91	0
	Hispanic	112	14	86	0
Voter Registration:	Not Registered	246	13	87	0
	Democrat	381	12	88	1
	Republican	270	17	83	0
	Independent	209	13	87	0
Church Type:	Protestant	492	14	85	0
	Catholic	313	14	86	0
Faith Perspective:	Evangelical	83	11	89	0
	Born Again	428	13	87	0
	Non-Christian	777	13	87	0

TABLE 94

In the last seven days, did you purchase a product you saw advertised on a televised home shopping channel?

		N	Yes	No	Don't Know
Total Responding		1206	4%	96%	0%
Gender:	Male	584	3	96	1
	Female	622	4	96	0
Age:	18 to 28	252	5	95	0
	29 to 47	514	3	97	0
	48 to 66	291	4	96	0
	67 to 98	120	4	94	2
Married:	Yes	659	3	97	0
	No	547	5	95	0
Have Kids Under 18:	Yes	513	5	95	0
	No	687	3	97	0
Household Income:	Under $25,000	382	4	96	0
	$25,000 to $50,000	438	5	94	1
	Over $50,000	227	3	97	0
Region:	Northeast	265	4	96	0
	South	398	3	97	1
	Midwest	279	4	96	0
	West	264	5	95	0
Education:	High School or Less	625	5	95	0
	Some College	325	2	98	0
	College Graduate	249	3	96	0
Ethnicity:	White	867	3	97	0
	Black	162	6	92	2
	Hispanic	112	5	95	0
Voter Registration:	Not Registered	246	2	97	0
	Democrat	381	5	95	0
	Republican	270	4	96	0
	Independent	209	3	96	1
Church Type:	Protestant	492	5	95	0
	Catholic	313	3	97	0
Faith Perspective:	Evangelical	83	5	94	1
	Born Again	428	3	96	0
	Non-Christian	777	4	96	0

TABLE 95

In the last seven days, did you borrow something from a public library?

		N	Yes	No	Don't Know
Total Responding		1206	14%	86%	0%
Gender:	Male	584	13	87	1
	Female	622	15	85	0
Age:	18 to 28	252	15	85	0
	29 to 47	514	17	82	1
	48 to 66	291	10	90	0
	67 to 98	120	6	94	0
Married:	Yes	659	15	84	1
	No	547	12	88	0
Have Kids Under 18:	Yes	513	19	81	1
	No	687	10	90	0
Household Income:	Under $25,000	382	9	90	1
	$25,000 to $50,000	438	17	83	0
	Over $50,000	227	15	85	0
Region:	Northeast	265	11	89	0
	South	398	16	84	0
	Midwest	279	12	86	1
	West	264	14	86	0
Education:	High School or Less	625	11	89	1
	Some College	325	15	85	0
	College Graduate	249	20	80	0
Ethnicity:	White	867	13	87	0
	Black	162	13	87	0
	Hispanic	112	24	72	4
Voter Registration:	Not Registered	246	6	94	0
	Democrat	381	16	84	0
	Republican	270	16	84	0
	Independent	209	17	83	0
Church Type:	Protestant	492	12	88	0
	Catholic	313	15	85	0
Faith Perspective:	Evangelical	83	13	87	0
	Born Again	428	14	86	0
	Non-Christian	777	14	86	1

TABLE 96

In the last seven days, did you read all or part of a book for pleasure, other than the Bible?

		N	Yes	No	Don't Know
Total Responding		1206	53%	47%	0%
Gender:	Male	584	49	51	0
	Female	622	57	43	0
Age:	18 to 28	252	45	55	0
	29 to 47	514	56	44	0
	48 to 66	291	53	47	0
	67 to 98	120	59	41	0
Married:	Yes	659	54	46	0
	No	547	52	48	0
Have Kids Under 18:	Yes	513	54	46	0
	No	687	53	47	0
Household Income:	Under $25,000	382	47	53	0
	$25,000 to $50,000	438	54	45	0
	Over $50,000	227	60	40	0
Region:	Northeast	265	52	48	0
	South	398	54	46	0
	Midwest	279	53	47	0
	West	264	53	47	0
Education:	High School or Less	625	42	58	0
	Some College	325	59	41	0
	College Graduate	249	72	28	0
Ethnicity:	White	867	56	44	0
	Black	162	47	53	0
	Hispanic	112	46	54	0
Voter Registration:	Not Registered	246	41	59	0
	Democrat	381	52	47	0
	Republican	270	61	39	0
	Independent	209	63	37	0
Church Type:	Protestant	492	56	44	0
	Catholic	313	51	49	0
Faith Perspective:	Evangelical	83	63	37	0
	Born Again	428	57	43	0
	Non-Christian	777	51	49	0

TABLE 97

In the last seven days, did you volunteer some of your free time to help a church?

		N	Yes	No	Don't Know
Total Responding		1206	25%	75%	0%
Gender:	Male	584	22	78	0
	Female	622	27	72	0
Age:	18 to 28	252	17	83	0
	29 to 47	514	24	76	0
	48 to 66	291	30	70	0
	67 to 98	120	27	72	1
Married:	Yes	659	30	70	0
	No	547	18	81	0
Have Kids Under 18:	Yes	513	29	71	0
	No	687	22	78	0
Household Income:	Under $25,000	382	23	76	0
	$25,000 to $50,000	438	28	72	0
	Over $50,000	227	24	76	0
Region:	Northeast	265	19	81	0
	South	398	31	68	1
	Midwest	279	23	77	0
	West	264	21	79	0
Education:	High School or Less	625	22	78	0
	Some College	325	26	73	0
	College Graduate	249	30	69	0
Ethnicity:	White	867	25	75	0
	Black	162	28	72	0
	Hispanic	112	17	83	0
Voter Registration:	Not Registered	246	11	89	0
	Democrat	381	26	74	0
	Republican	270	30	69	1
	Independent	209	27	73	0
Church Type:	Protestant	492	33	67	0
	Catholic	313	18	82	0
Faith Perspective:	Evangelical	83	55	45	0
	Born Again	428	40	60	0
	Non-Christian	777	16	84	0

TABLE 98

In the last seven days, did you volunteer some of your free time to help a nonprofit organization, other than a church?

		N	Yes	No	Don't Know
Total Responding		1206	21%	79%	0%
Gender:	Male	584	20	80	0
	Female	622	23	77	0
Age:	18 to 28	252	13	87	0
	29 to 47	514	21	79	0
	48 to 66	291	26	74	0
	67 to 98	120	24	76	0
Married:	Yes	659	23	77	0
	No	547	20	80	0
Have Kids Under 18:	Yes	513	21	79	0
	No	687	22	78	0
Household Income:	Under $25,000	382	20	80	0
	$25,000 to $50,000	438	21	79	0
	Over $50,000	227	25	75	0
Region:	Northeast	265	23	77	0
	South	398	22	78	0
	Midwest	279	19	81	0
	West	264	21	79	0
Education:	High School or Less	625	17	83	0
	Some College	325	23	77	0
	College Graduate	249	29	71	0
Ethnicity:	White	867	21	79	0
	Black	162	25	75	0
	Hispanic	112	26	74	0
Voter Registration:	Not Registered	246	11	89	0
	Democrat	381	24	76	0
	Republican	270	26	74	0
	Independent	209	24	76	0
Church Type:	Protestant	492	22	78	0
	Catholic	313	20	80	0
Faith Perspective:	Evangelical	83	24	76	0
	Born Again	428	21	79	0
	Non-Christian	777	22	78	0

Table 99

Compared to a year ago, are you currently spending more time, less time, or about the same amount of time at home with your family?

		N	More Time	Same Time	Less Time	Don't Know
Total Responding		604	38%	47%	14%	1%
Gender:	Male	294	42	43	14	0
	Female	309	34	51	14	1
Age:	18 to 28	124	41	26	33	0
	29 to 47	247	44	43	12	0
	48 to 66	144	33	62	5	0
	67 to 98	71	26	63	7	4
Married:	Yes	346	38	55	7	0
	No	257	38	37	23	1
Have Kids Under 18:	Yes	249	48	38	14	0
	No	352	31	54	14	1
Household Income:	Under $25,000	186	36	46	16	2
	$25,000 to $50,000	216	43	41	16	0
	Over $50,000	119	39	50	12	0
Region:	Northeast	137	37	47	16	0
	South	195	38	48	14	1
	Midwest	139	37	49	13	2
	West	133	42	44	14	0
Education:	High School or Less	313	39	46	15	0
	Some College	160	38	51	10	1
	College Graduate	127	37	45	16	1
Ethnicity:	White	435	35	51	13	1
	Black	81	46	35	19	0
	Hispanic	55	52	33	16	0
Voter Registration:	Not Registered	110	42	32	26	1
	Democrat	202	37	48	14	1
	Republican	132	36	52	12	1
	Independent	107	42	47	11	1
Church Type:	Protestant	252	38	51	10	1
	Catholic	153	41	43	16	0
Faith Perspective:	Evangelical	41	36	49	13	2
	Born Again	228	41	47	11	1
	Non-Christian	376	36	47	16	1

TABLE 100

Compared to a year ago, are you currently spending more time, less time, or about the same amount of time watching television?

		N	More Time	Same Time	Less Time	Don't Know
Total Responding		604	15%	47%	38%	0%
Gender:	Male	294	15	48	38	0
	Female	309	15	46	39	1
Age:	18 to 28	124	21	33	46	0
	29 to 47	247	11	46	42	0
	48 to 66	144	15	50	36	0
	67 to 98	71	18	63	19	0
Married:	Yes	346	8	53	39	0
	No	257	24	39	37	0
Have Kids Under 18:	Yes	249	11	42	46	0
	No	352	17	50	33	0
Household Income:	Under $25,000	186	20	48	31	1
	$25,000 to $50,000	216	11	48	40	0
	Over $50,000	119	10	46	44	0
Region:	Northeast	137	10	46	44	0
	South	195	14	47	39	1
	Midwest	139	17	50	32	1
	West	133	17	45	38	0
Education:	High School or Less	313	19	46	36	0
	Some College	160	9	55	34	1
	College Graduate	127	12	39	50	0
Ethnicity:	White	435	13	51	36	0
	Black	81	21	31	46	1
	Hispanic	55	21	33	47	0
Voter Registration:	Not Registered	110	22	37	40	1
	Democrat	202	14	46	40	0
	Republican	132	12	52	36	0
	Independent	107	13	49	38	0
Church Type:	Protestant	252	12	50	38	0
	Catholic	153	22	36	42	0
Faith Perspective:	Evangelical	41	3	50	47	0
	Born Again	228	12	43	44	1
	Non-Christian	376	16	49	35	0

TABLE 101

Compared to a year ago, are you currently spending more time, less time, or about the same amount of time with your friends?

		N	More Time	Same Time	Less Time	Don't Know
Total Responding		604	23%	48%	29%	0%
Gender:	Male	294	19	49	32	0
	Female	309	27	47	26	1
Age:	18 to 28	124	26	32	42	0
	29 to 47	247	21	49	30	0
	48 to 66	144	22	56	21	0
	67 to 98	71	25	55	19	2
Married:	Yes	346	20	51	29	0
	No	257	27	43	29	0
Have Kids Under 18:	Yes	249	24	41	35	0
	No	352	23	52	25	0
Household Income:	Under $25,000	186	27	43	30	0
	$25,000 to $50,000	216	22	46	31	1
	Over $50,000	119	22	50	28	0
Region:	Northeast	137	20	48	33	0
	South	195	19	50	30	1
	Midwest	139	25	48	27	0
	West	133	31	44	25	0
Education:	High School or Less	313	23	50	27	1
	Some College	160	26	40	33	0
	College Graduate	127	20	52	28	0
Ethnicity:	White	435	24	51	25	0
	Black	81	17	39	43	1
	Hispanic	55	29	32	39	0
Voter Registration:	Not Registered	110	26	37	36	1
	Democrat	202	24	50	26	0
	Republican	132	25	53	22	0
	Independent	107	20	43	37	0
Church Type:	Protestant	252	24	52	25	0
	Catholic	153	27	41	32	0
Faith Perspective:	Evangelical	41	25	48	27	0
	Born Again	228	24	46	31	0
	Non-Christian	376	23	49	28	0

TABLE 102

Compared to a year ago, are you currently spending more time, less time, or about the same amount of time working at your job?

		N	More Time	Same Time	Less Time	Don't Know
Total Responding		604	34%	40%	23%	3%
Gender:	Male	294	37	38	22	3
	Female	309	31	41	24	4
Age:	18 to 28	124	48	28	24	1
	29 to 47	247	41	42	16	1
	48 to 66	144	23	48	26	4
	67 to 98	71	10	38	42	10
Married:	Yes	346	28	46	22	4
	No	257	42	31	24	3
Have Kids Under 18:	Yes	249	38	45	16	1
	No	352	31	36	28	5
Household Income:	Under $25,000	186	39	29	29	3
	$25,000 to $50,000	216	29	45	22	4
	Over $50,000	119	37	44	18	2
Region:	Northeast	137	37	36	24	3
	South	195	30	46	21	3
	Midwest	139	37	32	25	6
	West	133	34	42	22	2
Education:	High School or Less	313	34	38	24	4
	Some College	160	30	40	28	3
	College Graduate	127	39	44	15	3
Ethnicity:	White	435	36	39	21	4
	Black	81	30	37	31	2
	Hispanic	55	33	48	19	0
Voter Registration:	Not Registered	110	38	42	19	2
	Democrat	202	31	39	26	4
	Republican	132	29	46	21	4
	Independent	107	39	35	26	0
Church Type:	Protestant	252	31	40	26	3
	Catholic	153	40	36	20	3
Faith Perspective:	Evangelical	41	21	48	22	9
	Born Again	228	35	42	19	4
	Non-Christian	376	33	38	25	3

TABLE 103

Compared to a year ago, are you currently spending more time, less time, or about the same amount of time participating in activities related to your church or place of religious involvement?

		N	More Time	Same Time	Less Time	Don't Know
Total Responding		604	17%	54%	27%	3%
Gender:	Male	294	14	58	25	3
	Female	309	19	50	30	2
Age:	18 to 28	124	15	41	41	4
	29 to 47	247	20	53	23	4
	48 to 66	144	14	63	22	0
	67 to 98	71	13	55	29	3
Married:	Yes	346	17	59	23	1
	No	257	16	47	32	5
Have Kids Under 18:	Yes	249	23	47	28	2
	No	352	12	58	27	3
Household Income:	Under $25,000	186	17	46	34	2
	$25,000 to $50,000	216	19	52	25	4
	Over $50,000	119	17	62	19	1
Region:	Northeast	137	17	50	29	4
	South	195	20	57	21	2
	Midwest	139	16	51	30	2
	West	133	12	56	30	2
Education:	High School or Less	313	14	53	29	3
	Some College	160	21	52	25	2
	College Graduate	127	17	57	26	1
Ethnicity:	White	435	18	56	24	2
	Black	81	18	44	34	4
	Hispanic	55	7	50	37	7
Voter Registration:	Not Registered	110	14	43	38	4
	Democrat	202	15	58	25	3
	Republican	132	21	56	23	1
	Independent	107	20	49	28	3
Church Type:	Protestant	252	16	58	24	1
	Catholic	153	18	51	27	4
Faith Perspective:	Evangelical	41	29	49	22	0
	Born Again	228	25	56	18	1
	Non-Christian	376	11	52	33	4

TABLE 104

Compared to a year ago, are you currently spending more time, less time, or about the same amount of time volunteering your time?

		N	More Time	Same Time	Less Time	Don't Know
Total Responding		604	20%	48%	30%	2%
Gender:	Male	294	20	50	28	2
	Female	309	21	46	32	2
Age:	18 to 28	124	21	36	43	0
	29 to 47	247	25	47	26	2
	48 to 66	144	15	56	28	0
	67 to 98	71	14	47	33	6
Married:	Yes	346	20	53	26	1
	No	257	20	41	36	3
Have Kids Under 18:	Yes	249	26	42	32	0
	No	352	16	52	29	3
Household Income:	Under $25,000	186	22	42	34	1
	$25,000 to $50,000	216	21	49	28	2
	Over $50,000	119	22	48	29	2
Region:	Northeast	137	16	48	36	0
	South	195	25	44	29	3
	Midwest	139	16	48	32	4
	West	133	22	54	24	1
Education:	High School or Less	313	20	49	29	2
	Some College	160	16	47	36	1
	College Graduate	127	25	49	26	1
Ethnicity:	White	435	20	51	28	2
	Black	81	18	33	45	4
	Hispanic	55	32	50	17	0
Voter Registration:	Not Registered	110	18	41	39	1
	Democrat	202	21	50	28	2
	Republican	132	24	45	29	2
	Independent	107	23	48	27	2
Church Type:	Protestant	252	20	47	33	0
	Catholic	153	19	49	30	1
Faith Perspective:	Evangelical	41	25	51	21	3
	Born Again	228	23	47	28	2
	Non-Christian	376	18	48	31	2

TABLE 105

Compared to a year ago, are you currently spending more time, less time, or about the same amount of time gaining additional formal education?

		N	More Time	Same Time	Less Time	Don't Know
Total Responding		604	23%	46%	28%	3%
Gender:	Male	294	24	47	26	2
	Female	309	22	45	29	3
Age:	18 to 28	124	44	26	30	0
	29 to 47	247	25	47	25	3
	48 to 66	144	11	60	26	3
	67 to 98	71	5	48	40	7
Married:	Yes	346	18	52	27	3
	No	257	30	38	28	3
Have Kids Under 18:	Yes	249	28	42	28	2
	No	352	20	49	28	3
Household Income:	Under $25,000	186	16	46	33	4
	$25,000 to $50,000	216	28	42	28	2
	Over $50,000	119	25	52	21	2
Region:	Northeast	137	24	46	30	0
	South	195	24	43	28	5
	Midwest	139	13	48	35	5
	West	133	31	50	18	1
Education:	High School or Less	313	21	47	30	3
	Some College	160	25	44	28	3
	College Graduate	127	26	49	23	2
Ethnicity:	White	435	19	47	31	4
	Black	81	23	53	23	1
	Hispanic	55	51	28	21	0
Voter Registration:	Not Registered	110	27	42	29	2
	Democrat	202	20	49	26	4
	Republican	132	24	51	22	3
	Independent	107	25	38	36	1
Church Type:	Protestant	252	20	51	26	4
	Catholic	153	29	38	32	1
Faith Perspective:	Evangelical	41	24	49	18	9
	Born Again	228	25	50	21	4
	Non-Christian	376	22	44	32	2

TABLE 106

Compared to a year ago, are you currently spending more time, less time, or about the same amount of time exercising or working out physically?

		N	More Time	Same Time	Less Time	Don't Know
Total Responding		604	32%	44%	23%	1%
Gender:	Male	294	36	45	18	1
	Female	309	28	43	27	2
Age:	18 to 28	124	40	40	20	0
	29 to 47	247	40	35	23	2
	48 to 66	144	19	52	27	2
	67 to 98	71	20	58	20	3
Married:	Yes	346	28	47	23	2
	No	257	38	39	22	1
Have Kids Under 18:	Yes	249	36	38	24	1
	No	352	29	48	22	1
Household Income:	Under $25,000	186	26	44	28	2
	$25,000 to $50,000	216	37	43	18	2
	Over $50,000	119	39	40	20	0
Region:	Northeast	137	37	40	23	0
	South	195	31	43	23	3
	Midwest	139	31	43	24	2
	West	133	29	49	21	1
Education:	High School or Less	313	35	43	21	1
	Some College	160	25	49	24	2
	College Graduate	127	34	39	26	1
Ethnicity:	White	435	31	44	24	2
	Black	81	28	36	33	3
	Hispanic	55	53	47	0	0
Voter Registration:	Not Registered	110	26	43	29	2
	Democrat	202	38	40	22	1
	Republican	132	31	48	19	2
	Independent	107	32	43	24	1
Church Type:	Protestant	252	27	50	21	1
	Catholic	153	43	34	23	0
Faith Perspective:	Evangelical	41	34	45	21	0
	Born Again	228	31	44	23	2
	Non-Christian	376	32	44	23	1

TABLE 107

Compared to a year ago, are you currently spending more time, less time, or about the same amount of time reading for pleasure?

		N	More Time	Same Time	Less Time	Don't Know
Total Responding		604	31%	45%	23%	1%
Gender:	Male	294	24	49	27	0
	Female	309	38	41	20	1
Age:	18 to 28	124	34	25	40	1
	29 to 47	247	30	45	25	1
	48 to 66	144	33	54	13	0
	67 to 98	71	33	52	13	1
Married:	Yes	346	29	51	20	0
	No	257	35	36	28	1
Have Kids Under 18:	Yes	249	33	40	27	0
	No	352	30	48	21	1
Household Income:	Under $25,000	186	32	40	27	1
	$25,000 to $50,000	216	31	47	21	1
	Over $50,000	119	29	49	22	0
Region:	Northeast	137	32	45	23	0
	South	195	31	46	21	1
	Midwest	139	32	43	25	1
	West	133	30	45	26	0
Education:	High School or Less	313	28	44	28	1
	Some College	160	38	46	16	1
	College Graduate	127	33	46	21	0
Ethnicity:	White	435	31	48	19	1
	Black	81	44	27	29	0
	Hispanic	55	13	46	42	0
Voter Registration:	Not Registered	110	28	38	34	0
	Democrat	202	35	45	19	1
	Republican	132	32	49	18	1
	Independent	107	31	44	25	0
Church Type:	Protestant	252	30	48	21	1
	Catholic	153	31	44	25	0
Faith Perspective:	Evangelical	41	38	39	18	6
	Born Again	228	33	44	22	1
	Non-Christian	376	30	46	24	0

TABLE 108

Compared to a year ago, are you currently spending more time, less time, or about the same amount of time listening to the radio?

		N	More Time	Same Time	Less Time	Don't Know
Total Responding		604	30%	51%	18%	1%
Gender:	Male	294	32	51	17	0
	Female	309	29	50	19	1
Age:	18 to 28	124	55	28	17	0
	29 to 47	247	25	54	20	1
	48 to 66	144	27	59	15	0
	67 to 98	71	15	59	20	6
Married:	Yes	346	26	58	15	1
	No	257	37	40	22	1
Have Kids Under 18:	Yes	249	31	49	20	1
	No	352	30	52	17	1
Household Income:	Under $25,000	186	33	42	23	2
	$25,000 to $50,000	216	29	56	15	1
	Over $50,000	119	33	51	16	0
Region:	Northeast	137	38	41	22	0
	South	195	25	52	22	1
	Midwest	139	33	53	12	1
	West	133	28	56	15	1
Education:	High School or Less	313	32	49	18	1
	Some College	160	29	54	16	1
	College Graduate	127	29	51	19	0
Ethnicity:	White	435	30	54	14	1
	Black	81	37	38	25	0
	Hispanic	55	26	45	28	0
Voter Registration:	Not Registered	110	40	38	21	1
	Democrat	202	26	55	18	1
	Republican	132	26	58	15	1
	Independent	107	34	48	18	0
Church Type:	Protestant	252	26	56	17	1
	Catholic	153	33	45	21	1
Faith Perspective:	Evangelical	41	16	62	22	0
	Born Again	228	29	53	17	1
	Non-Christian	376	31	49	19	1

TABLE 109

Compared to a year ago, are you currently spending more time, less time, or about the same amount of time discussing the meaning and challenges of life with family and others?

		N	More Time	Same Time	Less Time	Don't Know
Total Responding		604	34%	48%	16%	2%
Gender:	Male	294	30	51	17	3
	Female	309	38	45	15	1
Age:	18 to 28	124	36	30	32	2
	29 to 47	247	39	50	9	1
	48 to 66	144	28	58	13	1
	67 to 98	71	21	53	22	4
Married:	Yes	346	30	55	13	2
	No	257	39	38	21	2
Have Kids Under 18:	Yes	249	38	45	16	1
	No	352	31	50	17	2
Household Income:	Under $25,000	186	30	45	22	3
	$25,000 to $50,000	216	39	48	12	1
	Over $50,000	119	34	49	17	0
Region:	Northeast	137	31	50	19	0
	South	195	34	47	15	3
	Midwest	139	32	49	17	3
	West	133	39	46	14	1
Education:	High School or Less	313	32	47	18	2
	Some College	160	35	48	15	2
	College Graduate	127	38	48	13	1
Ethnicity:	White	435	33	51	15	2
	Black	81	35	40	21	4
	Hispanic	55	50	36	14	0
Voter Registration:	Not Registered	110	43	36	19	2
	Democrat	202	33	51	15	2
	Republican	132	33	53	11	3
	Independent	107	32	42	25	1
Church Type:	Protestant	252	33	52	13	2
	Catholic	153	36	50	14	0
Faith Perspective:	Evangelical	41	29	66	4	0
	Born Again	228	43	47	9	1
	Non-Christian	376	29	48	21	3

TABLE 110

If you had to name the two or three most serious needs or problems you face in your life today, what would those needs or problems be for you, personally?

		N	Financial	Job	Time/ Stress	Family	Educ- ation	Health	Spiritual
Total Responding		1206	39%	16%	8%	12%	6%	12%	2%
Gender:	Male	571	40	19	9	8	5	9	2
	Female	616	36	13	9	15	7	15	1
Age:	18 to 28	244	44	22	9	6	12	5	3
	29 to 47	501	42	17	12	15	6	6	2
	48 to 66	285	32	15	5	13	2	23	1
	67 to 98	115	15	1	3	7	1	26	1
Married:	Yes	636	34	15	11	15	4	12	1
	No	570	45	17	6	9	7	12	2
Have Kids Under 18:	Yes	536	48	17	12	17	8	6	2
	No	668	32	15	5	8	4	17	1
Household Income:	Under $25,000	382	39	17	4	12	6	15	1
	$25,000 to $50,000	438	40	19	9	9	7	11	3
	Over $50,000	227	37	16	15	15	4	12	1
Region:	Northeast	252	45	17	11	9	5	12	2
	South	391	37	17	9	11	7	12	2
	Midwest	268	35	13	7	14	6	15	1
	West	262	31	16	7	14	4	13	1
Education:	High School or Less	642	42	14	6	12	4	12	1
	Some College	319	40	18	8	12	8	11	1
	College Graduate	241	31	18	14	12	6	14	2
Ethnicity:	White	853	36	15	8	12	4	13	1
	Black	184	56	17	10	11	10	9	0
	Hispanic	109	45	20	10	13	7	10	1
Voter Registration:	Not Registered	246	43	16	8	7	7	9	1
	Democrat	387	41	16	10	11	5	15	0
	Republican	264	37	14	5	15	5	10	1
	Independent	206	36	19	9	13	7	11	3
Church Type:	Protestant	492	36	15	8	14	3	15	2
	Catholic	312	40	11	11	12	6	11	1
Faith Perspective:	Evangelical	83	45	8	8	13	6	6	4
	Born Again	431	45	14	10	14	6	14	4
	Non-Christian	781	36	17	8	11	5	12	0

TABLE 111

Do you agree or disagree that there is no such thing as absolute truth; two people could define truth in totally conflicting ways but both could still be correct? Do you (agree/disagree) strongly or somewhat?

		N	Agree Strongly	Agree Somewhat	Disagree Somewhat	Disagree Strongly	Don't Know
Total Responding		1206	32%	39%	10%	15%	4%
Gender:	Male	584	30	40	9	16	5
	Female	622	33	39	10	14	4
Age:	18 to 28	252	32	46	10	9	3
	29 to 47	514	29	41	9	17	3
	48 to 66	291	34	37	10	15	5
	67 to 98	120	32	26	11	19	11
Married:	Yes	659	30	38	9	18	5
	No	547	34	41	10	11	4
Have Kids Under 18:	Yes	513	30	39	12	15	3
	No	687	32	40	8	15	5
Household Income:	Under $25,000	382	30	41	11	12	5
	$25,000 to $50,000	438	31	38	10	17	4
	Over $50,000	227	36	37	7	18	2
Region:	Northeast	265	26	47	11	12	5
	South	398	32	34	10	19	5
	Midwest	279	30	42	11	13	4
	West	264	39	38	6	14	4
Education:	High School or Less	625	32	39	10	14	6
	Some College	325	31	42	9	14	3
	College Graduate	249	31	38	10	18	3
Ethnicity:	White	867	30	41	10	15	4
	Black	162	39	26	11	18	6
	Hispanic	112	30	49	10	11	0
Voter Registration:	Not Registered	246	30	47	6	12	5
	Democrat	381	36	37	11	13	4
	Republican	270	27	37	10	21	5
	Independent	209	33	37	12	16	2
Church Type:	Protestant	492	29	38	8	18	6
	Catholic	313	30	45	10	12	3
Faith Perspective:	Evangelical	83	14	28	10	46	2
	Born Again	428	25	37	12	23	4
	Non-Christian	777	35	41	8	11	5

TABLE 112

Do you agree or disagree that the important thing in a relationship is not how much time you spend together, but the quality of the time spent together? Do you (agree/disagree) strongly or somewhat?

		N	Agree Strongly	Agree Somewhat	Disagree Somewhat	Disagree Strongly	Don't Know
Total Responding		1206	68%	22%	6%	3%	1%
Gender:	Male	584	68	22	6	3	1
	Female	622	68	21	6	4	1
Age:	18 to 28	252	68	25	4	3	1
	29 to 47	514	64	24	7	4	1
	48 to 66	291	74	17	5	3	2
	67 to 98	120	72	21	5	0	3
Married:	Yes	659	64	23	7	4	2
	No	547	73	20	3	2	1
Have Kids Under 18:	Yes	513	62	25	7	4	2
	No	687	73	19	4	3	1
Household Income:	Under $25,000	382	74	17	3	3	2
	$25,000 to $50,000	438	70	22	5	2	1
	Over $50,000	227	59	27	11	3	0
Region:	Northeast	265	67	24	7	1	1
	South	398	71	21	4	2	2
	Midwest	279	65	21	6	5	3
	West	264	69	21	6	4	0
Education:	High School or Less	625	73	18	5	3	2
	Some College	325	66	24	4	4	1
	College Graduate	249	57	29	10	3	1
Ethnicity:	White	867	66	24	6	3	1
	Black	162	74	18	5	3	0
	Hispanic	112	80	9	1	6	4
Voter Registration:	Not Registered	246	70	22	3	2	2
	Democrat	381	72	20	4	3	1
	Republican	270	61	25	8	4	1
	Independent	209	70	22	7	1	0
Church Type:	Protestant	492	67	22	7	3	1
	Catholic	313	74	18	5	2	1
Faith Perspective:	Evangelical	83	50	28	13	9	0
	Born Again	428	67	21	7	5	1
	Non-Christian	777	69	22	5	2	2

TABLE 113

Do you agree or disagree that the values and lifestyles shown in movies and television programs generally reflect the way most people live and think these days? Do you (agree/disagree) strongly or somewhat?

		N	Agree Strongly	Agree Somewhat	Disagree Somewhat	Disagree Strongly	Don't Know
Total Responding		1206	15%	20%	22%	40%	3%
Gender:	Male	584	14	21	21	41	3
	Female	622	15	20	23	40	2
Age:	18 to 28	252	14	27	31	26	2
	29 to 47	514	12	20	23	42	3
	48 to 66	291	17	18	19	44	3
	67 to 98	120	21	16	10	48	6
Married:	Yes	659	12	20	21	45	2
	No	547	18	21	24	34	3
Have Kids Under 18:	Yes	513	12	23	24	40	2
	No	687	17	19	21	41	3
Household Income:	Under $25,000	382	19	24	18	35	3
	$25,000 to $50,000	438	13	23	21	41	2
	Over $50,000	227	7	14	31	47	1
Region:	Northeast	265	10	22	30	37	1
	South	398	19	21	17	39	4
	Midwest	279	14	20	25	39	3
	West	264	13	18	19	48	2
Education:	High School or Less	625	20	23	19	34	3
	Some College	325	9	19	22	47	2
	College Graduate	249	7	14	31	46	2
Ethnicity:	White	867	12	19	24	42	3
	Black	162	24	20	12	39	4
	Hispanic	112	23	27	20	30	0
Voter Registration:	Not Registered	246	13	29	21	33	4
	Democrat	381	18	22	23	35	2
	Republican	270	15	12	22	51	1
	Independent	209	10	18	20	48	4
Church Type:	Protestant	492	12	18	23	44	3
	Catholic	313	16	24	22	37	1
Faith Perspective:	Evangelical	83	17	18	13	51	1
	Born Again	428	14	22	18	43	2
	Non-Christian	777	15	19	24	39	3

TABLE 114

Do you agree or disagree that the main purpose in life is enjoyment and personal fulfillment? Do you (agree/disagree) strongly or somewhat?

		N	Agree Strongly	Agree Somewhat	Disagree Somewhat	Disagree Strongly	Don't Know
Total Responding		1206	30%	31%	21%	16%	2%
Gender:	Male	584	32	31	21	14	2
	Female	622	28	31	21	17	2
Age:	18 to 28	252	36	37	17	9	1
	29 to 47	514	24	32	23	19	2
	48 to 66	291	28	24	27	17	4
	67 to 98	120	47	24	9	16	4
Married:	Yes	659	28	28	23	19	3
	No	547	32	34	19	12	2
Have Kids Under 18:	Yes	513	26	34	22	17	2
	No	687	32	29	21	15	3
Household Income:	Under $25,000	382	33	27	20	17	2
	$25,000 to $50,000	438	27	32	25	15	2
	Over $50,000	227	28	34	21	16	2
Region:	Northeast	265	27	37	21	13	2
	South	398	32	27	19	19	3
	Midwest	279	30	29	23	16	2
	West	264	29	32	24	14	1
Education:	High School or Less	625	35	26	21	14	3
	Some College	325	24	39	20	17	0
	College Graduate	249	23	31	25	18	3
Ethnicity:	White	867	29	29	22	17	3
	Black	162	34	31	16	17	1
	Hispanic	112	30	36	25	6	3
Voter Registration:	Not Registered	246	37	29	17	14	3
	Democrat	381	32	31	24	11	2
	Republican	270	21	31	23	22	3
	Independent	209	29	32	20	17	1
Church Type:	Protestant	492	27	29	23	19	2
	Catholic	313	32	32	24	10	3
Faith Perspective:	Evangelical	83	10	27	11	52	0
	Born Again	428	23	27	25	24	1
	Non-Christian	777	34	33	20	11	3

TABLE 115

Do you agree or disagree that the news media are fair and objective in their reporting of the news? Do you (agree/disagree) strongly or somewhat?

		N	Agree Strongly	Agree Somewhat	Disagree Somewhat	Disagree Strongly	Don't Know
Total Responding		1206	9%	28%	28%	32%	3%
Gender:	Male	584	8	28	24	36	3
	Female	622	10	28	31	29	3
Age:	18 to 28	252	9	33	31	26	1
	29 to 47	514	7	28	28	33	3
	48 to 66	291	8	29	27	33	3
	67 to 98	120	17	20	19	37	7
Married:	Yes	659	6	27	28	35	3
	No	547	12	29	27	29	3
Have Kids Under 18:	Yes	513	8	28	30	32	3
	No	687	10	28	26	33	3
Household Income:	Under $25,000	382	15	30	25	26	3
	$25,000 to $50,000	438	6	26	30	37	2
	Over $50,000	227	4	29	29	36	3
Region:	Northeast	265	7	31	32	28	2
	South	398	7	26	27	37	4
	Midwest	279	13	27	30	26	4
	West	264	10	30	22	35	3
Education:	High School or Less	625	10	32	27	27	4
	Some College	325	8	25	26	39	3
	College Graduate	249	5	23	32	38	1
Ethnicity:	White	867	8	28	29	32	3
	Black	162	15	27	21	35	1
	Hispanic	112	10	23	30	34	3
Voter Registration:	Not Registered	246	11	36	26	25	3
	Democrat	381	13	30	28	26	4
	Republican	270	3	27	26	41	4
	Independent	209	6	19	30	44	0
Church Type:	Protestant	492	8	25	30	35	3
	Catholic	313	9	32	24	33	3
Faith Perspective:	Evangelical	83	10	8	37	42	3
	Born Again	428	7	22	30	37	3
	Non-Christian	777	10	31	27	29	3

TABLE 116

Do you agree or disagree that in times of personal crisis you are absolutely certain you can count on God to take care of you? Do you (agree/disagree) strongly or somewhat?

		N	Agree Strongly	Agree Somewhat	Disagree Somewhat	Disagree Strongly	Don't Know
Total Responding		1206	63%	22%	6%	7%	2%
Gender:	Male	584	54	27	8	10	2
	Female	622	71	17	5	5	1
Age:	18 to 28	252	52	31	6	9	2
	29 to 47	514	64	21	7	7	2
	48 to 66	291	66	19	6	8	1
	67 to 98	120	75	9	6	8	2
Married:	Yes	659	67	20	5	6	2
	No	547	58	24	8	9	2
Have Kids Under 18:	Yes	513	66	21	6	5	2
	No	687	60	22	7	9	2
Household Income:	Under $25,000	382	65	19	6	8	1
	$25,000 to $50,000	438	63	25	5	6	2
	Over $50,000	227	55	25	10	11	0
Region:	Northeast	265	51	27	9	12	2
	South	398	77	15	5	2	1
	Midwest	279	59	25	7	7	2
	West	264	56	24	6	12	2
Education:	High School or Less	625	68	21	3	6	2
	Some College	325	63	21	8	7	2
	College Graduate	249	51	24	12	12	1
Ethnicity:	White	867	63	23	6	7	2
	Black	162	77	9	4	10	0
	Hispanic	112	56	28	7	6	3
Voter Registration:	Not Registered	246	57	26	5	10	1
	Democrat	381	66	19	5	8	2
	Republican	270	68	21	5	4	1
	Independent	209	57	22	9	10	2
Church Type:	Protestant	492	73	16	6	4	2
	Catholic	313	59	28	5	7	1
Faith Perspective:	Evangelical	83	89	5	0	3	3
	Born Again	428	87	9	0	2	2
	Non-Christian	777	50	29	10	10	2

TABLE 117

Do you agree or disagree that life is too complex these days? Do you (agree/disagree) strongly or somewhat?

		N	Agree Strongly	Agree Somewhat	Disagree Somewhat	Disagree Strongly	Don't Know
Total Responding		1206	29%	35%	22%	12%	1%
Gender:	Male	584	24	34	26	14	1
	Female	622	34	36	19	10	1
Age:	18 to 28	252	32	33	26	8	1
	29 to 47	514	30	35	21	12	1
	48 to 66	291	28	38	19	13	1
	67 to 98	120	28	26	27	16	3
Married:	Yes	659	28	37	22	11	1
	No	547	30	32	22	14	1
Have Kids Under 18:	Yes	513	30	34	22	12	1
	No	687	29	35	22	13	1
Household Income:	Under $25,000	382	35	32	20	12	1
	$25,000 to $50,000	438	27	36	23	13	1
	Over $50,000	227	23	42	23	12	0
Region:	Northeast	265	31	37	21	11	1
	South	398	28	34	20	16	1
	Midwest	279	33	34	21	9	3
	West	264	25	34	28	11	1
Education:	High School or Less	625	32	37	19	11	2
	Some College	325	29	32	25	13	1
	College Graduate	249	24	34	26	15	1
Ethnicity:	White	867	30	36	22	11	2
	Black	162	25	36	21	18	0
	Hispanic	112	31	31	29	8	0
Voter Registration:	Not Registered	246	35	33	19	11	2
	Democrat	381	28	38	21	12	1
	Republican	270	28	34	26	12	1
	Independent	209	28	37	19	14	2
Church Type:	Protestant	492	30	34	23	12	2
	Catholic	313	32	37	19	11	2
Faith Perspective:	Evangelical	83	30	40	18	12	1
	Born Again	428	29	38	20	12	1
	Non-Christian	777	30	33	23	12	2

TABLE 118

Do you agree or disagree that sometimes it feels like life is not worth living? Do you (agree/disagree) strongly or somewhat?

		N	Agree Strongly	Agree Somewhat	Disagree Somewhat	Disagree Strongly	Don't Know
Total Responding		1206	6%	11%	11%	70%	1%
Gender:	Male	584	6	11	11	70	1
	Female	622	6	12	11	70	1
Age:	18 to 28	252	6	14	11	70	0
	29 to 47	514	6	10	13	70	1
	48 to 66	291	7	11	8	73	1
	67 to 98	120	9	13	9	64	5
Married:	Yes	659	4	10	10	75	1
	No	547	9	13	12	65	1
Have Kids Under 18:	Yes	513	7	10	11	71	1
	No	687	6	12	11	70	1
Household Income:	Under $25,000	382	10	14	11	63	2
	$25,000 to $50,000	438	5	10	10	75	1
	Over $50,000	227	5	8	10	76	1
Region:	Northeast	265	5	11	9	74	1
	South	398	5	12	14	69	1
	Midwest	279	7	11	11	67	3
	West	264	8	12	8	72	0
Education:	High School or Less	625	6	14	12	66	2
	Some College	325	7	9	7	76	1
	College Graduate	249	5	8	12	75	0
Ethnicity:	White	867	6	11	10	71	1
	Black	162	7	13	10	70	0
	Hispanic	112	7	9	21	63	0
Voter Registration:	Not Registered	246	11	18	11	58	2
	Democrat	381	6	9	11	73	1
	Republican	270	5	8	12	75	0
	Independent	209	4	11	9	76	0
Church Type:	Protestant	492	5	12	8	73	2
	Catholic	313	7	9	14	71	0
Faith Perspective:	Evangelical	83	4	7	7	81	2
	Born Again	428	5	10	8	77	0
	Non-Christian	777	7	12	12	66	2

TABLE 119

Do you agree or disagree that you, personally, have a responsibility to share what you have with others who are poor or struggling? Do you (agree/disagree) strongly or somewhat?

		N	Agree Strongly	Agree Somewhat	Disagree Somewhat	Disagree Strongly	Don't Know
Total Responding		1206	47%	41%	5%	5%	2%
Gender:	Male	584	41	45	7	6	1
	Female	622	53	38	4	3	2
Age:	18 to 28	252	41	48	7	4	0
	29 to 47	514	47	41	5	4	2
	48 to 66	291	50	39	4	6	1
	67 to 98	120	53	33	4	6	3
Married:	Yes	659	47	41	6	4	2
	No	547	47	42	5	5	1
Have Kids Under 18:	Yes	513	47	43	5	3	2
	No	687	47	40	6	6	1
Household Income:	Under $25,000	382	56	34	5	4	2
	$25,000 to $50,000	438	42	47	6	3	2
	Over $50,000	227	44	42	6	7	1
Region:	Northeast	265	44	46	6	4	1
	South	398	49	39	5	5	1
	Midwest	279	48	41	5	2	3
	West	264	45	40	5	8	2
Education:	High School or Less	625	47	40	5	6	2
	Some College	325	48	45	4	3	1
	College Graduate	249	47	39	7	4	2
Ethnicity:	White	867	46	42	5	5	2
	Black	162	60	34	3	4	0
	Hispanic	112	31	50	9	7	4
Voter Registration:	Not Registered	246	46	38	9	6	1
	Democrat	381	51	39	4	4	2
	Republican	270	51	39	5	4	1
	Independent	209	40	49	5	5	0
Church Type:	Protestant	492	51	38	6	3	2
	Catholic	313	45	45	5	5	1
Faith Perspective:	Evangelical	83	77	20	2	0	1
	Born Again	428	57	35	4	3	1
	Non-Christian	777	41	45	6	6	2

TABLE 120

Do you think abortions should be legal under any circumstances, legal only under certain circumstances, or illegal under all circumstances?

		N	Always Legal	Sometimes Legal	Always Illegal	Don't Know
Total Responding		601	29%	49%	17%	5%
Gender:	Male	288	28	53	15	4
	Female	313	29	45	20	6
Age:	18 to 28	126	35	44	17	3
	29 to 47	270	28	52	16	4
	48 to 66	147	22	51	18	8
	67 to 98	46	34	41	24	2
Married:	Yes	309	25	55	17	3
	No	292	33	43	18	6
Have Kids Under 18:	Yes	262	31	46	19	4
	No	336	27	51	16	5
Household Income:	Under $25,000	198	28	43	24	5
	$25,000 to $50,000	220	23	57	15	4
	Over $50,000	108	33	54	10	3
Region:	Northeast	126	42	41	15	2
	South	205	19	55	21	6
	Midwest	141	26	54	15	4
	West	130	35	41	17	7
Education:	High School or Less	307	23	50	22	5
	Some College	168	34	49	12	5
	College Graduate	123	36	48	13	3
Ethnicity:	White	432	28	52	15	5
	Black	79	30	37	28	5
	Hispanic	57	24	48	22	6
Voter Registration:	Not Registered	137	32	46	15	7
	Democrat	175	31	48	18	2
	Republican	140	20	51	24	5
	Independent	101	38	46	12	4
Church Type:	Protestant	236	23	54	17	6
	Catholic	162	29	45	24	3
Faith Perspective:	Evangelical	41	3	57	35	6
	Born Again	200	12	55	27	6
	Non-Christian	402	37	46	13	4

Table 121

What do you feel would be the best way for the public schools to handle matters related to birth control and sex education among students under the age of 18?

		N	A	B	C	D	E
Total Responding		601	28%	19%	28%	19%	6%
Gender:	Male	288	25	22	25	22	6
	Female	313	31	17	31	16	6
Age:	18 to 28	126	18	13	54	13	3
	29 to 47	270	31	23	26	15	5
	48 to 66	147	32	22	12	27	7
	67 to 98	46	31	8	20	31	11
Married:	Yes	309	35	20	19	21	5
	No	292	21	19	37	16	6
Have Kids Under 18:	Yes	262	32	18	32	13	5
	No	336	25	20	25	23	6
Household Income:	Under $25,000	198	24	15	33	19	9
	$25,000 to $50,000	220	31	22	26	20	2
	Over $50,000	108	30	26	27	12	4
Region:	Northeast	126	19	19	42	16	4
	South	205	34	15	26	18	7
	Midwest	141	22	25	24	21	7
	West	130	35	20	22	19	4
Education:	High School or Less	307	25	16	31	22	6
	Some College	168	36	22	24	12	6
	College Graduate	123	27	24	25	19	5
Ethnicity:	White	432	31	22	24	17	5
	Black	79	17	10	37	32	4
	Hispanic	57	21	3	49	14	14
Voter Registration:	Not Registered	137	19	20	40	14	6
	Democrat	175	29	20	29	22	1
	Republican	140	37	16	18	21	8
	Independent	101	27	24	28	18	4
Church Type:	Protestant	236	33	20	18	24	5
	Catholic	162	26	19	35	15	6
Faith Perspective:	Evangelical	41	58	0	3	35	3
	Born Again	200	40	17	13	25	5
	Non-Christian	402	22	21	36	15	6

A: The schools should teach a standard course on sex education, and promote sexual abstinence.

B: The schools should teach a standard course on sex education, and mention sexual abstinence as an option.

C. The schools should teach a standard course on sex education, and make condoms and other birth control devices available to students upon their request.

D: The schools should leave sex education up to parents, and should not make any condoms or birth control devices available to students.

E: Don't know.

TABLE 122

Do you think children under the age of 18 who want to live apart from their parents should be:

		N	Allowed to Under Any Circumstances	Allowed if Can Prove Abuse or Neglect by Family	Not Allowed to Under Any Circumstances	Don't Know
Total Responding		601	10%	68%	12%	10%
Gender:	Male	288	9	66	14	11
	Female	313	11	69	11	9
Age:	18 to 28	126	14	75	5	7
	29 to 47	270	10	70	11	9
	48 to 66	147	10	62	17	11
	67 to 98	46	5	57	27	11
Married:	Yes	309	6	69	14	10
	No	292	15	66	9	9
Have Kids Under 18:	Yes	262	9	70	11	10
	No	336	11	66	13	10
Household Income:	Under $25,000	198	12	68	11	9
	$25,000 to $50,000	220	10	70	13	7
	Over $50,000	108	5	68	12	15
Region:	Northeast	126	9	75	6	11
	South	205	9	73	11	7
	Midwest	141	12	61	18	9
	West	130	12	60	14	14
Education:	High School or Less	307	14	64	14	8
	Some College	168	7	70	15	8
	College Graduate	123	6	75	4	15
Ethnicity:	White	432	9	70	11	11
	Black	79	18	62	17	3
	Hispanic	57	17	61	14	8
Voter Registration:	Not Registered	137	17	70	4	9
	Democrat	175	10	68	15	7
	Republican	140	8	64	20	8
	Independent	101	8	71	9	13
Church Type:	Protestant	236	6	73	12	9
	Catholic	162	13	66	14	8
Faith Perspective:	Evangelical	41	0	90	6	5
	Born Again	200	7	76	11	6
	Non-Christian	402	12	64	12	12

TABLE 123

When it comes to penalties for committing premeditated murder, do you believe the government should:

		N	Make Death Penalty Mandatory	Make Long Sentence Without Parole Mandatory	Leave Penalty Up to Jury	Don't Know
Total Responding		601	47%	20%	25%	8%
Gender:	Male	288	55	10	27	8
	Female	313	40	28	23	9
Age:	18 to 28	126	54	20	21	6
	29 to 47	270	47	17	28	9
	48 to 66	147	40	24	25	10
	67 to 98	46	54	26	14	6
Married:	Yes	309	50	18	23	9
	No	292	43	22	27	7
Have Kids Under 18:	Yes	262	47	21	22	9
	No	336	47	19	27	8
Household Income:	Under $25,000	198	46	26	21	7
	$25,000 to $50,000	220	46	16	30	7
	Over $50,000	108	49	17	26	8
Region:	Northeast	126	50	21	23	6
	South	205	43	25	24	7
	Midwest	141	49	14	23	14
	West	130	47	15	30	8
Education:	High School or Less	307	46	20	25	9
	Some College	168	58	16	21	6
	College Graduate	123	34	23	32	11
Ethnicity:	White	432	50	17	25	8
	Black	79	40	40	19	1
	Hispanic	57	37	16	28	19
Voter Registration:	Not Registered	137	47	21	28	3
	Democrat	175	54	21	19	6
	Republican	140	42	15	32	12
	Independent	101	48	21	23	8
Church Type:	Protestant	236	46	19	28	7
	Catholic	162	52	15	24	9
Faith Perspective:	Evangelical	41	42	14	43	1
	Born Again	200	47	22	25	6
	Non-Christian	402	47	18	25	9

TABLE 124

There has been some discussion about a person's right to die, that is, their right to choose whether to continue living or to die. If a person has a disease that cannot be cured, do you feel:

		N	A	B	C	D	E
Total Responding		601	30%	24%	17%	22%	3%
Gender:	Male	288	30	25	18	20	4
	Female	313	30	23	15	24	2
Age:	18 to 28	126	26	24	24	25	0
	29 to 47	270	33	23	14	22	3
	48 to 66	147	24	27	16	21	4
	67 to 98	46	37	18	12	24	6
Married:	Yes	309	30	26	12	21	4
	No	292	29	21	22	23	2
Have Kids Under 18:	Yes	262	26	24	18	24	3
	No	336	32	23	15	21	3
Household Income:	Under $25,000	198	25	23	18	29	2
	$25,000 to $50,000	220	28	25	19	21	2
	Over $50,000	108	43	21	10	15	6
Region:	Northeast	126	32	22	23	20	0
	South	205	28	23	11	28	3
	Midwest	141	25	30	17	19	4
	West	130	35	19	18	20	5
Education:	High School or Less	307	27	24	18	25	2
	Some College	168	34	20	16	20	3
	College Graduate	123	29	29	14	20	3
Ethnicity:	White	432	31	24	14	21	3
	Black	79	24	11	17	40	5
	Hispanic	57	11	41	32	16	0
Voter Registration:	Not Registered	137	36	27	20	14	2
	Democrat	175	31	23	15	24	4
	Republican	140	24	23	14	27	4
	Independent	101	30	20	21	22	3
Church Type:	Protestant	236	26	26	12	25	5
	Catholic	162	33	26	18	17	3
Faith Perspective:	Evangelical	41	8	16	2	58	9
	Born Again	200	23	21	11	34	4
	Non-Christian	402	33	25	19	17	2

A: The doctors should be allowed to painlessly end the person's life if the person requests it.

B: The doctors should be allowed to painlessly end the person's life only if the person and the person's family request it.

C: The person should be allowed to have his or her life ended by any means he or she desires.

D: There are no circumstances under which an individual should be allowed to end his or her life.

E: Don't know.

TABLE 125

Do you feel that legalized casino gambling such as that in Las Vegas or Atlantic City should be:

		N	Legal Everywhere	Legal Only Where Legal Now	Illegal Everywhere	Don't Know
Total Responding		601	36%	40%	14%	10%
Gender:	Male	288	41	40	11	8
	Female	313	32	39	17	12
Age:	18 to 28	126	30	53	15	2
	29 to 47	270	40	40	12	8
	48 to 66	147	37	31	12	19
	67 to 98	46	28	29	31	12
Married:	Yes	309	32	41	15	12
	No	292	41	38	13	8
Have Kids Under 18:	Yes	262	35	44	14	7
	No	336	38	36	15	12
Household Income:	Under $25,000	198	36	39	17	8
	$25,000 to $50,000	220	35	44	14	7
	Over $50,000	108	43	38	9	10
Region:	Northeast	126	39	48	9	5
	South	205	34	29	22	15
	Midwest	141	38	38	12	12
	West	130	36	49	11	4
Education:	High School or Less	307	34	40	17	10
	Some College	168	40	40	12	8
	College Graduate	123	36	40	12	13
Ethnicity:	White	432	36	38	16	10
	Black	79	47	24	16	13
	Hispanic	57	28	61	6	6
Voter Registration:	Not Registered	137	47	35	12	6
	Democrat	175	37	38	13	13
	Republican	140	26	48	17	10
	Independent	101	37	39	17	7
Church Type:	Protestant	236	26	40	21	13
	Catholic	162	38	51	5	7
Faith Perspective:	Evangelical	41	6	33	54	6
	Born Again	200	24	39	28	9
	Non-Christian	402	42	40	8	10

TABLE 126

In the past 30 days, did you make a contribution to any type of charitable organization, including a church or synagogue?

		N	Yes	No	Don't Know
Total Responding		1206	64%	36%	0%
Gender:	Male	584	62	37	1
	Female	622	66	34	0
Age:	18 to 28	252	51	49	0
	29 to 47	514	62	38	1
	48 to 66	291	75	25	0
	67 to 98	120	72	27	1
Married:	Yes	659	73	26	1
	No	547	53	47	0
Have Kids Under 18:	Yes	513	62	38	0
	No	687	66	34	1
Household Income:	Under $25,000	382	54	46	0
	$25,000 to $50,000	438	67	32	0
	Over $50,000	227	76	23	1
Region:	Northeast	265	67	33	0
	South	398	63	37	1
	Midwest	279	65	34	1
	West	264	62	37	1
Education:	High School or Less	625	54	46	0
	Some College	325	73	26	0
	College Graduate	249	79	20	1
Ethnicity:	White	867	67	32	1
	Black	162	55	45	0
	Hispanic	112	48	52	0
Voter Registration:	Not Registered	246	42	58	0
	Democrat	381	67	33	1
	Republican	270	74	25	1
	Independent	209	71	29	0
Church Type:	Protestant	492	71	29	0
	Catholic	313	63	37	0
Faith Perspective:	Evangelical	83	82	18	0
	Born Again	428	77	22	0
	Non-Christian	777	57	43	0

TABLE 127

During the past year, did you donate money to colleges or other educational organizations? *(Base: Donated to a nonprofit in the past year.)*

		N	Yes	No	Don't Know
Total Responding		978	26%	74%	0%
Gender:	Male	454	28	72	0
	Female	524	25	75	0
Age:	18 to 28	182	22	78	0
	29 to 47	423	28	72	0
	48 to 66	246	27	73	0
	67 to 98	102	20	80	1
Married:	Yes	556	30	70	0
	No	421	22	78	0
Have Kids Under 18:	Yes	415	29	71	0
	No	559	25	75	0
Household Income:	Under $25,000	287	17	83	0
	$25,000 to $50,000	373	26	74	0
	Over $50,000	203	38	62	0
Region:	Northeast	225	26	74	0
	South	321	27	73	0
	Midwest	224	27	73	0
	West	206	25	75	0
Education:	High School or Less	461	18	82	0
	Some College	289	24	76	0
	College Graduate	223	47	53	0
Ethnicity:	White	733	25	75	0
	Black	125	39	61	0
	Hispanic	74	25	75	0
Voter Registration:	Not Registered	166	15	85	0
	Democrat	323	31	69	0
	Republican	233	30	70	0
	Independent	181	23	77	0
Church Type:	Protestant	418	31	69	0
	Catholic	255	23	77	0
Faith Perspective:	Evangelical	80	28	71	1
	Born Again	390	30	70	0
	Non-Christian	587	24	76	0

TABLE 128

During the past year, did you donate money to churches, synagogues or other houses of worship? *(Base: Donated to a nonprofit in the past year.)*

		N	Yes	No	Don't Know
Total Responding		978	74%	26%	0%
Gender:	Male	454	72	28	0
	Female	524	76	24	0
Age:	18 to 28	182	65	35	0
	29 to 47	423	72	28	0
	48 to 66	246	79	21	0
	67 to 98	102	77	23	0
Married:	Yes	556	81	19	0
	No	421	65	35	0
Have Kids Under 18:	Yes	415	77	23	0
	No	559	71	29	0
Household Income:	Under $25,000	287	69	31	0
	$25,000 to $50,000	373	76	24	0
	Over $50,000	203	77	23	0
Region:	Northeast	225	71	29	0
	South	321	79	21	0
	Midwest	224	79	21	0
	West	206	64	36	0
Education:	High School or Less	461	72	28	0
	Some College	289	75	25	0
	College Graduate	223	77	23	0
Ethnicity:	White	733	74	26	0
	Black	125	75	25	0
	Hispanic	74	72	28	0
Voter Registration:	Not Registered	166	63	36	0
	Democrat	323	71	29	0
	Republican	233	83	17	0
	Independent	181	73	27	0
Church Type:	Protestant	418	82	18	0
	Catholic	255	77	23	0
Faith Perspective:	Evangelical	80	91	9	0
	Born Again	390	86	14	0
	Non-Christian	587	66	34	0

TABLE 129

During the past year, did you donate money to religious organizations, other than churches or other houses of worship? *(Base: Donated to a nonprofit in the past year.)*

		N	Yes	No	Don't Know
Total Responding		978	27%	73%	1%
Gender:	Male	454	28	71	1
	Female	524	26	74	0
Age:	18 to 28	182	19	81	0
	29 to 47	423	23	77	1
	48 to 66	246	37	63	0
	67 to 98	102	29	68	3
Married:	Yes	556	31	69	0
	No	421	21	78	1
Have Kids Under 18:	Yes	415	25	75	0
	No	559	28	71	1
Household Income:	Under $25,000	287	23	76	1
	$25,000 to $50,000	373	30	69	1
	Over $50,000	203	24	76	1
Region:	Northeast	225	31	69	0
	South	321	22	77	1
	Midwest	224	27	73	0
	West	206	28	70	1
Education:	High School or Less	461	23	77	0
	Some College	289	31	68	1
	College Graduate	223	30	69	1
Ethnicity:	White	733	26	73	1
	Black	125	21	77	2
	Hispanic	74	37	63	0
Voter Registration:	Not Registered	166	16	84	0
	Democrat	323	27	72	1
	Republican	233	35	64	1
	Independent	181	27	73	0
Church Type:	Protestant	418	31	68	1
	Catholic	255	28	72	0
Faith Perspective:	Evangelical	80	44	56	0
	Born Again	390	33	66	0
	Non-Christian	587	22	77	1

TABLE 130

During the past year, did you donate money to political parties or advocacy organizations? *(Base: Donated to a nonprofit in the past year.)*

		N	Yes	No	Don't Know
Total Responding		978	21%	79%	1%
Gender:	Male	454	22	78	0
	Female	524	20	79	1
Age:	18 to 28	182	16	84	0
	29 to 47	423	22	78	0
	48 to 66	246	18	81	2
	67 to 98	102	31	69	0
Married:	Yes	556	22	77	0
	No	421	19	80	1
Have Kids Under 18:	Yes	415	19	81	0
	No	559	22	77	1
Household Income:	Under $25,000	287	18	81	1
	$25,000 to $50,000	373	21	78	0
	Over $50,000	203	27	73	0
Region:	Northeast	225	22	78	0
	South	321	20	79	0
	Midwest	224	19	80	0
	West	206	22	76	2
Education:	High School or Less	461	16	83	1
	Some College	289	18	82	0
	College Graduate	223	34	65	1
Ethnicity:	White	733	21	79	0
	Black	125	21	79	0
	Hispanic	74	23	73	4
Voter Registration:	Not Registered	166	10	89	0
	Democrat	323	27	72	1
	Republican	233	25	74	0
	Independent	181	19	81	1
Church Type:	Protestant	418	25	75	0
	Catholic	255	22	77	1
Faith Perspective:	Evangelical	80	15	84	1
	Born Again	390	20	80	0
	Non-Christian	587	21	78	1

TABLE 131

During the past year, did you donate money to health-care or medical-research organizations? *(Base: Donated to a nonprofit in the past year.)*

		N	Yes	No	Don't Know
Total Responding		978	44%	55%	1%
Gender:	Male	454	41	58	1
	Female	524	47	53	0
Age:	18 to 28	182	36	63	1
	29 to 47	423	43	56	0
	48 to 66	246	52	48	0
	67 to 98	102	42	58	0
Married:	Yes	556	46	53	0
	No	421	41	58	1
Have Kids Under 18:	Yes	415	43	57	0
	No	559	45	54	1
Household Income:	Under $25,000	287	43	57	0
	$25,000 to $50,000	373	42	57	1
	Over $50,000	203	47	53	1
Region:	Northeast	225	44	55	1
	South	321	40	59	0
	Midwest	224	51	49	0
	West	206	43	57	0
Education:	High School or Less	461	39	60	1
	Some College	289	46	54	0
	College Graduate	223	51	48	1
Ethnicity:	White	733	46	53	1
	Black	125	34	66	0
	Hispanic	74	51	49	0
Voter Registration:	Not Registered	166	35	64	1
	Democrat	323	45	55	0
	Republican	233	46	53	1
	Independent	181	46	54	0
Church Type:	Protestant	418	43	56	1
	Catholic	255	54	46	1
Faith Perspective:	Evangelical	80	40	60	0
	Born Again	390	42	57	0
	Non-Christian	587	45	54	1

TABLE 132

During the past year, did you donate money to wildlife or environmental organizations? *(Base: Donated to a nonprofit in the past year.)*

		N	Yes	No	Don't Know
Total Responding		978	29%	71%	0%
Gender:	Male	454	30	70	0
	Female	524	28	71	1
Age:	18 to 28	182	23	76	1
	29 to 47	423	32	67	0
	48 to 66	246	28	71	1
	67 to 98	102	26	74	0
Married:	Yes	556	31	68	0
	No	421	26	73	1
Have Kids Under 18:	Yes	415	30	70	0
	No	559	28	71	1
Household Income:	Under $25,000	287	22	78	0
	$25,000 to $50,000	373	30	70	0
	Over $50,000	203	37	62	0
Region:	Northeast	225	32	68	0
	South	321	24	75	0
	Midwest	224	30	70	0
	West	206	32	67	1
Education:	High School or Less	461	25	75	0
	Some College	289	29	70	1
	College Graduate	223	38	62	0
Ethnicity:	White	733	31	68	0
	Black	125	10	88	1
	Hispanic	74	28	72	0
Voter Registration:	Not Registered	166	22	77	0
	Democrat	323	24	76	0
	Republican	233	30	70	0
	Independent	181	42	56	1
Church Type:	Protestant	418	30	69	1
	Catholic	255	34	66	0
Faith Perspective:	Evangelical	80	24	74	2
	Born Again	390	26	74	1
	Non-Christian	587	31	68	0

TABLE 133

During the past year, did you donate money to community-development organizations? *(Base: Donated to a nonprofit in the past year.)*

		N	Yes	No	Don't Know
Total Responding		978	31%	69%	1%
Gender:	Male	454	30	69	1
	Female	524	31	68	1
Age:	18 to 28	182	26	73	1
	29 to 47	423	33	67	0
	48 to 66	246	31	68	2
	67 to 98	102	32	67	1
Married:	Yes	556	34	65	1
	No	421	26	73	0
Have Kids Under 18:	Yes	415	33	67	1
	No	559	29	70	1
Household Income:	Under $25,000	287	28	72	0
	$25,000 to $50,000	373	31	68	1
	Over $50,000	203	35	64	1
Region:	Northeast	225	30	70	0
	South	321	30	69	1
	Midwest	224	36	64	1
	West	206	27	72	1
Education:	High School or Less	461	29	70	1
	Some College	289	30	70	0
	College Graduate	223	35	64	1
Ethnicity:	White	733	30	69	1
	Black	125	37	63	0
	Hispanic	74	32	68	0
Voter Registration:	Not Registered	166	26	74	0
	Democrat	323	33	65	1
	Republican	233	32	68	1
	Independent	181	28	71	0
Church Type:	Protestant	418	29	69	2
	Catholic	255	30	70	0
Faith Perspective:	Evangelical	80	22	78	0
	Born Again	390	29	71	1
	Non-Christian	587	32	67	1

TABLE 134

During the past year, did you donate money to music, art or cultural organizations?
(Base: Donated to a nonprofit in the past year.)

		N	Yes	No	Don't Know
Total Responding		978	15%	85%	0%
Gender:	Male	454	15	85	0
	Female	524	15	84	1
Age:	18 to 28	182	12	88	0
	29 to 47	423	14	86	0
	48 to 66	246	18	82	0
	67 to 98	102	18	82	0
Married:	Yes	556	15	85	0
	No	421	15	85	0
Have Kids Under 18:	Yes	415	12	88	0
	No	559	17	82	0
Household Income:	Under $25,000	287	13	87	0
	$25,000 to $50,000	373	15	85	0
	Over $50,000	203	20	80	0
Region:	Northeast	225	14	85	0
	South	321	16	84	0
	Midwest	224	17	83	0
	West	206	13	86	0
Education:	High School or Less	461	11	89	0
	Some College	289	16	83	1
	College Graduate	223	23	77	0
Ethnicity:	White	733	16	83	0
	Black	125	15	85	0
	Hispanic	74	6	94	0
Voter Registration:	Not Registered	166	12	88	0
	Democrat	323	16	84	0
	Republican	233	16	83	1
	Independent	181	16	84	0
Church Type:	Protestant	418	16	83	1
	Catholic	255	13	87	0
Faith Perspective:	Evangelical	80	11	89	0
	Born Again	390	12	88	0
	Non-Christian	587	17	82	0

TABLE 135

Do you consider yourself to be Protestant, Catholic, Jewish, or of some other religious faith?

		N	Prot-estant	Cath-olic	Jewish	Other	Atheist/ No Faith	Chris-tian	Don't Know
Total Responding		1206	39%	26%	2%	23%	5%	3%	2%
Gender:	Male	584	36	25	3	23	6	4	3
	Female	622	41	27	1	24	4	2	2
Age:	18 to 28	252	19	32	1	31	10	4	2
	29 to 47	514	33	28	1	28	4	3	3
	48 to 66	291	58	21	3	13	4	1	0
	67 to 98	120	63	20	4	9	2	0	3
Married:	Yes	659	44	24	2	21	3	3	3
	No	547	32	28	2	27	8	2	1
Have Kids Under 18:	Yes	513	32	27	1	27	5	5	2
	No	687	43	25	3	21	5	1	2
Household Income:	Under $25,000	382	37	27	2	22	6	4	2
	$25,000 to $50,000	438	41	23	1	28	4	3	1
	Over $50,000	227	41	28	5	18	6	1	1
Region:	Northeast	265	29	38	4	17	5	5	2
	South	398	44	19	2	29	3	2	2
	Midwest	279	44	25	2	19	6	0	3
	West	264	35	25	1	25	8	4	1
Education:	High School or Less	625	37	28	1	23	4	4	3
	Some College	325	41	22	3	27	5	1	0
	College Graduate	249	41	26	4	18	7	2	2
Ethnicity:	White	867	46	25	2	20	4	2	2
	Black	162	30	9	1	47	9	4	1
	Hispanic	112	4	65	4	8	6	6	7
Voter Registration:	Not Registered	246	25	31	1	28	9	3	3
	Democrat	381	41	26	3	23	4	2	1
	Republican	270	52	26	1	17	2	2	0
	Independent	209	37	24	4	25	7	2	2
Church Type:	Protestant	492	95	0	0	0	0	5	0
	Catholic	313	0	100	0	0	0	0	0
Faith Perspective:	Evangelical	83	72	1	0	20	0	8	0
	Born Again	428	53	18	0	24	1	3	1
	Non-Christian	777	31	30	3	23	7	2	3

TABLE 136

In the last seven days, did you attend a service at a church or synagogue, other than a special event such as a wedding or funeral?

		N	Yes	No	Don't Know
Total Responding		604	42%	58%	0%
Gender:	Male	294	35	65	0
	Female	309	49	51	0
Age:	18 to 28	124	33	67	0
	29 to 47	247	41	58	1
	48 to 66	144	50	50	0
	67 to 98	71	45	55	0
Married:	Yes	346	48	52	0
	No	257	34	65	1
Have Kids Under 18:	Yes	249	49	51	0
	No	352	37	63	0
Household Income:	Under $25,000	186	38	62	0
	$25,000 to $50,000	216	47	53	1
	Over $50,000	119	43	57	0
Region:	Northeast	137	45	54	1
	South	195	48	52	0
	Midwest	139	38	62	0
	West	133	33	67	0
Education:	High School or Less	313	39	61	0
	Some College	160	45	55	0
	College Graduate	127	47	53	0
Ethnicity:	White	435	43	57	0
	Black	81	45	55	0
	Hispanic	55	29	71	0
Voter Registration:	Not Registered	110	34	66	0
	Democrat	202	45	54	1
	Republican	132	45	55	0
	Independent	107	42	58	0
Church Type:	Protestant	252	46	54	0
	Catholic	153	48	51	1
Faith Perspective:	Evangelical	41	70	30	0
	Born Again	228	60	40	0
	Non-Christian	376	31	69	0

TABLE 137

In the last seven days, did you read from the Bible, other than when you were at a church or synagogue?

		N	Yes	No	Don't Know
Total Responding		1206	37%	62%	0%
Gender:	Male	584	33	66	0
	Female	622	41	58	1
Age:	18 to 28	252	28	71	0
	29 to 47	514	36	64	0
	48 to 66	291	45	54	1
	67 to 98	120	45	53	2
Married:	Yes	659	41	59	0
	No	547	33	67	1
Have Kids Under 18:	Yes	513	40	60	0
	No	687	35	64	1
Household Income:	Under $25,000	382	46	53	1
	$25,000 to $50,000	438	36	63	1
	Over $50,000	227	29	71	0
Region:	Northeast	265	32	68	0
	South	398	48	52	0
	Midwest	279	34	65	1
	West	264	29	69	1
Education:	High School or Less	625	38	61	1
	Some College	325	36	64	0
	College Graduate	249	37	63	0
Ethnicity:	White	867	35	65	0
	Black	162	54	46	0
	Hispanic	112	38	62	0
Voter Registration:	Not Registered	246	28	72	0
	Democrat	381	43	56	1
	Republican	270	39	60	0
	Independent	209	36	64	0
Church Type:	Protestant	492	48	52	1
	Catholic	313	26	74	0
Faith Perspective:	Evangelical	83	85	15	0
	Born Again	428	61	39	0
	Non-Christian	777	24	75	1

TABLE 138

In the last seven days, did you attend a Sunday School class at a church?

		N	Yes	No	Don't Know
Total Responding		1206	21%	79%	0%
Gender:	Male	584	19	81	0
	Female	622	23	77	0
Age:	18 to 28	252	17	83	0
	29 to 47	514	22	78	0
	48 to 66	291	22	78	0
	67 to 98	120	20	80	0
Married:	Yes	659	26	74	0
	No	547	15	85	0
Have Kids Under 18:	Yes	513	25	75	0
	No	687	18	82	0
Household Income:	Under $25,000	382	23	77	0
	$25,000 to $50,000	438	23	77	0
	Over $50,000	227	17	83	0
Region:	Northeast	265	12	88	0
	South	398	30	70	0
	Midwest	279	18	82	0
	West	264	19	81	0
Education:	High School or Less	625	21	79	0
	Some College	325	21	79	0
	College Graduate	249	21	79	0
Ethnicity:	White	867	20	80	0
	Black	162	25	75	0
	Hispanic	112	26	74	0
Voter Registration:	Not Registered	246	12	88	0
	Democrat	381	23	77	0
	Republican	270	26	74	0
	Independent	209	23	77	0
Church Type:	Protestant	492	28	72	0
	Catholic	313	9	91	0
Faith Perspective:	Evangelical	83	59	41	0
	Born Again	428	37	63	0
	Non-Christian	777	12	88	0

TABLE 139

In the last seven days, did you participate in a small group that meets regularly for Bible study, prayer or Christian fellowship, not including a Sunday School or 12-step group?

		N	Yes	No	Don't Know
Total Responding		1206	12%	87%	1%
Gender:	Male	584	9	90	1
	Female	622	15	84	1
Age:	18 to 28	252	11	89	0
	29 to 47	514	11	88	1
	48 to 66	291	12	87	1
	67 to 98	120	18	81	1
Married:	Yes	659	14	84	1
	No	547	10	90	1
Have Kids Under 18:	Yes	513	13	86	1
	No	687	12	87	1
Household Income:	Under $25,000	382	12	86	1
	$25,000 to $50,000	438	15	85	0
	Over $50,000	227	9	90	0
Region:	Northeast	265	11	89	0
	South	398	15	84	1
	Midwest	279	11	87	2
	West	264	11	89	0
Education:	High School or Less	625	11	88	1
	Some College	325	14	85	0
	College Graduate	249	12	87	1
Ethnicity:	White	867	12	87	0
	Black	162	16	84	0
	Hispanic	112	4	90	6
Voter Registration:	Not Registered	246	8	92	0
	Democrat	381	14	86	1
	Republican	270	15	84	1
	Independent	209	12	88	0
Church Type:	Protestant	492	16	84	0
	Catholic	313	6	93	1
Faith Perspective:	Evangelical	83	42	56	2
	Born Again	428	24	76	0
	Non-Christian	777	6	93	1

Table 140

In the last seven days, did you watch a television show that featured a church service, Christian teaching or some other type of Christian activity?

		N	Yes	No	Don't Know
Total Responding		1206	35%	65%	0%
Gender:	Male	584	32	68	0
	Female	622	37	62	0
Age:	18 to 28	252	28	72	0
	29 to 47	514	32	68	0
	48 to 66	291	42	58	0
	67 to 98	120	44	56	0
Married:	Yes	659	32	68	0
	No	547	37	62	0
Have Kids Under 18:	Yes	513	31	69	0
	No	687	37	62	0
Household Income:	Under $25,000	382	38	61	0
	$25,000 to $50,000	438	35	65	0
	Over $50,000	227	28	72	0
Region:	Northeast	265	31	69	0
	South	398	43	57	0
	Midwest	279	33	67	0
	West	264	28	72	0
Education:	High School or Less	625	40	60	0
	Some College	325	31	68	0
	College Graduate	249	26	73	0
Ethnicity:	White	867	31	69	0
	Black	162	53	47	0
	Hispanic	112	41	59	0
Voter Registration:	Not Registered	246	29	71	0
	Democrat	381	43	57	0
	Republican	270	30	70	0
	Independent	209	31	69	0
Church Type:	Protestant	492	41	59	0
	Catholic	313	28	72	0
Faith Perspective:	Evangelical	83	62	38	0
	Born Again	428	52	48	0
	Non-Christian	777	25	75	0

TABLE 141

In the last seven days, did you listen to a radio program that featured Christian preaching or teaching?

		N	Yes	No	Don't Know
Total Responding		1206	27%	73%	0%
Gender:	Male	584	25	75	0
	Female	622	28	72	0
Age:	18 to 28	252	20	80	0
	29 to 47	514	25	75	0
	48 to 66	291	31	69	0
	67 to 98	120	38	62	0
Married:	Yes	659	29	71	0
	No	547	24	76	0
Have Kids Under 18:	Yes	513	26	74	0
	No	687	28	72	0
Household Income:	Under $25,000	382	35	65	0
	$25,000 to $50,000	438	26	74	0
	Over $50,000	227	18	82	0
Region:	Northeast	265	25	75	0
	South	398	34	66	0
	Midwest	279	25	75	0
	West	264	19	81	0
Education:	High School or Less	625	29	70	0
	Some College	325	27	73	0
	College Graduate	249	19	81	0
Ethnicity:	White	867	23	77	0
	Black	162	50	50	0
	Hispanic	112	24	76	0
Voter Registration:	Not Registered	246	18	82	0
	Democrat	381	35	65	0
	Republican	270	26	74	0
	Independent	209	24	76	0
Church Type:	Protestant	492	36	64	0
	Catholic	313	15	85	0
Faith Perspective:	Evangelical	83	70	30	0
	Born Again	428	44	56	0
	Non-Christian	777	17	83	0

TABLE 142

In the last seven days, did you read a book about the Bible or about Christian principles or activities?

		N	Yes	No	Don't Know
Total Responding		1206	27%	73%	0%
Gender:	Male	584	24	76	0
	Female	622	30	70	0
Age:	18 to 28	252	23	77	0
	29 to 47	514	24	76	0
	48 to 66	291	31	69	0
	67 to 98	120	36	64	0
Married:	Yes	659	29	71	0
	No	547	24	76	0
Have Kids Under 18:	Yes	513	29	71	0
	No	687	25	74	0
Household Income:	Under $25,000	382	34	66	0
	$25,000 to $50,000	438	26	74	0
	Over $50,000	227	19	81	0
Region:	Northeast	265	24	75	0
	South	398	31	68	0
	Midwest	279	26	73	0
	West	264	23	77	0
Education:	High School or Less	625	26	74	0
	Some College	325	29	71	0
	College Graduate	249	28	71	0
Ethnicity:	White	867	24	76	0
	Black	162	38	62	0
	Hispanic	112	29	71	0
Voter Registration:	Not Registered	246	17	82	1
	Democrat	381	30	70	0
	Republican	270	32	68	0
	Independent	209	24	76	0
Church Type:	Protestant	492	32	67	0
	Catholic	313	22	78	0
Faith Perspective:	Evangelical	83	59	41	0
	Born Again	428	42	58	0
	Non-Christian	777	19	81	0

TABLE 143

In the last seven days, did you listen to a radio station that plays only Christian music?

		N	Yes	No	Don't Know
Total Responding		1206	22%	78%	0%
Gender:	Male	584	22	77	1
	Female	622	22	78	0
Age:	18 to 28	252	17	83	0
	29 to 47	514	22	78	0
	48 to 66	291	25	74	1
	67 to 98	120	26	74	0
Married:	Yes	659	23	77	1
	No	547	22	78	0
Have Kids Under 18:	Yes	513	22	78	0
	No	687	22	77	1
Household Income:	Under $25,000	382	27	73	1
	$25,000 to $50,000	438	25	75	0
	Over $50,000	227	13	87	0
Region:	Northeast	265	17	83	0
	South	398	30	70	1
	Midwest	279	21	79	0
	West	264	16	83	1
Education:	High School or Less	625	23	76	1
	Some College	325	22	78	0
	College Graduate	249	18	82	0
Ethnicity:	White	867	19	81	0
	Black	162	44	54	1
	Hispanic	112	19	81	0
Voter Registration:	Not Registered	246	15	85	0
	Democrat	381	27	73	1
	Republican	270	22	78	0
	Independent	209	24	76	0
Church Type:	Protestant	492	28	71	0
	Catholic	313	10	90	0
Faith Perspective:	Evangelical	83	56	44	0
	Born Again	428	36	63	0
	Non-Christian	777	14	86	0

TABLE 144

In the last seven days, did you read a magazine that is exclusively about Christianity or activities of special interest to Christians?

		N	Yes	No	Don't Know
Total Responding		1206	22%	78%	0%
Gender:	Male	584	18	81	0
	Female	622	25	74	0
Age:	18 to 28	252	14	86	0
	29 to 47	514	21	79	0
	48 to 66	291	28	72	0
	67 to 98	120	33	65	3
Married:	Yes	659	25	75	0
	No	547	19	81	1
Have Kids Under 18:	Yes	513	22	78	0
	No	687	22	78	1
Household Income:	Under $25,000	382	25	75	0
	$25,000 to $50,000	438	23	76	1
	Over $50,000	227	16	84	0
Region:	Northeast	265	20	80	1
	South	398	25	75	1
	Midwest	279	20	79	0
	West	264	22	78	0
Education:	High School or Less	625	24	76	1
	Some College	325	20	79	0
	College Graduate	249	20	80	0
Ethnicity:	White	867	22	78	0
	Black	162	25	74	1
	Hispanic	112	24	76	0
Voter Registration:	Not Registered	246	13	87	0
	Democrat	381	27	72	0
	Republican	270	23	76	0
	Independent	209	21	78	1
Church Type:	Protestant	492	30	70	0
	Catholic	313	20	80	0
Faith Perspective:	Evangelical	83	54	46	0
	Born Again	428	34	66	0
	Non-Christian	777	15	84	1

Table 145

Do you agree or disagree that the Bible is totally accurate in all of its teachings? Do you (agree/disagree) strongly or somewhat?

		N	Agree Strongly	Agree Somewhat	Disagree Somewhat	Disagree Strongly	Don't Know
Total Responding		1206	38%	21%	21%	15%	6%
Gender:	Male	584	32	22	22	18	6
	Female	622	43	19	20	12	6
Age:	18 to 28	252	32	30	20	14	4
	29 to 47	514	41	20	20	14	5
	48 to 66	291	43	14	23	14	6
	67 to 98	120	31	23	20	17	9
Married:	Yes	659	41	19	20	12	7
	No	547	34	23	22	17	4
Have Kids Under 18:	Yes	513	43	22	20	10	5
	No	687	34	20	21	18	6
Household Income:	Under $25,000	382	40	23	17	15	5
	$25,000 to $50,000	438	43	20	21	11	5
	Over $50,000	227	28	18	28	22	4
Region:	Northeast	265	28	22	22	23	6
	South	398	49	20	16	9	6
	Midwest	279	37	21	24	15	4
	West	264	34	21	24	14	7
Education:	High School or Less	625	45	22	18	9	6
	Some College	325	34	20	25	17	5
	College Graduate	249	26	19	23	26	6
Ethnicity:	White	867	37	19	23	15	6
	Black	162	49	26	11	10	3
	Hispanic	112	33	29	19	17	3
Voter Registration:	Not Registered	246	39	24	17	16	4
	Democrat	381	40	24	16	16	4
	Republican	270	40	18	23	11	8
	Independent	209	30	19	26	18	7
Church Type:	Protestant	492	48	18	17	12	4
	Catholic	313	24	27	27	16	6
Faith Perspective:	Evangelical	83	100	0	0	0	0
	Born Again	428	65	19	9	3	3
	Non-Christian	777	23	22	27	21	7

TABLE 146

Do you agree or disagree that you, personally, have a responsibility to tell other people your religious beliefs? Do you (agree/disagree) strongly or somewhat?

		N	Agree Strongly	Agree Somewhat	Disagree Somewhat	Disagree Strongly	Don't Know
Total Responding		1206	28%	17%	24%	29%	2%
Gender:	Male	584	25	18	28	28	1
	Female	622	30	17	21	31	2
Age:	18 to 28	252	27	13	30	31	0
	29 to 47	514	26	19	26	28	1
	48 to 66	291	30	19	18	30	3
	67 to 98	120	30	20	19	26	4
Married:	Yes	659	31	18	21	28	2
	No	547	24	17	27	31	1
Have Kids Under 18:	Yes	513	30	17	26	26	1
	No	687	26	18	22	32	2
Household Income:	Under $25,000	382	30	19	24	26	1
	$25,000 to $50,000	438	32	17	24	26	1
	Over $50,000	227	19	16	27	36	2
Region:	Northeast	265	22	14	28	36	0
	South	398	35	22	19	22	2
	Midwest	279	28	16	24	31	2
	West	264	22	15	29	32	2
Education:	High School or Less	625	30	19	23	26	2
	Some College	325	29	17	24	30	1
	College Graduate	249	21	14	27	37	2
Ethnicity:	White	867	27	17	24	30	2
	Black	162	43	18	17	20	1
	Hispanic	112	11	27	28	34	0
Voter Registration:	Not Registered	246	18	18	30	32	1
	Democrat	381	33	21	21	24	2
	Republican	270	32	14	20	31	3
	Independent	209	22	17	28	33	0
Church Type:	Protestant	492	36	20	18	22	3
	Catholic	313	16	17	31	36	1
Faith Perspective:	Evangelical	83	100	0	0	0	0
	Born Again	428	48	24	14	12	2
	Non-Christian	777	16	14	30	39	2

TABLE 147

Do you agree or disagree that religion is very important in your life? Do you (agree/disagree) strongly or somewhat?

		N	Agree Strongly	Agree Somewhat	Disagree Somewhat	Disagree Strongly	Don't Know
Total Responding		1206	62%	22%	9%	7%	1%
Gender:	Male	584	55	25	10	9	1
	Female	622	69	18	7	4	2
Age:	18 to 28	252	52	27	14	6	2
	29 to 47	514	61	23	8	8	0
	48 to 66	291	72	15	6	6	1
	67 to 98	120	70	15	6	6	2
Married:	Yes	659	65	21	7	6	1
	No	547	59	22	10	8	1
Have Kids Under 18:	Yes	513	67	20	8	5	0
	No	687	59	22	9	8	2
Household Income:	Under $25,000	382	66	20	7	6	1
	$25,000 to $50,000	438	62	21	11	6	0
	Over $50,000	227	53	27	8	11	1
Region:	Northeast	265	55	23	12	8	1
	South	398	74	15	5	4	1
	Midwest	279	59	26	10	4	1
	West	264	54	24	10	11	1
Education:	High School or Less	625	65	19	10	6	1
	Some College	325	62	23	7	7	1
	College Graduate	249	56	25	9	9	1
Ethnicity:	White	867	59	25	8	7	1
	Black	162	80	9	3	7	1
	Hispanic	112	61	14	22	3	0
Voter Registration:	Not Registered	246	55	25	11	8	2
	Democrat	381	66	20	8	5	1
	Republican	270	66	21	7	5	0
	Independent	209	61	21	8	10	0
Church Type:	Protestant	492	70	20	5	4	0
	Catholic	313	62	24	9	4	1
Faith Perspective:	Evangelical	83	94	6	0	0	0
	Born Again	428	83	12	3	1	0
	Non-Christian	777	50	27	12	10	2

TABLE 148

Do you agree or disagree that the devil, or Satan, is not a living being, but is a symbol of evil? Do you (agree/disagree) strongly or somewhat?

		N	Agree Strongly	Agree Somewhat	Disagree Somewhat	Disagree Strongly	Don't Know
Total Responding		1206	36%	23%	12%	22%	7%
Gender:	Male	584	33	27	13	20	6
	Female	622	38	20	11	24	8
Age:	18 to 28	252	37	28	14	13	8
	29 to 47	514	30	23	14	27	6
	48 to 66	291	42	22	8	23	6
	67 to 98	120	42	16	13	15	13
Married:	Yes	659	37	20	11	25	6
	No	547	34	27	13	18	8
Have Kids Under 18:	Yes	513	33	22	14	25	7
	No	687	38	24	11	20	7
Household Income:	Under $25,000	382	37	23	11	21	9
	$25,000 to $50,000	438	32	23	14	25	6
	Over $50,000	227	39	23	14	21	4
Region:	Northeast	265	40	29	8	18	5
	South	398	36	20	12	27	6
	Midwest	279	37	22	12	22	8
	West	264	30	23	19	19	10
Education:	High School or Less	625	37	23	13	21	6
	Some College	325	36	22	12	23	8
	College Graduate	249	32	26	11	24	7
Ethnicity:	White	867	36	23	12	24	5
	Black	162	42	17	14	18	8
	Hispanic	112	31	32	11	14	12
Voter Registration:	Not Registered	246	37	19	13	20	11
	Democrat	381	38	26	10	19	7
	Republican	270	31	19	15	30	5
	Independent	209	34	27	13	21	6
Church Type:	Protestant	492	34	21	12	28	6
	Catholic	313	46	27	10	14	3
Faith Perspective:	Evangelical	83	18	3	3	73	3
	Born Again	428	34	12	15	35	4
	Non-Christian	777	36	29	11	15	8

TABLE 149

Do you agree or disagree that if a person is generally good, or does enough good things for others during his or her life, he or she will earn a place in heaven? Do you (agree/disagree) strongly or somewhat?

		N	Agree Strongly	Agree Somewhat	Disagree Somewhat	Disagree Strongly	Don't Know
Total Responding		1206	37%	24%	12%	22%	5%
Gender:	Male	584	33	28	13	20	6
	Female	622	41	20	11	24	4
Age:	18 to 28	252	41	27	12	17	3
	29 to 47	514	36	25	11	24	4
	48 to 66	291	35	20	13	25	7
	67 to 98	120	38	23	15	18	6
Married:	Yes	659	34	23	13	25	4
	No	547	40	24	11	19	6
Have Kids Under 18:	Yes	513	35	25	14	23	4
	No	687	39	22	11	22	6
Household Income:	Under $25,000	382	40	21	12	24	4
	$25,000 to $50,000	438	30	28	13	24	4
	Over $50,000	227	39	21	14	18	8
Region:	Northeast	265	40	26	12	16	7
	South	398	36	17	11	31	4
	Midwest	279	35	30	11	21	4
	West	264	38	24	15	17	6
Education:	High School or Less	625	41	21	11	23	4
	Some College	325	32	29	14	20	5
	College Graduate	249	33	24	13	23	8
Ethnicity:	White	867	37	22	12	23	6
	Black	162	31	29	13	23	4
	Hispanic	112	48	24	6	21	0
Voter Registration:	Not Registered	246	40	21	10	25	4
	Democrat	381	38	26	13	18	6
	Republican	270	37	19	11	28	5
	Independent	209	32	24	15	24	5
Church Type:	Protestant	492	29	20	15	31	5
	Catholic	313	57	30	6	5	2
Faith Perspective:	Evangelical	83	0	0	0	100	0
	Born Again	428	24	18	17	38	2
	Non-Christian	777	44	27	9	13	7

TABLE 150

Do you agree or disagree that Jesus Christ made mistakes? Do you (agree/disagree) strongly or somewhat?

		N	Agree Strongly	Agree Somewhat	Disagree Somewhat	Disagree Strongly	Don't Know
Total Responding		1206	12%	24%	15%	38%	10%
Gender:	Male	584	14	23	18	34	10
	Female	622	11	25	13	42	10
Age:	18 to 28	252	14	28	19	32	7
	29 to 47	514	12	26	15	38	9
	48 to 66	291	9	19	13	47	12
	67 to 98	120	14	23	16	32	14
Married:	Yes	659	10	25	15	42	9
	No	547	15	24	16	34	11
Have Kids Under 18:	Yes	513	13	22	18	40	7
	No	687	11	26	14	37	12
Household Income:	Under $25,000	382	9	26	19	35	10
	$25,000 to $50,000	438	13	22	16	41	8
	Over $50,000	227	18	28	13	33	8
Region:	Northeast	265	14	26	19	29	11
	South	398	9	19	14	49	8
	Midwest	279	13	25	13	41	9
	West	264	14	30	16	29	12
Education:	High School or Less	625	11	25	17	38	10
	Some College	325	14	24	14	41	7
	College Graduate	249	13	24	14	35	14
Ethnicity:	White	867	12	27	14	38	10
	Black	162	11	14	21	47	8
	Hispanic	112	16	23	18	35	8
Voter Registration:	Not Registered	246	11	29	13	37	10
	Democrat	381	11	23	19	38	9
	Republican	270	15	21	10	43	11
	Independent	209	14	25	19	32	10
Church Type:	Protestant	492	10	23	14	46	8
	Catholic	313	16	31	18	27	8
Faith Perspective:	Evangelical	83	4	3	2	90	2
	Born Again	428	7	16	16	56	5
	Non-Christian	777	15	29	15	28	13

TABLE 151

Which of the following descriptions comes closest to what you, personally, believe about God:

		N	Every-one is God	God Is Powerful All-Knowing Creator	God Is Total Realization of Human Potential	There Are Many Gods, Each with Power/Auth.	God Is Higher State of Con-sciousness	There Is No Such Thing as God	Don't Know
Total Responding		1206	3%	67%	8%	3%	10%	2%	8%
Gender:	Male	584	4	60	8	5	11	3	9
	Female	622	3	73	8	2	8	1	6
Age:	18 to 28	252	3	63	13	2	12	3	4
	29 to 47	514	3	66	8	5	10	2	7
	48 to 66	291	2	71	6	2	8	2	9
	67 to 98	120	7	68	5	2	4	3	10
Married:	Yes	659	3	70	6	3	8	2	8
	No	547	4	62	10	4	12	2	7
Have Kids Under 18:	Yes	513	3	70	8	3	9	1	6
	No	687	4	64	8	3	10	3	8
Household Income:	Under $25,000	382	4	70	5	2	10	2	7
	$25,000 to $50,000	438	2	68	10	4	8	2	6
	Over $50,000	227	3	58	12	4	13	2	7
Region:	Northeast	265	2	56	13	4	14	4	7
	South	398	5	74	6	1	6	0	8
	Midwest	279	3	69	7	2	10	1	8
	West	264	3	63	7	7	10	3	6
Education:	High School or Less	625	3	70	6	3	10	1	7
	Some College	325	3	67	7	4	9	3	7
	College Graduate	249	4	57	13	2	11	3	11
Ethnicity:	White	867	3	65	9	3	11	2	7
	Black	162	7	76	4	1	6	0	5
	Hispanic	112	0	76	8	0	4	0	13
Voter Registration:	Not Registered	246	4	63	9	5	9	3	6
	Democrat	381	3	70	7	2	9	2	6
	Republican	270	2	74	7	2	9	1	5
	Independent	209	5	56	10	4	11	2	12
Church Type:	Protestant	492	3	75	7	3	7	1	5
	Catholic	313	4	66	8	2	12	1	5
Faith Perspective:	Evangelical	83	0	100	0	0	0	0	0
	Born Again	428	0	90	4	0	2	0	3
	Non-Christian	777	5	53	10	5	14	3	10

TABLE 152

Have you ever made a personal commitment to Jesus Christ that is still important in your life today?

		N	Yes	No	Don't Know
Total Responding		1206	64%	34%	2%
Gender:	Male	584	57	41	2
	Female	622	71	27	2
Age:	18 to 28	252	52	45	3
	29 to 47	514	66	32	2
	48 to 66	291	71	27	2
	67 to 98	120	64	34	2
Married:	Yes	659	69	28	3
	No	547	58	40	2
Have Kids Under 18:	Yes	513	67	32	1
	No	687	62	35	3
Household Income:	Under $25,000	382	66	33	1
	$25,000 to $50,000	438	64	35	1
	Over $50,000	227	65	34	1
Region:	Northeast	265	52	46	3
	South	398	73	25	2
	Midwest	279	66	33	2
	West	264	61	36	3
Education:	High School or Less	625	63	35	2
	Some College	325	69	29	2
	College Graduate	249	61	36	3
Ethnicity:	White	867	65	33	2
	Black	162	73	27	0
	Hispanic	112	51	44	4
Voter Registration:	Not Registered	246	55	42	3
	Democrat	381	70	29	1
	Republican	270	66	32	2
	Independent	209	61	36	3
Church Type:	Protestant	492	77	22	2
	Catholic	313	60	37	3
Faith Perspective:	Evangelical	83	100	0	0
	Born Again	428	100	0	0
	Non-Christian	777	44	52	3

Table 153

Which one of these statements comes closest to what you believe will happen to you after you die? *(Base: people who have made a personal commitment to Jesus Christ)*

		N	A	B	C	D	E	F	G	H
Total Responding		788	7%	9%	55%	9%	1%	12%	4%	3%
Gender:	Male	331	7	10	54	9	1	12	4	3
	Female	442	7	9	57	9	0	11	4	3
Age:	18 to 28	132	5	15	45	12	0	18	2	3
	29 to 47	341	6	8	61	8	1	11	4	2
	48 to 66	207	7	8	57	8	1	10	5	4
	67 to 98	77	17	8	46	10	0	9	6	4
Married:	Yes	455	7	8	59	9	1	9	4	3
	No	318	7	11	50	9	0	16	4	3
Have Kids Under 18:	Yes	343	7	8	59	9	1	9	5	3
	No	428	7	10	53	9	0	13	4	3
Household Income:	Under $25,000	250	10	9	49	9	0	13	6	4
	$25,000 to $50,000	280	5	9	62	8	2	11	3	2
	Over $50,000	148	5	12	58	9	0	10	5	1
Region:	Northeast	137	7	17	47	6	0	18	1	4
	South	291	5	4	69	5	0	8	5	2
	Midwest	183	10	11	49	9	1	12	2	5
	West	162	7	10	45	17	1	12	6	2
Education:	High School or Less	396	7	10	51	9	1	14	4	3
	Some College	225	7	9	61	8	0	8	4	3
	College Graduate	151	5	9	58	9	0	11	4	3
Ethnicity:	White	562	6	11	58	9	1	10	3	2
	Black	118	8	7	57	4	0	15	4	5
	Hispanic	57	10	2	35	22	0	15	8	7
Voter Registration:	Not Registered	136	11	14	49	7	0	13	4	2
	Democrat	268	6	10	58	9	0	10	3	3
	Republican	178	6	6	60	8	1	12	4	4
	Independent	128	7	8	56	11	2	13	2	1
Church Type:	Protestant	377	5	9	63	7	1	9	3	3
	Catholic	189	10	13	41	14	0	16	3	3
Faith Perspective:	Evangelical	83	0	0	100	0	0	0	0	0
	Born Again	428	0	0	100	0	0	0	0	0
	Non-Christian	345	16	21	0	20	1	26	9	7

A: When you die you will go to heaven because you have tried to obey the 10 Commandments.

B: When you die you will go to heaven because you are basically a good person.

C: When you die you will go to heaven because you have confessed your sins and have accepted Jesus Christ as your savior.

D: When you die you will go to heaven because God loves all people and will not let them perish.

E: When you die you will not go to heaven.

F: You do not know what will happen after you die.

G: Other.

H: Don't know.

Table 154

Have you ever felt as though you were in the presence of God? *(Base: Protestants and Catholics)*

		N	Yes	No	Don't Know
Total Responding		525	68%	29%	3%
Gender:	Male	241	63	35	2
	Female	284	72	24	4
Age:	18 to 28	98	60	36	4
	29 to 47	219	73	25	2
	48 to 66	132	63	32	6
	67 to 98	64	75	24	1
Married:	Yes	303	68	29	3
	No	221	69	28	3
Have Kids Under 18:	Yes	226	66	31	3
	No	298	69	27	4
Household Income:	Under $25,000	168	72	22	5
	$25,000 to $50,000	189	69	30	1
	Over $50,000	107	61	37	2
Region:	Northeast	118	66	32	2
	South	173	70	26	4
	Midwest	121	64	33	2
	West	113	70	25	5
Education:	High School or Less	277	70	26	5
	Some College	145	63	37	1
	College Graduate	100	70	28	3
Ethnicity:	White	387	66	31	3
	Black	68	69	26	6
	Hispanic	46	76	18	6
Voter Registration:	Not Registered	91	66	28	5
	Democrat	183	74	22	4
	Republican	123	69	31	0
	Independent	88	63	35	2
Church Type:	Protestant	252	71	28	2
	Catholic	154	63	32	5
Faith Perspective:	Evangelical	40	92	5	2
	Born Again	215	83	14	3
	Non-Christian	310	58	39	3

TABLE 155

How often have you felt you have been in God's presence? *(Base: Protestants and Catholics who have felt as though they have been in the presence of God)*

		N	Every Day	At Least Once Per Week	Occasion- ally	Once or Twice in Your Life	Don't Know
Total Responding		359	37%	9%	31%	19%	5%
Gender:	Male	152	37	9	28	19	7
	Female	204	37	8	32	19	3
Age:	18 to 28	59	40	4	28	24	3
	29 to 47	160	30	11	31	20	8
	48 to 66	83	41	10	29	17	3
	67 to 98	48	50	5	30	14	1
Married:	Yes	205	38	10	28	19	5
	No	152	36	7	34	18	5
Have Kids Under 18:	Yes	150	42	8	26	19	5
	No	206	33	9	34	19	5
Household Income:	Under $25,000	121	35	8	32	21	4
	$25,000 to $50,000	130	42	8	28	15	7
	Over $50,000	66	28	11	35	22	4
Region:	Northeast	78	50	8	20	13	8
	South	122	38	8	33	20	1
	Midwest	78	36	12	34	15	4
	West	79	23	7	34	28	8
Education:	High School or Less	193	36	9	29	19	7
	Some College	91	39	9	32	17	3
	College Graduate	70	38	8	31	21	2
Ethnicity:	White	257	33	11	34	19	3
	Black	47	64	4	15	11	6
	Hispanic	35	22	0	36	20	21
Voter Registration:	Not Registered	60	23	7	31	28	11
	Democrat	135	44	8	31	12	5
	Republican	85	34	11	32	20	3
	Independent	55	39	8	26	26	1
Church Type:	Protestant	178	37	8	31	18	6
	Catholic	96	34	8	28	23	6
Faith Perspective:	Evangelical	37	47	20	23	6	3
	Born Again	177	41	10	28	18	3
	Non-Christian	179	33	8	33	20	6

TABLE 156

How long has it been since the last time you felt you were in God's presence? *(Base: Protestants and Catholics who have felt as though they have been in the presence of God)*

		N	Within Past Week	Within Past Month	Within Last Six Months	Within Past Year	More than One Year Ago	Don't Know
Total Responding		359	51%	10%	9%	3%	16%	10%
Gender:	Male	152	49	13	9	2	18	9
	Female	204	53	8	9	5	15	11
Age:	18 to 28	59	55	12	5	4	21	4
	29 to 47	160	48	9	12	4	18	9
	48 to 66	83	50	14	7	2	12	15
	67 to 98	48	64	4	4	4	13	11
Married:	Yes	205	54	7	8	4	14	13
	No	152	48	14	10	3	19	6
Have Kids Under 18:	Yes	150	60	7	9	3	13	7
	No	206	45	13	9	3	18	12
Household Income:	Under $25,000	121	46	12	8	2	25	7
	$25,000 to $50,000	130	58	11	9	2	9	10
	Over $50,000	66	45	8	12	6	21	8
Region:	Northeast	78	62	10	13	1	8	6
	South	122	51	12	6	4	15	12
	Midwest	78	50	11	6	7	16	10
	West	79	43	6	12	2	26	11
Education:	High School or Less	193	52	11	7	3	16	10
	Some College	91	48	9	10	4	19	9
	College Graduate	70	52	10	12	2	14	10
Ethnicity:	White	257	48	12	9	4	17	9
	Black	47	75	1	3	3	7	11
	Hispanic	35	36	14	19	0	17	14
Voter Registration:	Not Registered	60	41	12	12	2	21	12
	Democrat	135	57	14	9	2	11	7
	Republican	85	52	7	10	5	14	12
	Independent	55	48	8	7	3	26	9
Church Type:	Protestant	178	49	12	9	3	17	10
	Catholic	96	53	12	9	2	18	6
Faith Perspective:	Evangelical	37	74	6	7	3	6	4
	Born Again	177	58	9	9	3	16	5
	Non-Christian	179	45	11	9	4	16	14

TABLE 157

When you attend worship services at your church, how often do you feel as though you are personally experiencing God's presence? *(Base: Protestants and Catholics who have felt as though they have been in the presence of God)*

		N	Always	Usually	Some-times	Rarely	Never	Don't Know
Total Responding		359	39%	18%	28%	7%	3%	5%
Gender:	Male	152	37	14	30	8	4	7
	Female	204	40	21	26	7	2	4
Age:	18 to 28	59	40	19	24	11	0	6
	29 to 47	160	34	18	28	7	7	6
	48 to 66	83	49	14	27	9	0	2
	67 to 98	48	40	19	34	0	0	7
Married:	Yes	205	37	20	29	7	3	4
	No	152	41	15	26	7	3	7
Have Kids Under 18:	Yes	150	37	17	29	9	3	5
	No	206	40	18	27	6	3	5
Household Income:	Under $25,000	121	39	16	27	6	6	6
	$25,000 to $50,000	130	40	22	26	7	1	5
	Over $50,000	66	33	15	33	14	2	3
Region:	Northeast	78	46	19	23	6	1	6
	South	122	39	14	30	7	3	7
	Midwest	78	39	23	25	6	3	4
	West	79	33	18	31	9	6	3
Education:	High School or Less	193	43	14	28	7	2	6
	Some College	91	39	23	24	8	4	3
	College Graduate	70	30	21	33	6	3	7
Ethnicity:	White	257	37	19	26	9	3	6
	Black	47	58	12	19	5	0	6
	Hispanic	35	26	16	52	0	6	0
Voter Registration:	Not Registered	60	34	13	27	9	8	9
	Democrat	135	43	19	27	5	2	3
	Republican	85	32	21	31	9	1	6
	Independent	55	39	16	29	6	3	7
Church Type:	Protestant	178	34	22	32	4	2	6
	Catholic	96	42	12	28	10	6	2
Faith Perspective:	Evangelical	37	37	34	20	0	0	9
	Born Again	177	47	23	22	4	0	4
	Non-Christian	179	31	13	33	10	6	7

TABLE 158

Are the worship services at your church boring? *(Base: Protestant or Catholic adults)*

		N	Yes	No	Don't Know
Total Responding		340	12%	86%	2%
Gender:	Male	136	15	85	0
	Female	204	10	87	3
Age:	18 to 28	62	20	80	0
	29 to 47	152	14	84	2
	48 to 66	90	5	91	4
	67 to 98	29	3	97	0
Married:	Yes	206	11	87	1
	No	134	13	85	2
Have Kids Under 18:	Yes	159	16	82	2
	No	180	8	90	2
Household Income:	Under $25,000	97	8	91	2
	$25,000 to $50,000	136	13	84	2
	Over $50,000	69	16	83	1
Region:	Northeast	68	17	79	4
	South	130	6	92	1
	Midwest	85	21	77	2
	West	58	4	96	0
Education:	High School or Less	164	10	88	2
	Some College	96	15	85	0
	College Graduate	78	12	83	4
Ethnicity:	White	260	14	84	1
	Black	47	1	97	2
	Hispanic	20	7	93	0
Voter Registration:	Not Registered	59	15	85	0
	Democrat	104	8	89	3
	Republican	89	11	88	1
	Independent	64	15	84	1
Church Type:	Protestant	173	9	89	2
	Catholic	102	19	81	0
Faith Perspective:	Evangelical	40	3	97	0
	Born Again	161	6	94	1
	Non-Christian	179	17	80	3

TABLE 159

Are the worship services at your church challenging? *(Base: Protestant or Catholic adults)*

		N	Yes	No	Don't Know
Total Responding		340	67%	29%	5%
Gender:	Male	136	66	31	3
	Female	204	67	27	6
Age:	18 to 28	62	56	42	2
	29 to 47	152	64	33	3
	48 to 66	90	79	16	5
	67 to 98	29	67	18	15
Married:	Yes	206	71	26	3
	No	134	60	33	7
Have Kids Under 18:	Yes	159	62	36	2
	No	180	71	22	6
Household Income:	Under $25,000	97	68	29	4
	$25,000 to $50,000	136	66	29	5
	Over $50,000	69	65	32	3
Region:	Northeast	68	62	32	6
	South	130	67	26	7
	Midwest	85	66	34	1
	West	58	74	24	2
Education:	High School or Less	164	69	28	3
	Some College	96	70	25	5
	College Graduate	78	60	34	6
Ethnicity:	White	260	69	26	5
	Black	47	65	32	3
	Hispanic	20	54	46	0
Voter Registration:	Not Registered	59	57	40	3
	Democrat	104	70	28	3
	Republican	89	71	24	6
	Independent	64	69	28	3
Church Type:	Protestant	173	79	17	5
	Catholic	102	49	48	3
Faith Perspective:	Evangelical	40	85	15	0
	Born Again	161	77	19	3
	Non-Christian	179	58	37	6

TABLE 160

Are the worship services at your church refreshing? *(Base: Protestant or Catholic adults)*

		N	Yes	No	Don't Know
Total Responding		340	90%	9%	1%
Gender:	Male	136	87	12	0
	Female	204	91	7	2
Age:	18 to 28	62	86	13	1
	29 to 47	152	94	5	1
	48 to 66	90	87	12	1
	67 to 98	29	88	9	3
Married:	Yes	206	91	8	1
	No	134	88	10	2
Have Kids Under 18:	Yes	159	91	7	2
	No	180	88	11	1
Household Income:	Under $25,000	97	89	9	2
	$25,000 to $50,000	136	91	8	1
	Over $50,000	69	86	13	1
Region:	Northeast	68	88	9	3
	South	130	91	8	1
	Midwest	85	85	14	2
	West	58	97	3	0
Education:	High School or Less	164	89	10	1
	Some College	96	92	8	0
	College Graduate	78	89	8	3
Ethnicity:	White	260	89	10	1
	Black	47	92	8	0
	Hispanic	20	100	0	0
Voter Registration:	Not Registered	59	90	8	2
	Democrat	104	92	5	3
	Republican	89	89	11	0
	Independent	64	82	17	1
Church Type:	Protestant	173	92	7	1
	Catholic	102	86	13	1
Faith Perspective:	Evangelical	40	100	0	0
	Born Again	161	95	5	0
	Non-Christian	179	85	13	2

TABLE 161

Are the worship services at your church Spirit-filled? *(Base: Protestant or Catholic adults)*

		N	Yes	No	Don't Know
Total Responding		340	85%	13%	2%
Gender:	Male	136	80	19	1
	Female	204	89	8	3
Age:	18 to 28	62	81	19	0
	29 to 47	152	86	11	3
	48 to 66	90	87	13	0
	67 to 98	29	90	0	10
Married:	Yes	206	85	13	2
	No	134	86	12	3
Have Kids Under 18:	Yes	159	83	14	3
	No	180	87	11	2
Household Income:	Under $25,000	97	83	12	5
	$25,000 to $50,000	136	83	15	2
	Over $50,000	69	86	14	0
Region:	Northeast	68	80	18	2
	South	130	82	15	4
	Midwest	85	91	7	1
	West	58	91	9	0
Education:	High School or Less	164	84	13	3
	Some College	96	87	11	2
	College Graduate	78	85	13	2
Ethnicity:	White	260	89	10	1
	Black	47	88	12	0
	Hispanic	20	45	39	16
Voter Registration:	Not Registered	59	78	17	5
	Democrat	104	83	13	3
	Republican	89	91	8	1
	Independent	64	84	16	0
Church Type:	Protestant	173	92	8	0
	Catholic	102	73	21	5
Faith Perspective:	Evangelical	40	100	0	0
	Born Again	161	92	5	3
	Non-Christian	179	79	19	2

TABLE 162

Are the worship services at your church outdated? *(Base: Protestant or Catholic adults)*

		N	Yes	No	Don't Know
Total Responding		340	13%	85%	1%
Gender:	Male	136	17	82	1
	Female	204	11	87	2
Age:	18 to 28	62	19	81	0
	29 to 47	152	13	85	2
	48 to 66	90	12	86	2
	67 to 98	29	11	89	0
Married:	Yes	206	14	85	0
	No	134	12	85	3
Have Kids Under 18:	Yes	159	16	83	1
	No	180	11	87	2
Household Income:	Under $25,000	97	9	88	3
	$25,000 to $50,000	136	16	83	1
	Over $50,000	69	16	84	0
Region:	Northeast	68	16	82	2
	South	130	16	84	1
	Midwest	85	12	87	1
	West	58	8	90	2
Education:	High School or Less	164	15	83	2
	Some College	96	11	89	0
	College Graduate	78	12	86	2
Ethnicity:	White	260	11	88	1
	Black	47	16	84	0
	Hispanic	20	46	54	0
Voter Registration:	Not Registered	59	15	85	0
	Democrat	104	11	86	3
	Republican	89	11	88	1
	Independent	64	18	82	0
Church Type:	Protestant	173	5	94	1
	Catholic	102	26	73	1
Faith Perspective:	Evangelical	40	1	99	0
	Born Again	161	7	92	1
	Non-Christian	179	19	79	2

TABLE 163

Are the worship services at your church life-transforming? *(Base: Protestant or Catholic adults)*

		N	Yes	No	Don't Know
Total Responding		340	58%	35%	6%
Gender:	Male	136	60	39	2
	Female	204	57	33	10
Age:	18 to 28	62	55	45	0
	29 to 47	152	52	40	7
	48 to 66	90	70	23	8
	67 to 98	29	57	29	15
Married:	Yes	206	60	33	7
	No	134	56	38	6
Have Kids Under 18:	Yes	159	53	39	7
	No	180	63	31	6
Household Income:	Under $25,000	97	55	37	8
	$25,000 to $50,000	136	62	34	5
	Over $50,000	69	58	39	3
Region:	Northeast	68	47	45	9
	South	130	62	30	8
	Midwest	85	55	38	7
	West	58	68	32	1
Education:	High School or Less	164	64	29	8
	Some College	96	52	43	5
	College Graduate	78	56	40	4
Ethnicity:	White	260	62	32	6
	Black	47	57	38	5
	Hispanic	20	31	54	16
Voter Registration:	Not Registered	59	53	40	8
	Democrat	104	56	38	6
	Republican	89	65	33	2
	Independent	64	57	34	9
Church Type:	Protestant	173	68	26	6
	Catholic	102	41	51	8
Faith Perspective:	Evangelical	40	89	9	2
	Born Again	161	70	22	9
	Non-Christian	179	48	47	5

TABLE 164

Are the worship services at your church embarrassing? *(Base: Protestant or Catholic adults)*

		N	Yes	No	Don't Know
Total Responding		340	3%	96%	1%
Gender:	Male	136	4	96	0
	Female	204	3	96	1
Age:	18 to 28	62	3	97	0
	29 to 47	152	3	95	1
	48 to 66	90	3	97	0
	67 to 98	29	0	100	0
Married:	Yes	206	4	96	0
	No	134	2	97	1
Have Kids Under 18:	Yes	159	4	95	1
	No	180	3	97	0
Household Income:	Under $25,000	97	4	96	0
	$25,000 to $50,000	136	4	94	1
	Over $50,000	69	1	98	1
Region:	Northeast	68	4	94	2
	South	130	4	96	0
	Midwest	85	3	97	0
	West	58	0	99	1
Education:	High School or Less	164	4	96	0
	Some College	96	2	98	0
	College Graduate	78	4	94	2
Ethnicity:	White	260	4	96	0
	Black	47	3	97	0
	Hispanic	20	0	100	0
Voter Registration:	Not Registered	59	4	95	1
	Democrat	104	3	96	1
	Republican	89	3	97	0
	Independent	64	6	94	0
Church Type:	Protestant	173	3	97	0
	Catholic	102	4	96	0
Faith Perspective:	Evangelical	40	3	97	0
	Born Again	161	3	97	0
	Non-Christian	179	4	95	1

TABLE 165

Are the worship services at your church participatory? *(Base: Protestant or Catholic adults)*

		N	Yes	No	Don't Know
Total Responding		340	82%	12%	6%
Gender:	Male	136	82	15	3
	Female	204	81	11	8
Age:	18 to 28	62	78	20	2
	29 to 47	152	84	12	4
	48 to 66	90	86	9	5
	67 to 98	29	72	3	25
Married:	Yes	206	83	12	6
	No	134	80	14	6
Have Kids Under 18:	Yes	159	81	13	6
	No	180	83	11	6
Household Income:	Under $25,000	97	83	12	5
	$25,000 to $50,000	136	81	13	6
	Over $50,000	69	82	14	5
Region:	Northeast	68	79	15	6
	South	130	79	12	8
	Midwest	85	83	14	3
	West	58	88	8	4
Education:	High School or Less	164	82	12	6
	Some College	96	83	13	4
	College Graduate	78	82	14	5
Ethnicity:	White	260	81	13	6
	Black	47	86	11	3
	Hispanic	20	93	7	0
Voter Registration:	Not Registered	59	81	10	9
	Democrat	104	81	12	6
	Republican	89	83	14	3
	Independent	64	90	6	4
Church Type:	Protestant	173	82	13	5
	Catholic	102	84	10	6
Faith Perspective:	Evangelical	40	92	3	4
	Born Again	161	85	10	6
	Non-Christian	179	79	15	6

TABLE 166

Are the worship services at your church disappointing? *(Base: Protestant or Catholic adults)*

		N	Yes	No	Don't Know
Total Responding		340	7%	90%	3%
Gender:	Male	136	7	92	1
	Female	204	7	89	4
Age:	18 to 28	62	6	94	0
	29 to 47	152	7	90	3
	48 to 66	90	9	89	2
	67 to 98	29	5	88	7
Married:	Yes	206	8	89	2
	No	134	5	91	4
Have Kids Under 18:	Yes	159	7	90	3
	No	180	7	90	3
Household Income:	Under $25,000	97	7	92	1
	$25,000 to $50,000	136	7	91	2
	Over $50,000	69	8	89	3
Region:	Northeast	68	7	86	6
	South	130	9	88	3
	Midwest	85	6	93	2
	West	58	4	95	1
Education:	High School or Less	164	7	91	2
	Some College	96	6	92	2
	College Graduate	78	9	87	5
Ethnicity:	White	260	7	91	2
	Black	47	10	84	5
	Hispanic	20	7	93	0
Voter Registration:	Not Registered	59	9	88	2
	Democrat	104	3	95	3
	Republican	89	8	91	2
	Independent	64	13	84	3
Church Type:	Protestant	173	6	92	2
	Catholic	102	9	88	3
Faith Perspective:	Evangelical	40	2	98	0
	Born Again	161	5	93	2
	Non-Christian	179	9	87	4

TABLE 167

Are the worship services at your church traditional? *(Base: Protestant or Catholic adults)*

		N	Yes	No	Don't Know
Total Responding		340	78%	19%	3%
Gender:	Male	136	74	22	3
	Female	204	80	17	3
Age:	18 to 28	62	77	20	3
	29 to 47	152	79	17	4
	48 to 66	90	75	24	1
	67 to 98	29	86	6	7
Married:	Yes	206	80	19	2
	No	134	75	19	6
Have Kids Under 18:	Yes	159	81	16	4
	No	180	75	22	3
Household Income:	Under $25,000	97	81	15	4
	$25,000 to $50,000	136	74	24	2
	Over $50,000	69	81	16	3
Region:	Northeast	68	76	19	4
	South	130	78	20	2
	Midwest	85	84	15	1
	West	58	69	23	8
Education:	High School or Less	164	80	16	4
	Some College	96	75	24	1
	College Graduate	78	75	19	6
Ethnicity:	White	260	77	20	3
	Black	47	76	22	2
	Hispanic	20	93	0	7
Voter Registration:	Not Registered	59	80	20	0
	Democrat	104	76	18	6
	Republican	89	81	16	3
	Independent	64	75	23	2
Church Type:	Protestant	173	76	21	3
	Catholic	102	83	13	4
Faith Perspective:	Evangelical	40	72	28	0
	Born Again	161	79	19	2
	Non-Christian	179	76	19	5

TABLE 168

Are the worship services at your church modern or contemporary? *(Base: Protestant or Catholic adults)*

		N	Yes	No	Don't Know
Total Responding		340	70%	23%	6%
Gender:	Male	136	76	21	3
	Female	204	67	25	8
Age:	18 to 28	62	76	21	4
	29 to 47	152	72	24	4
	48 to 66	90	62	31	7
	67 to 98	29	77	8	15
Married:	Yes	206	69	27	4
	No	134	72	18	10
Have Kids Under 18:	Yes	159	70	24	6
	No	180	70	23	7
Household Income:	Under $25,000	97	72	22	5
	$25,000 to $50,000	136	70	24	6
	Over $50,000	69	71	27	2
Region:	Northeast	68	79	13	9
	South	130	62	30	9
	Midwest	85	69	26	5
	West	58	82	18	0
Education:	High School or Less	164	70	25	5
	Some College	96	75	21	5
	College Graduate	78	67	25	9
Ethnicity:	White	260	73	23	4
	Black	47	59	24	17
	Hispanic	20	54	39	7
Voter Registration:	Not Registered	59	87	9	3
	Democrat	104	61	30	9
	Republican	89	75	23	2
	Independent	64	66	29	5
Church Type:	Protestant	173	71	21	7
	Catholic	102	75	23	3
Faith Perspective:	Evangelical	40	54	42	3
	Born Again	161	65	28	7
	Non-Christian	179	75	20	5

TABLE 169

Are the worship services at your church inspiring? *(Base: Protestant or Catholic adults)*

		N	Yes	No	Don't Know
Total Responding		340	92%	6%	3%
Gender:	Male	136	91	7	2
	Female	204	92	5	4
Age:	18 to 28	62	91	9	0
	29 to 47	152	93	5	2
	48 to 66	90	90	6	4
	67 to 98	29	91	3	6
Married:	Yes	206	92	6	3
	No	134	91	5	4
Have Kids Under 18:	Yes	159	90	6	3
	No	180	92	5	3
Household Income:	Under $25,000	97	91	8	1
	$25,000 to $50,000	136	93	5	2
	Over $50,000	69	90	5	5
Region:	Northeast	68	80	12	8
	South	130	94	4	2
	Midwest	85	93	5	2
	West	58	96	3	1
Education:	High School or Less	164	93	5	2
	Some College	96	92	6	2
	College Graduate	78	88	6	6
Ethnicity:	White	260	92	5	3
	Black	47	90	8	2
	Hispanic	20	100	0	0
Voter Registration:	Not Registered	59	92	5	3
	Democrat	104	93	4	3
	Republican	89	92	6	3
	Independent	64	88	9	3
Church Type:	Protestant	173	95	3	2
	Catholic	102	88	8	4
Faith Perspective:	Evangelical	40	100	0	0
	Born Again	161	97	3	1
	Non-Christian	179	87	8	5

TABLE 170

Are the worship services at your church just a performance? *(Base: Protestant or Catholic adults)*

		N	Yes	No	Don't Know
Total Responding		340	13%	83%	5%
Gender:	Male	136	14	82	4
	Female	204	12	83	5
Age:	18 to 28	62	21	79	0
	29 to 47	152	9	89	2
	48 to 66	90	12	80	8
	67 to 98	29	19	67	14
Married:	Yes	206	10	86	4
	No	134	18	78	5
Have Kids Under 18:	Yes	159	11	86	3
	No	180	15	79	6
Household Income:	Under $25,000	97	10	82	8
	$25,000 to $50,000	136	14	83	2
	Over $50,000	69	12	83	5
Region:	Northeast	68	14	80	6
	South	130	12	82	6
	Midwest	85	9	88	3
	West	58	21	78	1
Education:	High School or Less	164	12	81	7
	Some College	96	14	85	1
	College Graduate	78	11	85	4
Ethnicity:	White	260	14	82	4
	Black	47	3	88	8
	Hispanic	20	7	93	0
Voter Registration:	Not Registered	59	10	85	5
	Democrat	104	10	86	4
	Republican	89	17	80	3
	Independent	64	13	80	7
Church Type:	Protestant	173	11	87	2
	Catholic	102	16	77	7
Faith Perspective:	Evangelical	40	0	100	0
	Born Again	161	8	89	3
	Non-Christian	179	17	77	6

TABLE 171

Overall, how satisfied are you with your ability to worship God at your church? *(Base: Protestant or Catholic adults)*

		N	Very Satisfied	Somewhat Satisfied	Not Too Satisfied	Not at All Satisfied	Don't Know
Total Responding		340	66%	30%	3%	0%	1%
Gender:	Male	136	62	32	6	0	0
	Female	204	68	29	2	0	1
Age:	18 to 28	62	58	34	8	0	0
	29 to 47	152	61	36	2	0	1
	48 to 66	90	70	24	5	0	1
	67 to 98	29	89	11	0	0	0
Married:	Yes	206	67	30	2	0	0
	No	134	63	30	5	0	2
Have Kids Under 18:	Yes	159	62	35	2	0	1
	No	180	69	26	5	0	1
Household Income:	Under $25,000	97	71	24	5	0	0
	$25,000 to $50,000	136	62	34	3	0	1
	Over $50,000	69	60	34	5	1	1
Region:	Northeast	68	54	38	5	1	2
	South	130	73	24	4	0	0
	Midwest	85	59	36	3	1	1
	West	58	73	26	1	0	1
Education:	High School or Less	164	65	32	2	0	1
	Some College	96	65	31	4	0	0
	College Graduate	78	67	25	5	1	2
Ethnicity:	White	260	65	31	3	0	1
	Black	47	88	6	6	0	0
	Hispanic	20	38	55	7	0	0
Voter Registration:	Not Registered	59	66	30	4	0	0
	Democrat	104	73	24	1	0	2
	Republican	89	62	35	2	0	0
	Independent	64	55	36	9	1	0
Church Type:	Protestant	173	72	27	0	0	1
	Catholic	102	54	40	6	0	0
Faith Perspective:	Evangelical	40	85	15	0	0	0
	Born Again	161	77	20	2	0	0
	Non-Christian	179	55	39	5	0	2

Appendix III

About the Barna Research Group, Ltd.

The Barna Research Group was started in 1984 by George and Nancy Barna to provide full-service marketing research capabilities to Christian ministries. During its decade of service to ministries, the company has worked with numerous ministries, ranging from churches of all sizes to parachurch ministries in all facets of ministry endeavor. Clients have included parachurch organizations such as American Bible Society, Billy Graham Evangelistic Association, Biola University, Campus Crusade for Christ, CBN, Compassion International, Dallas Theological Seminary, Focus on the Family, Fuller Theological Seminary, Moody Bible Institute, Navigators, Prison Fellowship, Thomas Nelson Publishers, Trinity Broadcasting, Word Inc., World Vision and many others. Churches served range from large congregations (Willow Creek Community Church, Eastside Foursquare, New Venture Christian Fellowship) to start-up churches.

Barna Research Group has also served a wide variety of nonreligious clients, especially those in the nonprofit industry and the mass media. Those clients have included The Disney Channel, Turner Broadcasting, Southwestern Bell Telephone, the U.S. Army, C.A.R.E., United Cerebral Palsy, Boys and Girls Clubs and many others.

The vision for ministry of the Barna Research Group is to "enable Christian ministries to make better decisions by providing current, accurate and reliable information in bite-sized pieces at affordable prices." Toward this end, Barna Research Group provides a variety of services and products to clients. Those resources include custom research, syndicated research reports, books, audiotapes, videotapes, in-person presentations, standardized diagnostic tools and seminars.

For further information about George Barna or the Barna Research Group, please contact them at P.O. Box 4152, Glendale, CA 91222-0152 or call 818-241-9300. A full listing of the books, research reports, audio and videotapes, and the diagnostic tools currently available will be sent upon request.